MathLink®

This book introduces the basic concepts of *MathLink* and explains how to extend *Mathematica* using *MathLink*. *MathLink* provides a simple and powerful way to write programs that communicate with *Mathematica*, and it provides access to a wide range of network resources. Writing network programs is the most demanded skill in the Internet age, and *MathLink* provides a sophisticated level of network programming to the nonprogrammer, scientist, engineer, and student.

The text assumes that the reader is already familiar with *Mathematica*. *Mathematica*'s powerful "problem-oriented" programming language – which includes symbolic and numerical computation and excellent graphics capabilities – enables users to write compact and elegant programs that are much shorter than in conventional languages.

Source code for a range of practical examples – ranging from elementary to advanced – is examined in detail, allowing readers to easily adapt the code to suit their own practical needs. The purpose of this book is to show how to write *MathLink* programs and how to apply *MathLink* in a variety of situations.

The book includes a CD-ROM that contains the source code for all the routines used within the book, a help browser-enabled electronic text of the book, QuickTime, Metrowerks' CodeWarrior Lite, and the *MathLink* Developer Kit from Wolfram Research. This valuable CD-ROM provides a complete environment for developing your own *MathLink* programs.

Chikara Miyaji is on the research staff in the Institute of Sports Sciences at the University of Tsukuba, Japan. His main research area is sports biomechanics, especially the simulation of human movement, an interesting example of which is a "swimming robot" controlled by *Mathematica*. As a research tool, Miyaji has used *Mathematica* since version 1.2, and he has used *MathLink* since its first release.

Paul Abbott received his Ph.D. in theoretical physics from the University of Western Australia in 1987. He worked for Wolfram Research Inc. from 1989 to 1991 as a member of the Applications Department and, in 1992, gained an appointment as a computational physicist in the Department of Physics at the University of Western Australia. Abbott does research in the areas of wavelets and few-body atomic physics, and he has general interest in problems in computational and mathematical physics. He has more than ten years of experience with *Mathematica* and has been an editor of *The Mathematica Journal* since its inception in 1990.

MathLink®

Network Programming with *Mathematica*®

Chikara Miyaji
University of Tsukuba

Paul Abbott
University of Western Australia

CAMBRIDGE
UNIVERSITY PRESS

PUBLISHED BY THE PRESS SYNDICATE OF THE UNIVERSITY OF CAMBRIDGE
The Pitt Building, Trumpington Street, Cambridge, United Kingdom

CAMBRIDGE UNIVERSITY PRESS
The Edinburgh Building, Cambridge CB2 2RU, UK
40 West 20th Street, New York, NY 10011-4211, USA
10 Stamford Road, Oakleigh, VIC 3166, Australia
Ruiz de Alarcón 13, 28014 Madrid, Spain
Dock House, The Waterfront, Cape Town 8001, South Africa

http://www.cambridge.org

First published 2001

Printed in the United States of America

Typeface Times 11/14 pt.   *System* Mathematica   [AU]

A catalog record for this book is available from the British Library.

Library of Congress Cataloging in Publication Data
Miyaji, Chikara.
   Mathlink : network programming with Mathematica / Chikara Miyaji, Paul Abbott.
      p.   cm.
   ISBN 0-521-64172-1 – ISBN 0-521-64598-0
      1. Internet programming.   2. Mathematica (Computer file)   I. Abbott, Paul, 1960–   II. Title.
   QA76.625. M59   2000
   510′.288′53769 – dc21   00-033749

ISBN 0 521 64172 1 hardback
ISBN 0 521 64598 0 paperback

For the latest updates and corrections, visit:
ftp:/ /ftp.physics.uwa.edu.au/NetworkProgramming
or email to:
NetworkProgramming@physics.uwa.edu.au

I dedicate this book to my parents, Kanichi and Sonoko Miyaji, who always support and encourage my challenges.

Chikara

To my parents, Charles (Bud) Abbott and Jean Abbott, for convincing me of the importance of always finishing projects that I start.

Paul

Contents

Preface

Introduction

This book is about network programming for *Mathematica*. *MathLink* provides a simple and powerful way to write programs that communicate with *Mathematica,* and it provides access to a wide range of network resources. Writing network programs is the most demanded skill in the Internet age, and *MathLink* provides a sophisticated level of network programming to the nonprogrammer, scientist, engineer, and student.

The reader should be already familiar with *Mathematica*. *Mathematica'*s powerful "problem-oriented" programming language—which includes symbolic and numerical computation and excellent graphics capabilities—enables users to write compact and elegant programs that are much shorter than in conventional languages.

Nevertheless some readers will find *Mathematica* insufficient because it lacks a convenient interface for their particular problem: How do you import digital or analog electrical signals into *Mathematica*? Can you control a robot using *Mathematica*? Is there an easy and direct way to analyze digital images generated by an electron microscope?

MathLink can help in these situations. Using *MathLink* you can easily write programs that communicate with *Mathematica*. Since most electronic devices are connected to, or controlled by, a computer, it is straightforward to interface them to *Mathematica*. Once your device is connected to *Mathematica*, you can manipulate the data within *Mathematica*. In fact, all phases of research—experiment, data analysis, simulation, animation, and documentation —can be done using *Mathematica*. It is advantageous to think of *Mathematica* as an "integrated environment" rather than just as "a system for doing mathematics". The key to this integrated network programming environment is *MathLink*.

In general, it can be very difficult to write programs that rely on network communication. Most scientists and engineers do not want to write their own TCP/IP communication programs. However, using *MathLink* makes such communication as simple as possible. You only need to write the main part of the program; the rest is automatically handled by *MathLink*. The program then communicates with *Mathematica* through the network, and the data can then be processed within *Mathematica*. There are two points you should bear in mind when writing *MathLink* programs:

[1] **General overview of data transfer:** Since data transfer over the network using *MathLink* is transparent it is easy to lose sight of how the data are actually being transferred. Nevertheless it is important to have a general overview of the data transfer process when writing a network program.

[2] **Suitable design:** One needs to decide how to share the work between *MathLink* (calling external programs) and *Mathematica* (using high-level functions). This design decision can result in programs that vary greatly in complexity and efficiency.

If you understand these two points, you can easily write *MathLink* programs and take advantage of their power. Of course, the best way to learn these things is to read through the following examples, run them, and modify them to meet your own needs.

Rationale

This book introduces the basic concepts of *MathLink* and explains how to extend *Mathematica* using *MathLink*. Source code for a range of practical examples—ranging from simple to complicated—is examined in detail. These examples are quite useful as they stand but, since the reader can also modify them to meet their own specific needs, it is quite likely that readers will think of ways of modifying the code presented here in ways the authors did not even contemplate.

The purpose of this book is to show how to write *MathLink* programs and how to apply *MathLink* in a variety of situations. It is possible to build user-specific network environments using *MathLink*.

Book Overview

This book consists of two parts: Basics and Applications. The fundamentals of *MathLink*—templates, data transfer model, and transfer time—are explained in Basics. The Applications section demonstrates a wide range of *MathLink* application programs including a QuickTime movie interface and an interactive graphics program.

Basics

Chapter 1. Preliminaries

This chapter describes the *MathLink* Developer's Kit (MLDK), *MathLink* library, C compilers for various platforms, and provides instructions for installation off the CD-ROM.

Chapter 2. Connecting the Front End and the Kernel

This chapter explains *MathLink* basics using various front end and kernel connection methods, and also presents some simple background on networks. Readers who are unfamiliar with C should be able to easily understand this chapter because it only uses *Mathematica* functions.

Chapter 3. Compiling AddTwo

Here we build the **AddTwo** sample project. Modifying the source code, the data format of *MathLink* is then discussed. The *MathLink* template mechanism is also described.

Chapter 4. Transfer Time Using *MathLink*

When you design a *MathLink* program, it is important to know how long it takes for data transfer. This chapter introduces *MathLink* list transfer, builds a tool for measuring transfer time, and does some experimentation about data transfer on various computers.

Chapter 5. Debugging *MathLink* Programs

In general, programs require debugging. This chapter describes this process for *MathLink* programs and demonstrates other debugging methods including print statements and the use of dialogs.

Applications

Chapter 6. *TurtleGraphics*

Although *Mathematica* has excellent graphics, it does not include real-time graphics. In this chapter, a real-time graphics program using Macintosh's QuickDraw toolbox is created and the *TurtleGraphics* application is implemented using this program.

Chapter 7. Cellular Automata

In this chapter, a graphics program that shows cellular automata in real time is created as an extension of Chapter 6. Also, the extension of these programs to make them work with multiple windows is described.

Chapter 8. *MovieDigitizer*

Here a *MathLink* interface to QuickTime movies is described, making *Mathematica* an analysis tool for movies.

Chapter 9. Object-oriented Programming

After introducing an object-oriented programming (OOP) style for *Mathematica*—heavily used in later chapters—*Class* and *Inheritance* are discussed.

Chapter 10. Creating an Event-driven Mechanism

In this chapter, we build `Serializer`. This application enables *MathLink* template programs to send events to the kernel *asynchronously*. Using `Serializer` we can send events from *multiple MathLink* programs to one kernel. The event format and event sending mechanism of `Serializer` is described in detail since `Serializer` is a fundamental tool for later chapters.

Chapter 11. Creating a Window Object

Combining real-time graphics, the event-sending mechanism, and OOP, a window object is created. Using this synergy we can define the response to events through simple *Mathematica* functions. As an example of this approach, a free-hand drawing application is implemented using just a few lines of *Mathematica* code.

Chapter 12. Window Object Applications

In this chapter, we make two applications using window objects developed in Chapter 11. The first is *Sketch*, a simple application that allows one to draw points and lines in a window. The second is an interactive interface to the *Forest Fire* simulation of Section 7.3. The purpose of this chapter is to show how easy it is to customize window objects for special purposes.

Chapter 13. Writing an Interactive Graphics System

In this chapter we introduce *point*, *line*, and *curve* objects as window objects. Using the event-driven mechanism introduced in Chapter 11, these objects provide real-time interactive graphics that the current front end does not support. Two applications—interactive geometry and interactive curve fitting—are demonstrated. Coupling *Mathematica*'s power with interactive graphics makes it easy to create sophisticated graphics applications.

Chapter 14. Interactive Geometry

In this chapter, we expand the interactive graphics described in Chapter 13 to a full-scale *Interactive Geometry* package. This package enables the user to construct geometrical systems and manipulate geometrical objects by mouse interactively, which is similar to the commercial packages such as Cabri or SketchPad. Also, we describe how our OOPS is used to implement the *Interactive Geometry* package.

Chapter 15. Communication between *Mathematica* Sessions

This chapter shows how to link multiple Serializer sessions. Such a link enables us to send expressions between *Mathematica* sessions and assists cooperative work. For example, a user can copy and paste cell expressions to another session over the network, or exchange messages with other users. Hence Serializer becomes a communication tool between *Mathematica* sessions and is one powerful extension of this simple *MathLink* application.

Reading Guide

This book is designed for a wide audience—from the beginner who is new to *MathLink* programming to the expert programmer who has written sophisticated *MathLink* applications. The reader is expected to have some experience with *Mathematica* functional programming (see Section 2.2 of *The Mathematica Book*) and a working knowledge of the C language, but no complicated mathematical functions are used. Since different readers have varying interests and backgrounds, this section provides a guide to reading this book.

For the Novice Programmer

We suggest that you follow the sequence indicated in Figure P.1. After setting up the MLDK and a C compiler, using the information from Chapter 1, Chapter 2 introduces the concept of *MathLink* and explains some *MathLink* basics without C programming. Work through Chapters 3 and 4 to get experience compiling *MathLink* programs. Following that, read Chapter 6 and try modifying the code presented there. The debugging information in Chapter 5 will also be helpful.

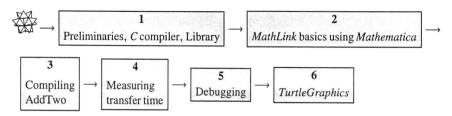

Figure P.1. Guide for the novice programmer.

For the Experienced Programmer

If you have had some experience with *MathLink* programming, follow the sequence indicated in Figure P.2. First read Chapters 2, 4, and 5. These should provide a deeper understanding about *MathLink* and template programming. Then try out one of the sample programs in Chapters 6, 7, or 8. Chapter 9 introduces a style of object-oriented programming which is then used in the "interactive graphics" applications of Chapters 10, 11, 12, 13, and 14.

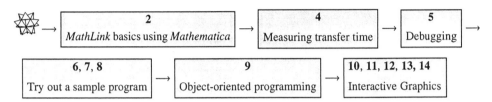

Figure P.2. Guide for the experienced programmer.

For the Expert Programmer

Experts might want to follow the sequence indicated in Figure P.3. Taken together, Chapters 9, 10, 11, 12, 13, and 14 form a large and unique *MathLink* application for interactive graphics from which even the expert programmer should be able to glean some useful ideas. A good exercise for the expert would be to write a new interactive graphics front end along the lines presented in these chapters. Finally, Chapter 15 hints at some interesting applications of notebook to notebook communication.

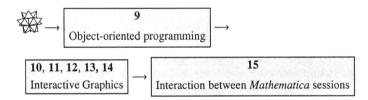

Figure P.3. Guide for the expert programmer.

Notational Conventions

In this book, various kind of programming are used—C programs, *Mathematica* functions, and *MathLink* templates. To avoid confusion we adopt the following notational conventions. Definitions and important concepts are displayed within a framed cell with a gray background, for example,

> ⚠ *MathLink* provides a general interface for external programs to communicate with *Mathematica*.

Compiled *MathLink* applications are denoted, for example, as follows: `Serializer`. *MathLink* projects are denoted using word capitalization, for example, as follows: **AddTwo**. To refer to a C function in the text, parentheses are added to the name of the function, for example, `main()`, and Courier font is used. A program listing of C functions appears as follows:

```
sendexpression()
{
    MLPutSymbol(eventlink,"hello");
    MLEndPacket(eventlink);
    MLFlush(eventlink);
}
```

Mathematica functions or symbols are denoted by appending square brackets to the function name, for example, **start[]**, and Courier Bold font is used. Program listings of *Mathematica* functions are displayed as follows:

```
Map[(#[move, {x_, y_}] :=
       (fitcurve[setdata, fitpoints[data]]; #[setposition, {x, y}])) &, data];
```

Some History

The first edition of this book was written in Japanese by CM and published by Iwanami book publishers in 1997 (ISBN 4-00-007707-4 C3355). This edition is based on the Japanese edition: CM did a rough translation into English and PA reworked this. During the collaboration, both the contents of the manuscript and the programs themselves were revised and improved by the authors. Also, PA was responsible for formatting the Notebooks and producing the electronic version of the manuscript.

Acknowledgments

It would have been impossible to complete this book without help from many people. The authors would like to thank everyone who helped make this book possible and give special thanks to the editor, Dr. Alan Harvey.

CM would like to acknowledge the following people and their contributions:

First of all, I want to thank my co-author PA. Without his help it would have been impossible to write the English edition of my book. Also, many programs in this book were improved by his suggestions. The depth of our collaboration is evidenced by the exchange of more than five hundred email messages.

Thanks to the staff at Wolfram Research who provided a number of valuable suggestions while I was there in 1996 as a visiting scholar and again in 1998. In particular, I want to thank the *MathLink* development team — Shawn Sheridan and Kevin Leuthold. Their assistance greatly improved the programs and helped refine a number of concepts. Also I would like to thank Chris Carlson, John Fultz, Theodore Gray, Todd Gayley, Mike Rasberry, and Tom Wickham-Jones for their suggestions and comments on my programs.

The MovieDigitizer and Interactive Graphics programs are based on material I presented at the 1995 and 1997 International *Mathematica* Symposiums (IMS). I would like to thank the IMS attendees and organizers who provided many helpful suggestions and warm encouragement.

Thanks to Prof. Richard Gaylord who tested some of my programs as an application of his book *Modeling Nature: Cellular Automata Simulations with Mathematica*. From his viewpoint as a *Mathematica* specialist and as the first user of my programs he gave me several valuable suggestions and I was very much encouraged that he liked my programs. Also I would like to thank him for his permission to use his "Life Game" and "Fire Animation" programs in this book.

I discussed the ideas of my programs with my colleague, Hiroshi Kimura, right from the beginning. Also he tested my ideas under the NEXTSTEP environment. I want to thank him very much.

Thanks also to the following people: Prof. Bruno Buchburger (RISC), Prof. Dana Scott (CMU), Dr. Mariusz Jankowski (University of Southern Maine), Dr. Bruno Autin (CERN), Dr. Yuji Itaya (Asahi University), Dr. Kiyoshi Yoda (Mitsubishi Research Lab), Junzo Sato (Tsukuba Business School), Koji Nakagawa (RISC), and Yuji Ohgi (Keio University). Of course, it is difficult to list all the people who help write a book so I apologize if I have omitted anyone.

PA would like to thank CM for the invitation to work on this exciting project. I first became aware of CM's programs at IMS'95 and I could see that he was doing some very interesting work. To get the widest possible audience for his ideas, it was important for the programs to be documented and fully explained and, as a long-time *Mathematica* user, I was keen for him to write a book on *MathLink*.

This book has taken quite some time to finalize, partially because our collaboration has been a long-distance one, with only three face-to-face meetings: Rovaniemi and Chicago in 1997, and then Perth in 1998. However, we have managed to communicate quite effectively by email, and exchanging *Mathematica* Notebooks made the editing process quite smooth. Using CVS (concurrent versions system) helped keep the difficult task of editing the manuscript under control and was vital with more than one author working on the manuscript at the same time.

I want to thank Shari Chappell for her editorial support and Kevin Leuthold for not only checking and improving the code but for general comments on the manuscript. Assistance from Lou D'Andria and Andre Kuzniarek on the use of the AuthorTools package (available from http://developer.wolfram.com/tools/AT/), used for the production of both the printed manuscript and the electronic book, was greatly appreciated.

Chikara Miyaji
Paul Abbott
May 2000

Foreword

A strong sign of *Mathematica*'s more and more widespread use is the growing demand for communication between *Mathematica* and the outside world. Reading data and outputting results is only the first step, easily accomplished with *Mathematica*'s input and output functions; it is the interaction that matters: reacting to a mouse click on a custom front end, or to the arrival of new data on a live data feed. The more success *Mathematica* enjoys, the more it becomes invisible to the end user. There is simply no time on the busy trading floor of a bank to enter formulas, or even to type on a keyboard. The sophisticated calculations *Mathematica* can do need to be triggered at the push of a button on the screen, and real-time data must be read concurrently. Consequently, even a simple application has at least three programs that need to talk to each other: a front end, the *Mathematica* kernel, and a back-end data source.

However, getting programs to talk to each other is a tedious task. Different operating systems, programming languages, and compilers all add to the practical problems of actually getting it to work. The establishment of a standard communication protocol, *MathLink*, is the first ingredient of the solution, one that Wolfram Research has taken early in the development of *Mathematica*. Not only is the protocol used internally to *Mathematica*, for the communication between the front end and the kernel, but it allows the kernel to communicate with data sources, Web servers, existing program libraries, or custom front ends.

The API, or—simply put—the .so or .dll and .h files and a development kit are the second part of the solution. Remarkably, such a kit has always been a standard part of every *Mathematica* version published. However, it hasn't been used as much as we had anticipated.

For a more widespread and easier use of the tools provided, a third component is necessary: tutorials, how-to's, nontrivial examples, all presented in a readable, yet accurate style. *MathLink: Network Programming with Mathematica* fills this requirement well. If all you need is a working program, and you do not care about the gory details of compiling and linking several components into one program, you will see step by step how to proceed. Chances are, however, you will get interested in learning *how* things work; in this case, you simply continue reading, and with the help of the many informative diagrams, the mysteries of asynchronous event-driven programs will rise above the mist of arcane communication protocols, operating-system shortcomings, and limitations of traditional programming languages. Interprocess communication will suddenly look easy.

The authors have succeeded in accommodating all major operating systems and still keeping most of their code portable. The key to portability is to keep the *MathLink* interface layer thin and do as much as possible within *Mathematica*. Even if it were not for portability, programming in *Mathematica* is much more fun and productive than is using a low-level language such as C, Java, or Visual Basic. My customers have always wondered how I could develop applications so quickly; please don't tell them my secret.

Roman E. Maeder
June 2000

Chapter 1 — Preliminaries

MathLink — the communication standard which allows higher-level communication between *Mathematica* and external programs — was introduced with the release of *Mathematica* Version 2.0. Prior to this, the kernel and front end communicated using the *MathTalk* protocol. With Version 2.0 *MathTalk* was replaced by *MathLink*, which is not only used for communication between the front end and kernel, but also enables general programs to communicate with the kernel. This chapter describes the:

[1] *MathLink* Developer's Kit (MLDK);

[2] *MathLink* library;

[3] C compilers for various platforms; and

[4] instructions for installation off the CD-ROM.

1.1. *MathLink* Developer's Kit — MLDK

The *MathLink* Developer's Kit (MLDK) is a collection of tools to build programs which use *MathLink* to communicate with the kernel. The applications in this book are written in C and are built using the MLDK which is bundled with *Mathematica*. The MLDK includes:

[1] the *MathLink* library;

[2] header file (`mathlink.h`);

[3] compile time libraries for various compilers;

[4] sample source programs;

[5] `mprep` (or SAmprep).

Currently, MLDK is available for Macintosh (PowerPC/68k), Microsoft Windows 95/98/NT4, SunOS (Sparc) 4.1.2 or higher, Solaris 2.4 or higher, Ultra Sparc 64bit optimized, HP-UX (HP-PA RISC) 10.00 or higher, AIX (PS/6000), Irix, Digital (DEC AXP 64 bit optimized), and Linux for PC. For the latest version of MLDK, visit www.wolfram.com/support/MathLink/. The CD-ROM accompanying this book includes the latest MLDK for Macintosh, Linux for PC, and Microsoft Windows.

1.2. *MathLink* Library

MathLink functionality is provided by the *MathLink* library, and all *MathLink* programs access this library as indicated in Figure 1.1. In many cases, the *MathLink* library is provided as a dynamic and shared library. Because of this, *MathLink* programs need to access the *MathLink* library at runtime. If *Mathematica* has been installed on a computer, the *MathLink* library has also been installed because the front end needs it. However, if the *MathLink* library does not exist on a particular computer, one needs to install the *MathLink* library manually. In such cases, one should refer to the target system's MLDK documentation.

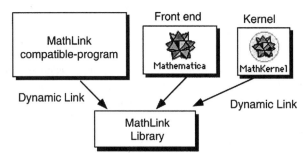

Figure 1.1. The *MathLink* library is accessed from various *MathLink* programs.

This book uses revision 7 of the *MathLink* library, which was current at the time this manuscript was completed (Nov 1999). The *MathLink* library is backward compatible, and supports all functionality of older revisions, that is, *MathLink* programs built using an older revision will work with any newer revision. Also, it is possible to build *MathLink* programs using the library of a newer revision which will be compatible with earlier revisions if only the older functionality is used. Such issues are discussed in the MLDK documentation.

User programs can access the *MathLink* library through functions such as `MLReady(stdlink)` and `MLTransferExpression(link1,link2)`. These functions are part of the *MathLink* API (Application Program Interface) shown in Figure 1.2. At the time of writing, more than 60 API functions are documented in *The Mathematica Book*.

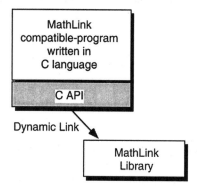

Figure 1.2. A *MathLink* program accesses the *MathLink* library through API functions.

1.3. Development Languages

One can write *MathLink* programs using *Mathematica* functions only. Alternatively, it is possible to write *MathLink* programs using various programming languages.

The *MathLink* API is defined using C functions. All programs in this book, and the example programs in the MLDK, are written in C. The `mprep` application in the MLDK reads a template file which defines the relationship between a *Mathematica* function and its corresponding C function by its format, and generates C source code which calls the *MathLink* C API.

The large number of readily available C compilers, and the fact that mprep presently only works with C, makes C the most suitable language in which to write *MathLink* programs. However, the C API and header file can be used with C++ compilers. Moreover, APIs for other languages can be built by wrapping the C API as indicated in Figure 1.3. A Java API and VisualBasic API for Microsoft Windows are provided in the MLDK. On *MathSource* (www.mathsource.com) one can find APIs for Perl, MatLab, Python, and Tc/Tkl. A Fortran API is presently under development. In late 1999, Wolfram Research released *J/Link*—a toolkit that integrates *Mathematica* and Java—available from www.wolfram.com/solutions/mathlink/jlink/.

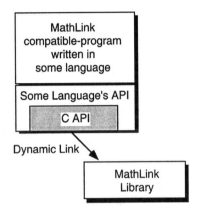

Figure 1.3. *MathLink* API for another language.

1.4. C Compiler for MLDK

To build a *MathLink* program written in C, one needs a C compiler. A wide range of C compilers exist and each has a different linking mechanism and library format. Although the *MathLink* library is dynamically linked at runtime, the compiler must resolve *MathLink* library API names at compile time. For this reason, a stub library is provided in the MLDK. The user can compile *MathLink* programs using the stub library. In the MLDK, stub libraries for popular C compilers are included. C compilers which can be used for *MathLink* development on typical platforms are listed below.

1.4.1. Macintosh

Presently, two compilers can be used to develop *MathLink* programs on the Macintosh:

    [1] MPW (Macintosh Programmer's Workshop) by Apple;

    [2] Metrowerks CodeWarrior C/C++.

The examples in this book are compiled using the CodeWarrior C compiler, but it is not difficult to compile them under the MPW C compiler.

1.4.2. Microsoft Windows

For Microsoft Windows, there are five compilers for developing *MathLink* programs:

[1] Microsoft Visual C++;

[2] Borland C/C++;

[3] Symantec C/C++;

[4] Watcom C/C++;

[5] Metrowerks CodeWarrior C/C++ for 95/98/NT.

1.4.3. Unix

For Unix systems, usually a C compiler is supplied by the manufacturer. Third-party C compilers and free compilers, such as the GNU C compiler (`gcc`), are also available.

1.5. MLDK under Unix

Let's examine the *MathLink* directories for Unix systems. The example below is for *Mathematica* 4.0 installed on a machine running Linux.

The *MathLink library*, header file, and `mprep` program are put in the `AddOns` directory when *Mathematica* is installed. The top *Mathematica* directory (`$TopDirectory`) consists of the following directories:

```
% ls
AddOns/          Documentation/   Registration/
Configuration/   Executables/     SystemFiles/
```

Changing directory into the *MathLink* directory for this system,

```
% cd AddOns/MathLink/DevelopersKits/Linux/
```

one sees that it includes three subdirectories.

```
% ls
CompilerAdditions/   Documentation/       MathLinkExamples/
```

In `CompilerAdditions` one finds the *MathLink* library, `libML.a`, the `mathlink.h` header file, and the `mprep` program.

```
% ls CompilerAdditions
libML.a      mathlink.h   mcc*         mprep*
```

Sample programs are in the `MathLinkExamples` directory.

```
% ls MathLinkExamples
Makefile     addtwo.tm    bitops.tm    factor.c     factor3.c    reverse.tm
addtwo.c     bitops.c     counter.tm   factor2.c    quotient.c   sumalist.tm
```

The `Documentation` directory contains system-specific documentation.

1.6. Installing *MathLink* on a Personal Computer

Commencing with *Mathematica* Version 3.0, the MLDK is included on the installer CD-ROM. To install the MLDK, choose Custom Install and select MathLink Developer Kit. Figure 1.4 shows the `MathInstaller` dialog on a Macintosh.

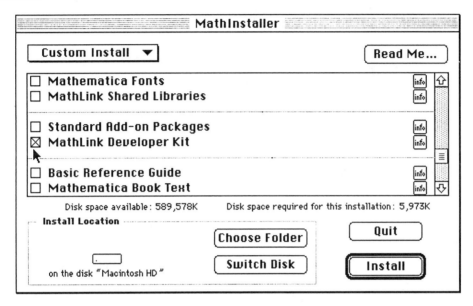

Figure 1.4. `MathInstaller` dialog on a Macintosh.

After finishing the installation, *MathLink* has been installed into the AddOns:MathLink:DevelopersKits folder as shown in   Figure 1.5. You then need to put the MathLinkLibraries and header files into the appropriate System and compiler directories. For example, if you are using the CodeWarrior C compiler on a PowerPC Macintosh, put MathLinkLibraries into the Extension folder, and move MathLink Compiler Additions into CodeWarrior's compiler folder. These procedures are described in the MLDK documentation.

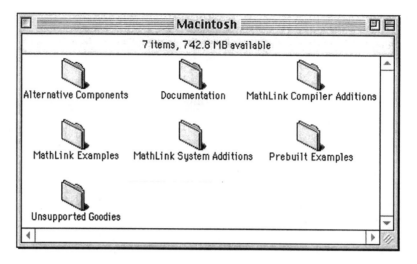

Figure 1.5. *MathLink* Developer's Kit for a Macintosh.

1.7. Installing the CD-ROM

The CD-ROM accompanying this book includes the items shown in Figure 1.6. Instructions for installing the required components are presented in the following subsections.

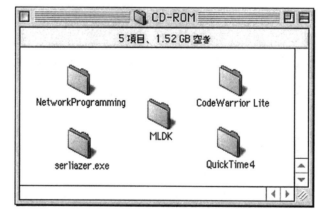

Figure 1.6. Contents of the CD-ROM.

1.7.1. NetworkProgramming

The NetworkProgramming directory contains the packages used in the following chapters and also the online documentation. Put this directory into *Mathematica*'s AddOns/Applications directory and then choose **Rebuild Help Index** from the **Help** menu. You can then search or browse the online documentation of this book as shown in Figure 1.7.

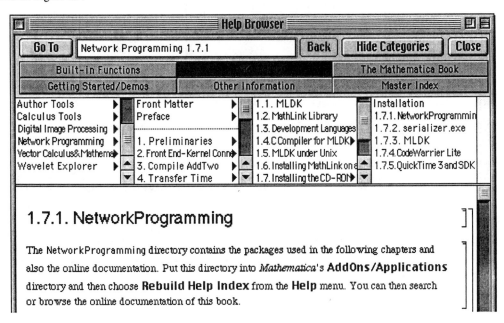

Figure 1.7. Browsing the online documentation of this book.

1.7.2. serializer.exe

Macintosh, Linux, and Microsoft Windows versions of the executable program serializer.exe are located in appropriately named subfolders of the **serializer.exe** folder on the CD-ROM. Move serializer.exe to the directory where the front end and kernel are located as shown in Figure 1.8. This directory can be easily found by evaluating **$HomeDirectory**.

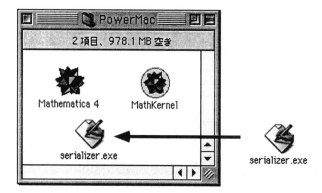

Figure 1.8. Move `serializer.exe` to `$HomeDirectory`.

Using the **Add** dialog under the **Kernel Configuration Options...** menu, set the Kernel name field to Serializer and set Kernel Program to serializer.exe. as shown in Figure 1.9.

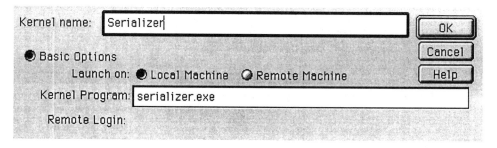

Figure 1.9. Setting Kernel name using the **Kernel Configuration Options...** menu.

1.7.3. MLDK

The CD-ROM includes the latest version of the MLDK for Macintosh, Windows, and Linux. If you do not have the latest version of the MLDK, follow the installation instructions on the CD-ROM.

1.7.4. Installing CodeWarrior Lite

The CD-ROM accompanying this book includes a copy of Metrowerks CodeWarrior Lite for MacOS and Windows95/NT4. CodeWarrior Lite can compile all source codes included on the CD-ROM so, if you do not already have a C compiler, you can try out the code here using this compiler. Note that there are some limitations on this compiler:

• users can modify source code but cannot create any new files or projects;

• only 68k projects can be compiled under MacOS;

• the Windows version only supports Windows95/NT4.

To install CodeWarrior Lite under MacOS (refer to Figure 1.10):

[1] First, double-click on CW LITE IDE Installer to install CodeWarrior Lite IDE;

[2] Then double-click on CW LITE C_CPP Installer to install the CodeWarrior Lite C compiler;

[3] Move the MathLink Compiler Additions folder (part of MLDK) to CodeWarrior Lite's MacOS Support folder;

[4] Create a Source folder in Metrowerks Standard Library:MSL C:MSL Mac and move console.stubs.c file to this folder.

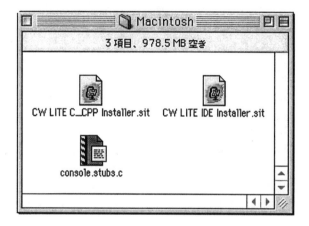

Figure 1.10. CodeWarrior Lite installer directory for a Macintosh.

To install CodeWarrior Lite under Windows:

[1] First, launch CW_Lite_Tools.exe to install CodeWarrior Lite IDE;

[2] Then launch CW_Lite_C.exe to install the CodeWarrior Lite C compiler;

[3] Move the include directory in MathLink Compiler Additions to CodeWarrior Lite's Win32-x86 Support/Headers directory;

[4] Move the lib directory in MathLink Compiler Additions to CodeWarrior Lite's Win32-x86 Support/Libraries directory.

1.7.5. Installing QuickTime 4 and SDK

The CD-ROM accompanying this book includes Apple's QuickTime 4 and its SDK (Software Developer's Kit) for both MacOS and Windows95/98/NT. The programs in Chapter 8 use the QuickTime 4 library. There are two parts to the installation process—installing the runtime libraries and installing the compile-time libraries and headers in the SDK.

For Macintosh users, QuickTime 4 is pre-installed under MacOS 9 or later. You only need to install QuickTime 4 if you are running an older version of the MacOS. If you are using a C compiler you do not need to install Quick-Time as it is pre-installed.

Here are the installation instructions for QuickTime 4 and its SDK for Windows95/NT:

[1] First, launch `nph-qt4reg.pl` to install QuickTime 4.0 on your system;

[2] Then unpack the `QuickTime_4.1.2_SDK_Windows.zip` archive.

[3] Move the CIncludes and ComponentIncludes subdirectories to CodeWarrior Lite's Win32-x86 Support/Headers directory;

[4] Move the Libraries subdirectory of qtwsdk to CodeWarrior Lite's Win32-x86 Support/Libraries directory.

At this time there is no QuickTime for Linux.

1.8. Related Reading

For general aspects of *Mathematica* programming, the following three books are very helpful.

[1] Maeder, R., *Programming in Mathematica*, Third Edition, Addison-Wesley, Reading, MA, 1997. URL: http://store.wolfram.com/view/ISBN020185449X.

[2] Gaylord, R.J., Kamin, S.N. and Wellin, P.R., *An Introduction to Programming with Mathematica*, Second Edition, Springer/TELOS, New York, 1996. URL: http://store.wolfram.com/view/ISBN0387944346.

[3] Wagner, D.B, *Power Programming with Mathematica: The Kernel*, McGraw-Hill, New York, 1996. URL: http://store.wolfram.com/view/ISBN007912237X.

The Notebook front end is described in:

[4] Glynn, J. and Gray, T., *The Beginner's Guide to Mathematica Version 3*, Cambridge University Press, New York, 1997. URL: http://store.wolfram.com/view/ISBN0521622026 or http://www.mathware.com/Books/Mathematica_Books/Mathematica_Guide/mathematica_guide.html.

For C programming and programming in general, have a look at the following books.

[5] Kernigham, B.W. and Plauger, P.J., *Software Tools*, Addison-Wesley, Reading, MA, 1976.

[6] Kernigham, B.W. and Plauger, P.J., *Software Tools in Pascal*, Addison-Wesley, Reading, MA, 1976.

[7] Abelson, H. and Sussman, G.J., *Structure and Interpretation of Computer Programs*, Second Edition, MIT Press, Cambridge, MA, 1996.

1.9. Summary

This chapter introduces the *MathLink* Developer's Kit, *MathLink* library, and C compilers on various platforms, and gives the installation instructions for the CD-ROM. Source code and applications for Macintosh, Microsoft Windows, and Linux are included on the CD-ROM. In the following chapters, to avoid being verbose, descriptions usually focus on the Macintosh version of each program. The Microsoft Windows and Linux versions work in an identical fashion.

Chapter 2 — Connecting the Front End and the Kernel

This chapter explains *MathLink* basics using various front end and kernel connection methods, and also presents some simple background on networks. Readers who are unfamiliar with C should be able to easily understand this chapter because it only uses *Mathematica* functions.

Chapter highlights include:

[1] *MathLink* basics, demonstrated using a range of Notebook front end and kernel connections;

[2] how to write simple *Mathematica* programs to exchange expressions using nine basic *MathLink* functions: **LinkConnect, LinkCreate, LinkReadyQ, LinkRead, LinkReadHeld, LinkWrite, LinkWriteHeld, LinkActivate**, and **LinkClose**;

[3] a packet monitor, which monitors packet transfer between the front end and kernel.

2.1. What Is *MathLink*?

Computers on a network can communicate with other computers as indicated in Figure 2.1. For example, your home computer can get information from another computer using the Internet. The basics of such information exchange consists of communication between programs.

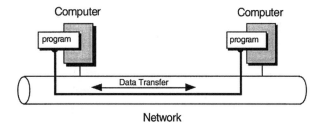

Figure 2.1. Programs exchanging information on a network.

MathLink uses such a program to program connection to transfer *Mathematica* expressions. The basic idea of *MathLink* is described as (see Section 2.12.1 of *The Mathematica Book*):

> ⚠ *MathLink* is a mechanism for exchanging *Mathematica* expressions between programs.

To communicate with each other, programs must know how to identify other programs and computers on the network. Also there must be rules for exchanging information. These rules are known as a *protocol*. For example, the Internet uses the TCP/IP protocol and Macintosh computers use the AppleTalk protocol to exchange information. *MathLink* is built upon these network protocols.

> ⚠ | *Protocol*: The rule or procedures governing the exchange of information on a network.
> *TCP/IP*: Protocol used on the Internet.
> *AppleTalk*: Macintosh communication protocol.

You can write programs that exchange expressions with the kernel using the mechanisms provided by *MathLink*. Such a program is *MathLink*-compatible; in this book, we shall call it a *MathLink program*.

MathLink programs create a bidirectional message channel to exchange expressions. This channel is called a *link* or *MathLink connection*.

More information on *MathLink* is available in *The Mathematica Book*, Sections 1.11.10 and 2.12, from the **Help** menu by entering *MathLink* into the **Master Index...**, and on the web (www.mathsource.com/Content/-Enhancements/MathLink). For Macintosh and Microsoft Windows, sample projects demonstrating how to use *MathLink* with several popular compilers are documented under **AddOns...** in the **Help** menu (see the Building listing).

2.2. Front End and the Kernel

Mathematica consists of two programs. One is the *front end*, which handles user input, and the other is the *kernel*, which does the computation (see Figure 2.2). These two programs communicate using *MathLink*. The most frequently used *MathLink* connection is this connection between the front end and the kernel. Every time you evaluate an expression it is sent to the kernel and returned to the front end through a *MathLink* connection.

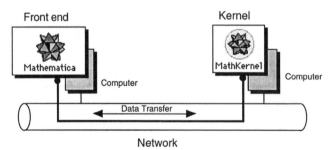

Figure 2.2. Front end and kernel transferring data on a network.

These two programs—the front end and kernel—do not need to be running on the same machine. Only a network connection between them is needed. If the kernel and front end are running on the same machine the kernel is a *local kernel*. If the kernel is running somewhere else on the network it is a *remote kernel*.

If you run the front end on a personal computer and the kernel on a workstation, you can enjoy the PC's friendly interface along with the computational performance of a more powerful workstation. The front end, itself a *MathLink* program—in fact, one of the most complicated *MathLink* programs ever written—transfers expressions to the kernel via a *MathLink* connection using the TCP/IP transfer protocol as shown in Figure 2.3.

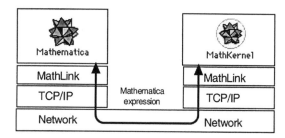

Figure 2.3. A *MathLink* connection between a front end and a kernel.

The basic connection procedure is identical on various computers. Machine-specific information about setting up a remote kernel is available: see Getting Started (Microsoft Windows), Getting Started (X/Unix), or Getting Started (Macintosh) in the Help Browser.

2.3. LinkMode: Listen and Connect

In this section, we examine the LinkMode option and its Listen and Connect arguments by demonstrating how to set up a connection between a front end and a remote (Unix) kernel.

Choose **Kernel Configuration Options...** from the **Kernel** menu. The dialog box shown in Figure 2.4 will appear. Click on the Add button and set Basic Options to Remote Machine and set the Kernel name: field to Remote. This name will then appear in **Start Kernel** submenu of **Kernel** menu.

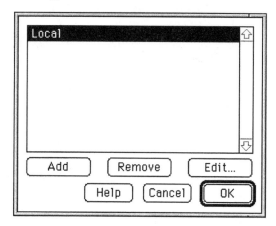

Figure 2.4. The **Kernel Configuration Options...** dialog box.

Now choose Advanced Options in the dialog. This field defines the *MathLink* connection settings for the front end. By default, the setting for Arguments to MLOpen is

```
-LinkMode Listen -LinkProtocol TCP -LinkOptions MLDontInteract
```

A second field in the dialog contains the command and options used when invoking the kernel. Under Microsoft Windows, the `Shell command to launch kernel` field is, by default, set to

```
winrsh -m -q -h -l "username" 'math -mathlink -LinkMode Connect -LinkName
"`linkname`"'
```

Similarly, on a Macintosh, the default settings for the `Communications Toolbox Login` are

```
^:username\r^:password\r^>"math" -mathlink -LinkMode Connect -LinkName
"`$LinkName`"
```

Note that the `Advanced Options` field contains the `LinkMode` option with argument `Listen`, and both `Shell command to launch kernel` and the `Communications Toolbox Login` contain the `LinkMode` option with argument `Connect`. The other options — `LinkProtocol` and `LinkName` — are discussed in the following sections.

Readers with access to a remote Unix kernel need to follow the system-specific procedures for connecting Macintosh and Windows front ends to remote kernels. After doing this, connecting a remote kernel (e.g., one running on the author's Unix machine with IP address 130.158.113.96) to a front end (running on the author's Macintosh with IP address 130.158.113.98) is simply a matter of choosing the **Remote** kernel item from the **Start Kernel** menu. This action automatically launches a kernel on the remote (Unix) host, using a command of the following form:

```
math -mathlink -LinkMode Connect -LinkName "2062@130.158.113.98"
```

The `LinkName` argument has been replaced with the string 2062@130.158.113.98, which indicates the port number 2062 (see Section 2.4) and the IP address of the front end process.

A *MathLink* connection is a peer to peer connection. This means that there is no distinction between the connected programs: both can send and receive packets.

⚠ | *Peer to peer connection*: A connection type in which both ends have an equal role and functionality.

However, at connection time, two different sides exist: one is the connecting side and the other is the listening side. We distinguish between the connecting side and listening side using the `Connect` and `Listen` arguments to the `LinkMode` option.

⚠ | Listening side: Argument to `LinkMode` is `Listen`. `-LinkCreate` is equivalent to `-LinkMode Listen`
Connecting side: Argument to `LinkMode` is `Connect`. This side will connect to the listening side.

To establish a *MathLink* connection, one program opens a link using `Listen`, and the other program connects to it using `Connect`. From the previous discussion we see that the front end uses `Listen` and the kernel uses `Connect`. The steps in this process are as follows:

[1] The front end opens a link using `-LinkMode Listen -LinkProtocol TCP -LinkOptions MLDontInteract`, as shown in Figure 2.5. The `LinkProtocol` option is `TCP` because Unix uses TCP/IP as its default protocol.

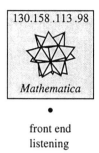

front end
listening

Figure 2.5. The front end starts listening.

[2] The front end sends commands to login on the remote machine, and then launches the remote kernel using `Connect` to connect to the front end (see Figure 2.6):

```
math -mathlink -LinkMode Connect -LinkName "2062@130.158.113.98"
```

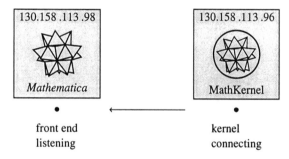

front end   kernel
listening   connecting

Figure 2.6. The kernel connects to the front end.

In this example, the connecting side is the kernel, and the listening side is the front end. Once the connection is established, the front end and kernel can exchange expressions with each other.

2.4. Port Number

In Section 2.3, the argument to the `LinkName` option was `2062@130.158.113.98` where `130.158.113.98` is the IP address, and `2062` is the *port number* (see Section 2.12.6 of *The Mathematica Book*). The port number is required because the host name is insufficient to fully identify the connection since several programs can be running on a single machine. Under the TCP/IP protocol, port numbers greater than 1024 are available to users.

⚠   *Port Number*: A number that uniquely identifies a connection at an IP address. For a TCP/IP connection, both a host name or IP Address and a port number are required.

In the following example, we use `MacTCPWatcher` (a Macintosh shareware application available from http://hyperarchive.lcs.mit.edu/) to examine the connection process between a front end and a remote kernel. Unfortunately, the authors are not aware of a comparable shareware Windows application.

[1] Launch the front end and select **Remote** from the **Start Kernel** submenu of the **Kernel** menu. This action causes a `telnet` window to appear. In `MacTCPWatcher` the **Open Transport Connections** window (Figure 2.7) shows the port numbers and programs currently running. The first line shows that a `telnet` connection is established on port 2063 to the remote host 130.158.113.96. Port 2062 was opened by the front end and is listening for a connection.

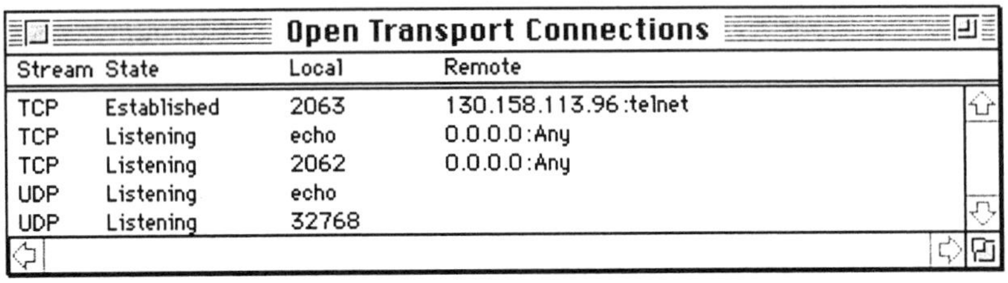

Stream	State	Local	Remote
TCP	Established	2063	130.158.113.96 :telnet
TCP	Listening	echo	0.0.0.0 :Any
TCP	Listening	2062	0.0.0.0 :Any
UDP	Listening	echo	
UDP	Listening	32768	

Figure 2.7. The front end is listening on port 2062. `telnet` is running on port 2063.

[2] After the remote kernel has been launched (with the `LinkName` argument set to `"2062@130.158.113.98"`), the **Open Transport Connections** window (Figure 2.8) shows that three connections are established: `telnet` is running on port 2063 and ports 2062 and 2064 are used by the *MathLink* connection. Port 2062 was opened by the `LinkName` argument. Port 2064 is used internally. In general, *MathLink* connections use two ports for their communication.

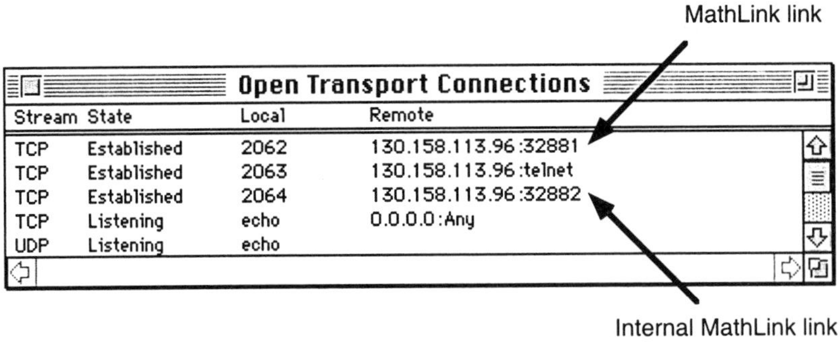

MathLink link

Stream	State	Local	Remote
TCP	Established	2062	130.158.113.96 :32881
TCP	Established	2063	130.158.113.96 :telnet
TCP	Established	2064	130.158.113.96 :32882
TCP	Listening	echo	0.0.0.0 :Any
UDP	Listening	echo	

Internal MathLink link

Figure 2.8. The connection is established.

By default, the command to invoke the kernel from the front end includes the option `-LinkName` `` `linkname` `` (`` `$LinkName` `` under the `MacOS`). The front end replaces the argument to `-LinkName` by the actual port number and its IP address. In this example, it was replaced by `2062@130.158.113.98`.

2.5. Using *Mathematica* Functions

Under the **Kernel Configuration Options...** menu, select **Remote** and hit the **Edit...** button. In succession, click on the `Basic Options`, `Remote Machine`, and `Advanced Options` radio buttons. Delete `-LinkOptions MLDontInteract` from `Arguments to MLOpen:` and all the lines for invoking the remote kernel. The `Advanced Options` settings should now look like Figure 2.9.

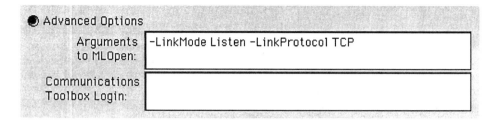

Figure 2.9. `Advanced Options` settings.

Note that, unlike Unix, `TCP` is *not* the default protocol on Macintosh or Windows machines so you need to include the `-LinkProtocol TCP` option as an argument to `MLOpen`.

Click **OK** twice and then choose **Remote** from the **Start Kernel** menu. A front end connection dialog like Figure 2.10 will appear:

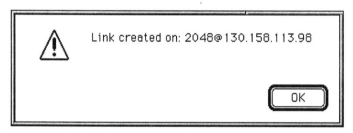

Figure 2.10. Front end connection dialog.

This dialog shows that the front end opened port 2048 and is awaiting a connection. The front end connection dialog did not appear in Section 2.3 because of the `MLDontInteract` option.

Because there is no `Toolbox Login:` argument, no `telnet` window appears (nor `winrsh` under Microsoft Windows). This means that the user must run the kernel manually. The argument to the `-LinkName` option must be the same as that displayed in the front end connection dialog (see Figure 2.10). On a Unix workstation we invoke the command below:

```
% math -mathlink -LinkMode Connect -LinkName "2048@130.158.113.98"
```

The resulting *MathLink* connection is equivalent to the automatic connection established in Section 2.3. We did not need to include the `-LinkProtocol TCP` option because this is the default protocol under Unix.

Note that it is also possible to establish the *MathLink* connection just using *Mathematica* functions:

```
% math
Mathematica 3.0 for Digital Unix
Copyright 1988-97 Wolfram Research, Inc.
 -- Terminal graphics initialized --

In[1]:=$ParentLink=LinkConnect["2048@130.158.113.98"]
```

Here we use **LinkConnect** to connect to the *MathLink* link and set this to be **$ParentLink**. After establishing the connection, the kernel's input and output go through this link and the front end can exchange expressions with the kernel.

> ⚠ **LinkConnect**[*name*] connects to *MathLink* link whose name is *name*.

> ⚠ **$ParentLink** is the *MathLink* **LinkObject** currently used for input and output by the kernel in a particular session.

It is possible to exchange the role of Listen and Connect. The only difference is which side is listening and which side is connecting. The output from the following command shows that the kernel is waiting on the port 32895.

```
% math -mathlink -LinkMode Listen
Link created on: 32895@130.158.113.96
```

This is analogous to the dialog that the front end displayed (c.f. Figure 2.10). Modifying the Arguments to MLOpen: (c.f. Figure 2.9) as shown in Figure 2.11 and choosing **Remote** from the **Start Kernel** menu again establishes the connection.

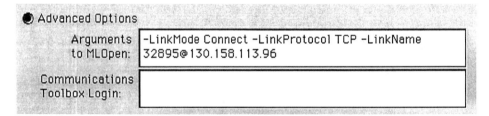

Figure 2.11. Connecting the front end to a kernel running on 32895@130.158.113.96.

It is also possible to switch the role of Create and Connect. After starting up a kernel (see Figure 2.12), **LinkCreate[]** opens a link and waits:

```
% math
Mathematica 3.0 for Digital Unix
Copyright 1988-97 Wolfram Research, Inc.
 -- Terminal graphics initialized --

In[1]:=$ParentLink=LinkCreate["32895"]
```

Figure 2.12. Setting a **$ParentLink** using **LinkCreate**.

> ⚠ **LinkCreate**[*name*] opens a link called *name*, which other programs can connect to.

Nothing is returned on the kernel side because the output has been switched to the new link. After setting the Arguments to MLOpen: as in Figure 2.11, and establishing the connection (by choosing **Remote** from the **Start Kernel** menu), you can enter expressions from the front end. To return to the kernel session, you need to unset **$ParentLink** (using **$ParentLink**=.) from the front end.

2.6. Kernel to Kernel Connection

It is possible to establish a kernel to kernel connection using **LinkCreate[]** and **LinkConnect[]** functions in a similar fashion to the examples in Section 2.5. First, we add new kernel entry, Kernel2, using the **Add** dialog under the **Kernel Configuration Options...** menu. Under Microsoft Windows or Unix, set the Kernel name field to Kernel2. Unlike other operating systems, the MacOS does not permit programs to be run twice at the same time. Since the default settings for Kernel2 are identical to those of the Local kernel, in the Finder duplicate the Math-Kernel application and rename it to Kernel2. Then use the **Kernel Configuration Options...** menu to set both the Kernel name and Kernel Program fields to Kernel2 as shown in Figure 2.13. Checking the Append name to In/Out prompts check-box causes the kernel name to be displayed in the cell label.

Figure 2.13. Kernel2 configuration using **Kernel Configuration Options...** for Macintosh.

Now, evaluate the following input cell.

```
(Kernel2) In[1]:=  whoami = "Kernel2"

(Kernel2) Out[1]=  Kernel2
```

In these examples, to make it clear which kernel will be evaluating specific input cells, we have introduced a new style—called **Kernel2**—which displays input expressions with a gray background. Also, the Evaluator for this cell style is set to be Kernel2 as can be seen from the CellLabel. Alternatively, the Evaluator option for any cell can be seen (and controlled) by selecting the cell, using the **Option Inspector...** under the **Format** menu, entering Evaluator, and hitting return.

The following cell's evaluator is the default kernel, Local. We see that **whoami** doesn't return Kernel2.

```
(Local) In[1]:=  whoami

(Local) Out[1]=  whoami
```

We assign the value of **whoami** to be **"Local"**.

(Local) In[2]:= **whoami = "Local"**

(Local) Out[2]= Local

Now, create a link on Kernel2, and name it **k2**,

(Kernel2) In[2]:= **k2 = LinkCreate["5000"]**

(Kernel2) Out[2]= LinkObject[5000, 2, 2]

and connect to this link from Local using **LinkConnect**, and name the link **loc**.

(Local) In[3]:= **loc = LinkConnect["5000"]**

(Local) Out[3]= LinkObject[5000, 2, 2]

In this example, we have used the link name **"5000"**. Note that, if your default **LinkProtocol** is **TCP**, **"5000"** is interpreted as a port number, otherwise it is interpreted as a link name for the default **LinkProtocol**. Note that the MacOS has **PPC** as its default **LinkProtocol** and Microsoft Windows uses **FileMap**.

Both **k2** and **loc** returned a LinkObject but, at this stage, both sides are just negotiating which partner to communicate with. After this step, both links must be activated to enable communication. **LinkActivate[]** activates a LinkObject. **LinkActivate[]** needs the other side to be activated, so initially **LinkActivate[]** will block until the other side activates it.

⚠   **LinkActivate**[*link*] activates *link* for reading and writing.

On Kernel2, evaluation of the following expression will be blocked until the other end activates it.

(Kernel2) In[3]:= **LinkActivate[k2]**

(Kernel2) Out[3]= LinkObject[5000, 2, 2]

Evaluation of the following input expression on Local causes input expressions on *both* Kernel2 and Local to get return values.

(Local) In[4]:= **LinkActivate[loc]**

(Local) Out[4]= LinkObject[5000, 2, 2]

Now both links are activated and it is possible to send expressions between the kernels. First, we send an expression from Kernel2.

(Kernel2) In[4]:= **LinkWrite[k2, Hold[1 + 2]]**

This sends the expression **Hold[1+2]** from Kernel2 to Local using **LinkWrite[]** as shown in Figure 2.14. Wrapping the expression with **Hold[]** prevents expression evaluation on the sender's kernel (Kernel2).

⚠   **LinkWrite**[*link, expr*] sends *expr* on *link*.

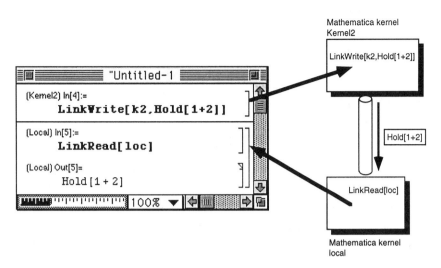

Figure 2.14. *MathLink* connection between kernels Local and Kernel2.

On Local, we evaluate the following expression and Hold[1+2] is returned:

(Local) In[5]:= **LinkRead[loc]**

(Local) Out[5]= Hold[1 + 2]

⚠ **LinkRead[***link***]** reads an expression from *link*.

Notice that **LinkWrite[]** just sends an expression on a link and no value is returned to Kernel2. Basically, *MathLink* can only send expressions and read expressions from links. If there is no expression on a link, **Link-Read[]** will wait until an expression arrives. To avoid this blocking, **LinkReadyQ[]** checks for expressions on links. It returns **True** if there is an expression on the link, or **False** if there is no expression on the link.

⚠ **LinkReadyQ[***link***]** returns **True** if an expression is on the *link*, otherwise it returns **False**.

Evaluate this expression on Local.

(Local) In[6]:= **LinkReadyQ[loc]**

(Local) Out[6]= False

False is returned because no expression was sent from Kernel2. Now send an expression from Kernel2.

(Kernel2) In[5]:= **LinkWrite[k2, Hold[1 - 3]]**

LinkReadyQ[] now returns **True**:

(Local) In[7]:= **LinkReadyQ[loc]**

(Local) Out[7]= True

and `Local` can read an expression:

(Local) In[8]:= **LinkRead[loc]**

(Local) Out[8]= Hold[1 - 3]

2.7. Exchanging Expressions between Kernels

Evaluating the following **While[]** loop on `Kernel2`,

(Kernel2) In[6]:= **While[True, If[LinkReadyQ[k2], LinkWrite[k2, LinkRead[k2]]]]**

reads expressions from link **k2**, evaluates them, and returns the result to **k2**. Expressions read by **LinkRead** are evaluated. Now send an expression from `Local`.

(Local) In[9]:= **LinkWrite[loc, Unevaluated[100!]]**

When sending an expression using **LinkWrite**, we wrap it with **Unevaluated[]** to prevent evaluation before transmission. Upon reading the link **loc**, we receive 100!, which is immediately evaluated.

(Local) In[10]:= **LinkRead[loc]**

(Local) Out[10]= 93326215443944152681699238856266700490715968264381621468592963895217599993229915608941463976156518286253679208272237582511852109168640000000000000000000000000

How do we exit this loop? Sending **Break[]** terminates the **While[]** loop.

(Local) In[11]:= **LinkWrite[loc, Unevaluated[Break[]]]**

This **While[]** loop is similar to the kernel's normal evaluation loop. The *Mathematica* Notebook front end sends expressions wrapped with **EnterExpressionPacket[]** or **EnterTextPacket[]** to the kernel. The link onto which the kernel reads and writes expressions is assigned to **$ParentLink**. For example, here is the **$ParentLink** of `Kernel2`.

(Kernel2) In[7]:= **$ParentLink**

(Kernel2) Out[7]= LinkObject[Mathematica 41, 1, 1]

After recording the current **$ParentLink** as **oldParentLink**,

(Kernel2) In[8]:= **oldParentLink = $ParentLink;**

we set **$ParentLink** to a newly created link.

(Kernel2) In[9]:= **$ParentLink = LinkOpen["6000", LinkMode → Listen]**

(Kernel2) test done.

This cell does not immediately return a value because the current **$ParentLink** has been altered. We connect a new link to `Kernel2`.

(Local) In[12]:= **kernel = LinkOpen["6000", LinkMode → Connect]**

(Local) Out[12]= LinkObject[6000, 3, 3]

To see what expressions are sent from `Kernel2` we read these expressions using **LinkRead[]** and then **Print** them out.

(Local) In[13]:= **While[LinkReadyQ[kernel], Print[LinkRead[kernel]]]**

ResumePacket[LinkObject[Mathematica 41, 1, 1]]

`ResumePacket[]` indicates that the front end and kernel session (`Kernel2`) have restarted on the newly assigned **$ParentLink**. We now run this command again:

(Local) In[14]:= **While[LinkReadyQ[kernel], Print[LinkRead[kernel]]]**

OutputNamePacket[Out[9]=]

ReturnExpressionPacket[
  BoxData[RowBox[{LinkObject, [, RowBox[{"6000", ,, 3, ,, 3}],]}], StandardForm]]

InputNamePacket[In[10]:=]

`OutputNamePacket[]` is the prompt for the return value. `ReturnExpressionPacket[]` is the returned expression for the previous input. This is the return value of the assignment (Kernel 2) In[9]:=. `InputNamePacket[]` is the prompt for the next input on the front end.

Now we send the expression **"1+2"**.

(Local) In[15]:= **LinkWrite[kernel, EnterTextPacket["1+2"]]**

(Local) In[16]:= **While[LinkReadyQ[kernel], Print[LinkRead[kernel]]]**

OutputNamePacket[Out[10]=]

ReturnExpressionPacket[BoxData[3, StandardForm]]

InputNamePacket[In[11]:=]

As in the previous example, `Kernel2` returns `OutputNamePacket[]`, followed by the return value 3, represented as `BoxData[3, StandardForm]` in the `ReturnExpressionPacket[]` as indicated in Figure 2.15.

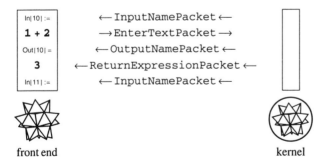

front end   kernel

Figure 2.15. Packet exchange for the evaluation of **1+2**.

Incidentally, the input line (see (Kernel 2) In[9]:= above) is still executing because no return expression has been sent to that link. To terminate this cell's evaluation, we send **OutputNamePacket[]**, **ReturnExpression-Packet[]**, and **InputNamePacket[]** to that link.

```
(Local) In[17]:=  LinkWrite[kernel, EnterTextPacket[
                    "LinkWrite[oldParentLink,OutputNamePacket[\"test\"]]"]];
                  LinkWrite[kernel, EnterTextPacket["LinkWrite[oldParentLink,
                    ReturnExpressionPacket[BoxData[\"done.\",StandardForm]]]"]];
                  LinkWrite[kernel, EnterTextPacket[
                    "LinkWrite[oldParentLink,InputNamePacket[\"test\"]]"]];
```

Now the execution of (Kernel 2) In[9]:= terminates and it gets the return value done.

Print[] sends expressions in a different way because the strings that the front end prints are a side-effect of **Print[]**, not its return value.

```
(Local) In[20]:=  Do[Print[hello], {3}]

                  hello

                  hello

                  hello
```

Here are the expressions underlying the **Print[]** command.

```
(Local) In[21]:=  LinkWrite[kernel, EnterTextPacket["Do[Print[hello],{2}]"]]
```

```
(Local) In[22]:=  While[LinkReadyQ[kernel], Print[LinkRead[kernel]]]

                  InputNamePacket[In[12]:= ]

                  InputNamePacket[In[13]:= ]

                  InputNamePacket[In[14]:= ]

                  ExpressionPacket[BoxData[hello, StandardForm]]

                  ExpressionPacket[BoxData[hello, StandardForm]]

                  InputNamePacket[In[15]:= ]
```

The packet ExpressionPacket[], sent by Kernel2, forces the front end to print.

2.8. A Packet Monitor

To see the packets exchanged between the front end and kernel, there is another tool available to us. After closing the links opened in the previous sections (by quitting the **Local** and **Kernel2** kernels under the **Quit Kernel** menu), choose **Serializer** in the **Start Kernel** menu. (This assumes that you have installed serializer.exe following the instructions in Section 1.7.2.)

```
(Serializer) In[1]:=  1 + 1

(Serializer) Out[1]=  2
```

If you look at the list of programs currently executing you will find that both serializer.exe and MathKernel are running (serializer.exe also launches MathKernel). Next, evaluate the following expression to start a *packet monitor*.

(Serializer) In[2]:=   **PacketMonitor[]**

      < -k : FrontEnd`SetOptions[
        FrontEndObject[LinkObject[serializer.exe, 1, 1]] Rule[EvaluatorNames,
          List[Rule[Local, List[Rule[AppendNameToCellLabel, True]]], Rule[Serializer,
            List[Rule[AppendNameToCellLabel, True], Rule[Executable, serializer.exe]]],
          Rule[Kernel2, List[Rule[AppendNameToCellLabel, True],
            Rule[Executable, MathKernel2], Rule[MLOpenArguments,
              -LinkMode Launch -LinkName ' MathKernel2' - mathlink]]]]]]

      < -k : OutputNamePacket[Out[2]=]

(Serializer) Out[2]=   1

      < -k : ReturnExpressionPacket[BoxData[1, StandardForm]]

Now all evaluation packets exchanged between the front end and kernel are displayed. For example, let us follow the evaluation of **1+1**:

(Serializer) In[3]:=   **1 + 1**

      < -k : InputNamePacket[In[3] :=]

      f0 -> : EnterExpressionPacket[
        MakeExpression[BoxData[RowBox[List[1, +, 1]]], StandardForm]]

      < -k : OutputNamePacket[Out[3]=]

(Serializer) Out[3]=   2

      < -k : ReturnExpressionPacket[BoxData[2, StandardForm]]

"<-k: " indicates that the kernel sends the packet and "f0->: " indicates that the front end sends the packet. 'lere is the sequence of the packets:

    [1] the kernel sends InputNamePacket[In[3] :=], which tells the front end to use In[3]:= for the next input cell;

    [2] the front end sends EnterExpressionPacket[...] to the kernel to evaluate the expression **1+1**;

    [3] the kernel sends OutputNamePacket[Out[3]=], which tells the front end to use Out[3]:= for the output ceil;

    [4] the return value 2 is sent from the kernel using ReturnExpressionPacket[...].

Next, we look at the ExpressionPacket packets generated by a **Print** command:

(Serializer) In[3]:=   **Do[Print[boo], {2}]**

      < -k : InputNamePacket[In[3] :=]

      f0 -> : EnterExpressionPacket[MakeExpression[
        BoxData[RowBox[List[Do, [, RowBox[List[RowBox[List[Print, [, boo,]]],
          ,, RowBox[List[{, 2, }]]]],]]]], StandardForm]]

      boo

      < -k : ExpressionPacket[BoxData[boo, StandardForm]]

      boo

      < -k : ExpressionPacket[BoxData[boo, StandardForm]]

Here is a more interesting example. Let's find out what packets are sent between the front end and kernel by the **NotebookCreate[]** command.

```
(Serializer) In[4]:=  NotebookCreate[]

                <-k : InputNamePacket[In[4]:= ]

                f0 -> : EnterExpressionPacket[
                    MakeExpression[BoxData[RowBox[List[NotebookCreate, [, ]]]], StandardForm]]

                <-k : FrontEnd`NotebookCreateReturnObject[]

                f -> : NotebookObject[$FrontEnd, 17]

                <-k : OutputNamePacket[Out[4]= ]

                <-k : FrontEnd`Value[$VersionNumber]

                f -> : 4.0

                <-k : FrontEnd`Notebooks[]

                f -> : List[NotebookObject[$FrontEnd, 17],
                    NotebookObject[$FrontEnd, 10], NotebookObject[$FrontEnd, 7]]

                <-k : FrontEnd`AbsoluteOptions[NotebookObject[
                       FrontEndObject[LinkObject[serializer.exe, 1, 1]], 17] List[WindowTitle]]

                f -> : List[Rule[WindowTitle, Untitled-1]]

(Serializer) Out[4]=  NotebookObject[ <<Untitled-1>> ]

                <-k :
                    ReturnExpressionPacket[BoxData[InterpretationBox[RowBox[List[NotebookObject, [,
                        RowBox[List[<<, Untitled-1 , >>]], ]]], NotebookObject[
                        FrontEndObject[LinkObject[serializer.exe, 1, 1]], 17]], StandardForm]]
```

We see that the kernel asks the front end its **$VersionNumber**.

We will use this **PacketMonitor[]** function in later chapters to check our programs. We stop monitoring:

```
(Serializer) In[5]:=  PacketMonitor[]

                <-k : ReturnPacket[Null]

                f0 -> : EnterExpressionPacket[
                    MakeExpression[BoxData[RowBox[List[PacketMonitor, [, ]]]], StandardForm]]

(Serializer) Out[5]=  0
```

To end the session, choose **Serializer** in the **Quit Kernel** menu.

2.9. Summary

This chapter explained the basic concepts of *MathLink* and introduced various connection methods. The basic *MathLink* operations were demonstrated through nine *Mathematica* functions: **LinkConnect**, **LinkCreate**, **LinkActivate**, **LinkReadyQ**, **LinkRead**, **LinkReadHeld**, **LinkWrite**, **LinkWriteHeld**, and **LinkClose**. The **PacketMonitor** function—implemented using the Serializer program described in Chapter 10—displays the packets exchanged between the front end and kernel.

Chapter 3 — Compiling AddTwo

Building AddTwo, a sample program provided with the *MathLink* Developer's Kit (MLDK), on various platforms helps one to become familiar with the general principles of building *MathLink* programs. Readers should try compiling AddTwo in their own environment and try out the examples in this chapter so as to:

[1] get experience compiling programs under a range of environments;

[2] appreciate *MathLink*'s template concept and its format;

[3] learn *MathLink*'s type conversion, and size limitations.

In this chapter, you will meet the *Mathematica* function **Install[]**, and several *MathLink* Library API functions: MLGetInteger(), MLGetReal(), MLPutInteger(), MLPutReal(), MLGetString(), and MLDisownString().

3.1. Using *MathLink* Templates

A *MathLink template program*, built using a *MathLink template* (see Section 2.12.3 of *The Mathematica Book*), is a special *MathLink program* whose functions can be called from within *Mathematica* as *Mathematica* functions. A *MathLink template* is a file which defines the relationship between a *Mathematica* function and its corresponding C function by its format. The mprep program, which is included in the MLDK, reads the template and generates C source code corresponding to that template. This is half a ready-made program; you only need to write the specific function related to the template. In this book, we will use *MathLink templates* intensively, instead of writing entire C programs. This is the easiest way to create *MathLink* programs, and it is the most suitable approach for a wide variety of applications.

> ⚠ From the *MathLink template*, the user can make a *MathLink program* by which C functions are called from *Mathematica*. *MathLink programs* use the *MathLink library* to exchange expressions with the kernel through the *MathLink connection*.

To build *MathLink* template programs, the MLDK (appropriate for the user's platform) is required. The procedure to build *MathLink* programs from template files, shown schematically in Figure 3.1, are as follows:

[1] Write a template file (e.g., addtwo.tm);

[2] Write C functions which will be called from the template file (e.g., addtwo.c);

[3] Generate a C source file from the template using mprep(SAmprep) (e.g., addtwo.tm.c or addtwotm.c);

[4] Compile [2] and [3], and link them with the *MathLink* library to get an executable *MathLink* program.

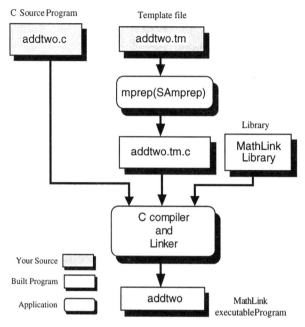

Figure 3.1. The process for building AddTwo.

When a *MathLink* executable program is invoked, it creates a *MathLink* connection to transfer information with the kernel. The *MathLink* program and the kernel can be running on different computers.

When the kernel begins the evaluation of **AddTwo[2,3]**, the parameters of the function, **2** and **3**, are transferred to AddTwo through the connection. Then these two values are sent to the C function addtwo() as its arguments, the function is executed, and the result, 5, is returned to the kernel. The computation process is indicated in Figure 3.2.

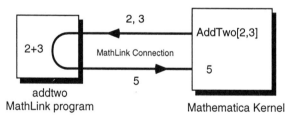

Figure 3.2. Computation process of **AddTwo[2,3]**.

This is similar to the communication between the front end and kernel. The front end prepares *Mathematica* expressions and transfers them to the kernel. The kernel evaluates each expression and transfers the result back to the front end.

3.2. Make AddTwo for Personal Computers

3.2.1 Preliminaries

When you install the CD-ROM accompanying this book, a `NetworkProgramming` directory is created in the `AddOns`Applications` directory. The `Chapter3` subdirectory contains the files related to this chapter (see Figure 3.3).

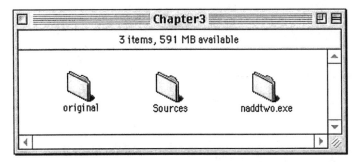

Figure 3.3. `Chapter3` directory in `AddOns`Applications`.

`Original` (see Figure 3.4) contains the unedited source code for AddTwo, which includes `addtwo.tm` and `addtwo.c`, copied from the MLDK examples, and project directories for the CodeWarrior compiler. `Sources` contains the source code for the programs in this chapter. `addtwo.tm` and `addtwo.c` are platform independent files which are used as the basis of these projects.

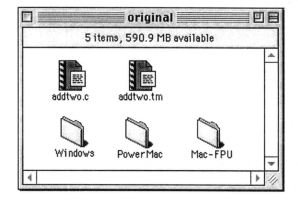

Figure 3.4. Contents of `Original`.

Three machine-specific project directories are included: the `PowerMac` project creates binaries for the PowerPC architecture, the `Windows` project creates Windows95/NT4 binaries, and the `Mac-FPU` project creates 68k binaries. Note that CodeWarrior Lite (see Section 1.7 for installation instructions) can compile only for 68k and Windows95/NT4.

3.2.2 Macintosh Project

The Mac-FPU (or PowerMac) folder (see Figure 3.5) contains the addtwo.mcp project file. This file manages all the source code and compilation procedures.

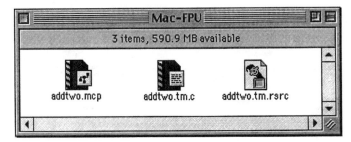

Figure 3.5. Contents of the Mac-FPU folder in the Original folder.

Figure 3.6. The addtwo.mcp project window for Macintosh.

addtwo.tm.c is a source file produced using SAmprep (see Figure 3.1), and addtwo.tm.rsrc is the resource file.

⚠ Macintosh Resource file: The resources for icons and dialog text strings, etc., of Macintosh applications are kept separate from the application program and are stored in the *resource fork* of a file.

Double-click on addtwo.mcp to launch CodeWarrior Lite IDE. This should open the project window as displayed in Figure 3.6.

The **sources** group contains the source files for this project; the **resources** group contains addtwo.tm.rsrc; the **Mac Libraries** group contains the libraries required for *any* Macintosh application; the **ANSI Libraries** group is needed for ANSI C library functions; and the **MathLink Libraries** group contains the compile-time *MathLink* library — mlimport.rsrc and mlimport.c — required for building *any* (Macintosh) *MathLink* program.

Choose **Make** from the **Project** menu to build the application. During compilation the message window shown in Figure 3.7 is displayed.

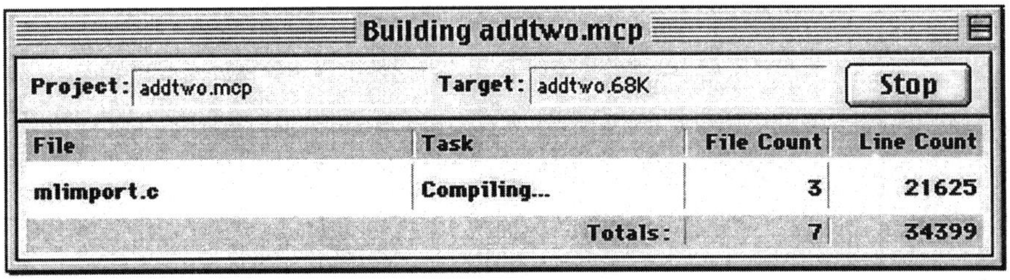

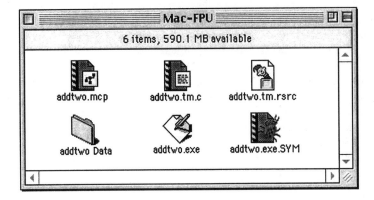

Figure 3.7. Building addtwo.mcp message window displayed during compilation.

After successful compilation, the addtwo.exe executable is created in the Mac-FPU folder (see Figure 3.8) and the byte count of objects appears in the **Code** and **Data** columns of the addtwo.mcp project window (c.f., Figure 3.6).

Figure 3.8. Mac-FPU folder after compilation.

The procedure for building addtwo.exe from the PowerMac and Windows projects is exactly the same. However, CodeWarrior Lite can compile only for 68k and Windows95/NT4.

If you change addtwo.tm you have to create addtwo.tm.c again (see Figure 3.1). To do this, launch SAmprep, open the modified addtwo.tm, and follow the instructions to create a new addtwo.tm.c. Then choose **Make** from the **Project** menu in CodeWarrior to build the new addtwo.exe executable.

3.2.3 Windows Project

The Original subdirectory of the CWLite/Windows directory contains the addtwo.mcp project file and addtwo.tm.c as shown in Figure 3.9.

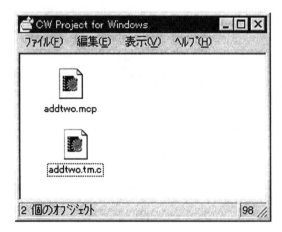

Figure 3.9. Contents of the Windows directory.

Double-click on addtwo.mcp to launch `CodeWarrior IDE` and open the project window (displayed in Figure 3.10). The Source group contains the source files for this project. MSL ANSI Libraries and Win32 SDK Libraries contain the libraries required for *any* Windows application. The compile-time *MathLink* library — ml32i1m.lib — is required for building *any* (Windows) *MathLink* program.

Choose **Make** from the **Project** menu to build the application. After successful compilation, the addtwo.exe executable is created in the Windows folder (see Figure 3.11) and the byte count of objects appears in the Code and Data columns of the addtwo.mcp project window (c.f., Figure 3.10).

If you change addtwo.tm you have to create addtwo.tm.c again (see Figure 3.1). To do this, run `mprep`, open the modified addtwo.tm, and follow the instructions to create a new addtwo.tm.c. Then choose **Make** from the **Project** menu in `CodeWarrior` to build the new `addtwo.exe` executable.

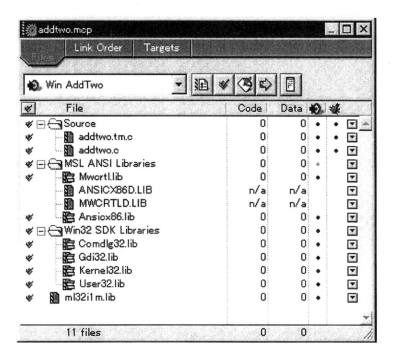

Figure 3.10. The addtwo.mcp project for Windows.

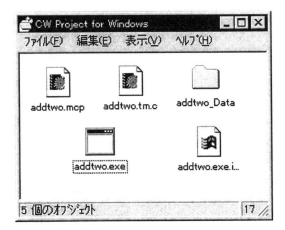

Figure 3.11. Windows directory after compilation.

3.2.4 Executing addtwo.exe

The execution procedures are identical under MacOS and Microsoft Windows. Launch `addtwo.exe` by double-clicking it. When the connection dialog displayed in Figure 3.12 appears, hit the OK button to start the program listening for a connection.

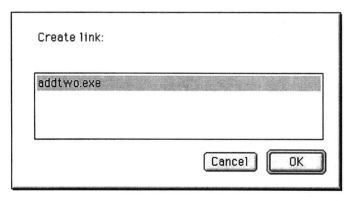

Figure 3.12. `addtwo.exe` connection dialog.

Now, connect to this link from *Mathematica* using the following command.

(Local) In[1]:= **lnk = Install[LinkConnect["addtwo.exe"]]**

(Local) Out[1]= LinkObject[addtwo.exe, 2, 2]

> ⚠ **Install[]** is a *Mathematica* function that prepares interaction between the kernel and *MathLink*-compatible external programs (built from *MathLink* templates).

Now we evaluate **AddTwo[2,3]**:

(Local) In[2]:= **AddTwo[2, 3]**

(Local) Out[2]= 5

Although **AddTwo[]** is not defined in *Mathematica*, 5 is returned. This is because **Install[]** defines **AddTwo[]**. The actual computation is done by the *MathLink*-compatible external program `addtwo.exe`.

3.3. Make AddTwo for Unix

Under Unix, there is a `MathLinkExamples` directory under the `AddOns/MathLink/DevelopersKits` hierarchy. From this directory, copy `Makefile`, `addtwo.c`, and `addtwo.tm` to your working directory.

```
% ls
Makefile  addtwo.c  addtwo.tm
```

Invoking `make addtwo` builds the executable program `addtwo`:

```
% make addtwo
.../mprep addtwo.tm > addtwotm.c
gcc -c -I... addtwotm.c
gcc -c -I... addtwo.c
gcc -I... addtwotm.o addtwo.o -L... -lML -lm -lsocket -lnsl -o addtwo
```

Instead of displaying the full directory path, we have used . . . to make this listing more concise. In this section, we use a Sun Microsystems Sparc5, running Solaris2, and gcc (the GNU C compiler). The steps involved are:

[1] mprep creates addtwotm.c from addtwo.tm;

[2] the C compiler compiles addtwotm.c and addtwo.c;

[3] the linker links the objects (addtwo.o and addtwotm.o) and libraries into the addtwo executable program.

The directory listing now reads

```
% ls
Makefile      addtwo.c      addtwo.tm     addtwotm.o
addtwo        addtwo.o      addtwotm.c
```

Now we run the executable program addtwo:

```
% addtwo
Create link:
```

It asks us to supply the TCP/IP port number for the *MathLink* connection. We set the port number to 5000:

```
Create link: 5000
```

To connect *Mathematica* to addtwo we use **Install[]**. The argument of **LinkConnect[]** consists of the port number (here 5000) and host name (here master.taiiku.tsukuba.ac.jp is the host on which addtwo is running):

```
% math
Mathematica 3.0 for Solaris
Copyright 1988-96 Wolfram Research, Inc.
 -- Terminal graphics initialized --

In[1]:= lnk = Install[LinkConnect["5000@master.taiiku.tsukuba.ac.jp"]]
Out[1]= LinkObject[5000@master.taiiku.tsukuba.ac.jp, 1, 1]
```

The evaluation of **AddTwo[2,3]** is computed by the addtwo program, and 5 is returned:

```
In[2]:= AddTwo[2,3]
Out[2]= 5
```

The two programs — addtwo and the kernel — can be running anywhere on the internet.

If you hit return when `Create link:` appears, a `Connect to link:` message will appear. In this case, the program will try to connect to the port that is listening for a connection. This mechanism is the same as the connection of the kernel and front end discussed in Section 2.5.

3.4. Source Files for AddTwo

In this section, we look more closely at the two source files — `addtwo.tm` and `addtwo.c` — which are located in the `Chapter3/Original` directory.

3.4.1 addtwo.tm

This file is a *MathLink* template, and defines the binding between the C function `addtwo()` and the *Mathematica* function **AddTwo[]**. The main part of `addtwo.tm` is

```
:Begin:
:Function:      addtwo
:Pattern:       AddTwo[i_Integer,j_Integer]
:Arguments:     {i,j}
:ArgumentTypes: {Integer, Integer}
:ReturnType:    Integer
:End:
```

All definitions start with `:Begin:` and end with `:End:`. The line

```
:Function: addtwo
```

declares a C function name, `addtwo`. This function will be called from **AddTwo[]**. The line

```
:Pattern:    AddTwo[i_Integer,j_Integer]
```

defines the *Mathematica* pattern **AddTwo[i_Integer,j_Integer]**. When an expression matches this pattern, replacement rules will apply to the arguments {i,j} in the `:Arguments:` list:

```
:Arguments: {i,j}
```

Data transferred to the C function, `addtwo`, are combined into a list. `:Arguments:` describes how to build up this list, in this case, {i,j}. When **AddTwo[2,3]** is evaluated, {2,3} will be sent. If {i+1,j-1} is in the `:Arguments:` field, {3,2} will be sent instead.

   `:ArgumentTypes:` defines the data types when the *MathLink* program gets data from the link. In our case,

```
:ArgumentTypes: {Integer, Integer}
```

means that two integer values will be extracted from the link. These values become parameters of the `addtwo()` function. Then, `addtwo()` is invoked and the return value is transferred back to the kernel according to next definition:

```
:ReturnType:     Integer
```

With this definition, the return value of addtwo() will be sent as an Integer to the link. The kernel receives it and supplies it as the return value of **AddTwo[]**. The process of this function call and data transfer is shown in Figure 3.13.

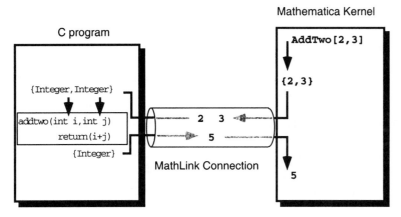

Figure 3.13. The process of **AddTwo[]** evaluation and internal data flow.

A *MathLink* connection can read and write *simultaneously*. In the figure, the *MathLink* connection pipe (which holds both a reading and writing stream) expresses this.

3.4.2 addtwo.c

The function addtwo(), defined in the file addtwo.c, is quite simple; it takes two integer parameters, and returns their sum.

```
extern int addtwo(int i, int j);
int addtwo(int i, int j)
{
    return(i + j);
}
```

3.5. Data Size

In *Mathematica*, you can have unlimited size integers. However, this is not true for *MathLink* programs. Let's try some examples. (Caution: the Macintosh version of addtwo.exe will terminate when $Failed is returned).

(Local) In[3]:= **AddTwo[2^{31} - 1, 0]**

(Local) Out[3]= 2147483647

(Local) In[4]:= **AddTwo[2^{31}, 0]**

(Local) Out[4]= $Failed

(Local) In[5]:= **AddTwo[-2^{31}, 0]**

(Local) Out[5]= -2147483648

(Local) In[6]:= **AddTwo[-2^{31} - 1, 0]**

(Local) Out[6]= $Failed

From the preceding examples, we deduce that *MathLink* is using 32 bit integers, that is, the integer range is $-2^{31} \le n \le 2^{31} - 1$. Since *MathLink* programs will run on various computers with differing integer representations, you may obtain different results for the above examples.

> ⚠ | The size of data that can be handled by *MathLink* programs depends on the operating system and compiler.

Also you should note that if $Failed is not returned, it does not guarantee that the answer is correct. It is also possible for addition to cause an overflow. Consider the following examples:

(Local) In[7]:= **AddTwo[2^{31} - 1, 1]**

(Local) Out[7]= -2147483648

(Local) In[8]:= **AddTwo[-2^{31}, -1]**

(Local) Out[8]= 2147483647

Since the *MathLink* program represents integers as signed numbers, the most significant bit represents the sign, and overflow affects this sign bit. Positive answers are returned as negative and vice versa. You should bear these points in mind when sending data to *MathLink* programs.

We disconnect addtwo.exe using **Uninstall[]**. The link is closed, and the application addtwo.exe is terminated.

(Local) In[9]:= **Uninstall[lnk]**

(Local) Out[9]= addtwo.exe

3.6. Template File and C Program for addtworeal

We now extend our application to compute the sum of two real numbers. We add the following lines to addtwo.tm:

```
:Begin:
:Function:      addtworeal
:Pattern:       AddTwoReal[i_, j_]
:Arguments:     {i,j}
:ArgumentTypes: {Real, Real}
:ReturnType:    Real
:End:
```

:ArgumentTypes:{Real, Real} indicates that addtworeal will get two arguments typed double. Using :ReturnType: Real tells **AddTwoReal[]** to return a real number. We also include the addtworeal() function, to calculate sum of real numbers, in addtwo.c:

```
extern double addtworeal(double i, double j);
double addtworeal(double i, double j)
{
    return(i + j);
}
```

The source code and executable program, naddtwo.exe, are included in subdirectories of the Chapter3 folder. After invoking naddtwo.exe (see Figure 3.14),

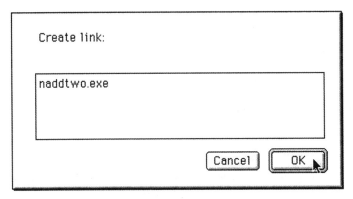

Figure 3.14. Invoking naddtwo.exe.

we connect to it as we did with addtwo.exe.

(Local) In[10]:= **lnk = Install["naddtwo.exe", LinkMode → Connect]**

(Local) Out[10]= LinkObject[naddtwo.exe, 3, 2]

(Local) In[11]:= **AddTwoReal[2.5, 3.4]**

(Local) Out[11]= 5.9

As expected, we get a real answer.

One should bear in mind the difference between a *Mathematica* **Real** and double in C. In *Mathematica*, real numbers are represented in two ways — machine-precision numbers and arbitrary-precision numbers. Once the data are transferred to C, real numbers depend on the representation of floating-point numbers in C. For example,

(Local) In[12]:= **AddTwoReal[1.79769 10³⁰⁸, 0.0]**

(Local) Out[12]= 1.79769×10^{308}

(Local) In[13]:= **AddTwoReal[1.79769 10³⁰⁹, 0.0]**

(Local) Out[13]= $Failed

> ⚠ The size of real numbers that can be handled depends on the machine floating-point number representation.

3.7. *Mathematica* **Pattern and Type Conversion**

We modify the `:Pattern:` template of **AddTwo[]** to the generic pattern **[i_,j_]** instead of using typed arguments:

```
:Begin:
:Function:      addtwo
:Pattern:       AddTwo[i_,j_]
:Arguments:     {i,j}
:ArgumentTypes: {Integer, Integer}
:ReturnType:    Integer
:End:
```

Then we rebuild the program as described in Section 3.2.2 (Macintosh), Section 3.2.3 (Windows), or Section 3.3 (Unix).

First we try sending integers to **AddTwoReal[]**:

(Local) In[14]:= **AddTwoReal[2, 3]**

(Local) Out[14]= 5.

In this case, a list of integers, **{2,3}**, is sent from the kernel to the link. When the list is transferred to the *MathLink* program, these two arguments are converted to `double`. Type conversion (coercion) takes place, and integers are converted to floating-point numbers.

Next we send reals to **AddTwo[]**:

(Local) In[15]:= **AddTwo[2.5, 0]**

(Local) Out[15]= 2

Here the real number, **2.5**, is converted to an integer when it is transferred to the link. 2 is returned because 2.5 is truncated.

Hence it is important to understand the characteristics of *MathLink* programs in which type conversions take place when data are transferred to or from the kernel.

It is possible to define (i.e., overload) a single *Mathematica* function that calls *different* C functions using pattern-matching. For example, consider the following template:

```
:Begin:
:Function:      addtwo
:Pattern:       AddTwo[i_, j_]
:Arguments:     { i, j }
:ArgumentTypes: { Integer, Integer }
:ReturnType:    Integer
:End:

:Begin:
:Function:      addtworeal
:Pattern:       AddTwo[i_Real, j_Real]
```

```
:Arguments:     { i, j }
:ArgumentTypes: { Real, Real }
:ReturnType:    Real
:End:
```

Here the C function addtworeal will be called if **AddTwo[]** is supplied with two **Real** arguments, otherwise addtwo will be called. When integer parameters are supplied, **AddTwo[]** returns the sum as an integer:

(Local) In[16]:= **AddTwo[2, 3]**

(Local) Out[16]= 5

With floating-point numbers:

(Local) In[17]:= **AddTwo[2.5, 3.0]**

(Local) Out[17]= 5.5

With mixed integer and floating-point arguments, the arguments are coerced (truncated) to be integers and an integer is returned:

(Local) In[18]:= **AddTwo[2.5, 3]**

(Local) Out[18]= 5

Now we add a template using :ArgumentTypes: {String, String}:

```
:Begin:
:Function:      addtwostring
:Pattern:       AddTwoString[i_,j_]
:Arguments:     {i,j}
:ArgumentTypes: {String, String}
:ReturnType:    Real
:End:
```

The C function argument must be a character pointer, char *s, because the string itself is saved by the *MathLink* library, and its pointer is passed to the C function:

```
extern double addtwostring(char *s1, char *s2);
double addtwostring(char *s1, char *s2)
{
    return(atof(s1)+atof(s2));
}
```

If you send two "numeric" strings to **AddTwoString[]**, it returns a real value:

(Local) In[19]:= **AddTwoString["1.2", "2.3"]**

(Local) Out[19]= 3.5

But, you can send **Integer**, or **Real** values to **AddTwoString[]**, and these are converted (coerced) properly:

(Local) In[20]:= **AddTwoString[1, 2]**

(Local) Out[20]= 3.

(Local) In[21]:= **AddTwoString[1.2, 2.3]**

(Local) Out[21]= 3.5

This means that the data object on the link can be read by the *MathLink* library as a **String**. We summarize these *MathLink* library type conversions (coercions) as follows:

[1] **Integer** and **Real** data on a link are read into the *MathLink* library as Integer or Real depending on :ArgumentTypes:.

[2] **String**, **Integer**, and **Real** data are correctly handled by the *MathLink* library using String in :ArgumentTypes:.

3.8. Exploring Template Files

To better understand *MathLink* type conversion, it is good to examine the file that mprep produces from the template. Compare the code that calls addtwo() and addtworeal() in addtwo.tm.c. The file that mprep generates is quite long; however, the relevant code is short. Here is the part that calls addtwo():

```
static int _tr0( MLINK mlp)
{    int res = 0;
     int _tp0;
     int _tp1;
     int _tp2;
     if ( ! MLGetInteger( mlp, &_tp1) ) goto L0;
     if ( ! MLGetInteger( mlp, &_tp2) ) goto L1;
     if ( ! MLNewPacket(mlp) ) goto L2;
     res = 1;
     _tp0 = addtwo(_tp1, _tp2);
     res = MLAbort ?
         MLPutFunction( mlp, "Abort", 0) : MLPutInteger( mlp, _tp0);
L2: L1:
L0: return res;
} /* _tr0 */
```

and here is the part that calls addtworeal():

```
static int _tr1( MLINK mlp)
{    int res = 0;
     double _tp0;
     double _tp1;
     double _tp2;
     if ( ! MLGetReal( mlp, &_tp1) ) goto L0;
     if ( ! MLGetReal( mlp, &_tp2) ) goto L1;
     if ( ! MLNewPacket(mlp) ) goto L2;
     res = 1;
     _tp0 = addtworeal(_tp1, _tp2);
     res = MLAbort ?
         MLPutFunction( mlp, "Abort", 0) : MLPutReal( mlp, _tp0);
L2: L1:
L0: return res;
} /* _tr1 */
```

The variables _tp0, _tp1, and _tp2 are automatically generated. They read data from the link mlp using MLGetInteger() or MLGetReal(). These *MathLink* functions are documented in Section A.11.1 of *The Mathematica Book*. The two variables, _tp1 and _tp2, will become the parameters of the functions, addtwo() or addtworeal(). The return values of these functions are returned onto the link by MLPutInteger() or MLPutReal(). These *MathLink* library functions read or write the data on the link, and the data conversions (indicated in Figure 3.15) take place at this point.

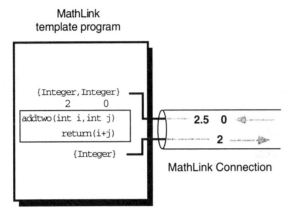

Figure 3.15. Data conversion in the *MathLink* program.

The C source code corresponding to addtwostring follows next. In this case, MLGetString() is used to read the data, and at this point the data conversion takes place. After the call to addtwostring, MLDisownString() is used to free-up the memory which MLGetString() allocated.

```
static int _tr2(MLINK mlp)
{
    int res = 0;
    int _tp0;
    kcharp_ct _tp1;
    kcharp_ct _tp2;
    if ( ! MLGetString( mlp, &_tp1) ) goto L0;
    if ( ! MLGetString( mlp, &_tp2) ) goto L1;
    if ( ! MLNewPacket(mlp) ) goto L2;

    _tp0 = addtwostring(_tp1, _tp2);

    res = MLAbort ?
        MLPutFunction( mlp, "Abort", 0) : MLPutInteger( mlp, _tp0);
L2: MLDisownString(mlp, _tp2);
L1: MLDisownString(mlp, _tp1);

L0: return res;
}
```

3.9. Evaluation Process

Here is the definition of **AddTwo[]**:

```
(Local) In[22]:=   ToString[Definition[AddTwo]]
```

```
(Local) Out[22]=   AddTwo[i_Real, j_Real] := ExternalCall[
                       LinkObject[naddtwo.exe, 3, 2], CallPacket[2, {i, j}]]

                   AddTwo[i_, j_] := ExternalCall[
                       LinkObject[naddtwo.exe, 3, 2], CallPacket[0, {i, j}]]
```

Evaluating **AddTwo[2,3]** calls **ExternalCall[]** with argument **CallPacket[0,{2,3}]**. **ExternalCall[]** is a system function that reads and writes expressions on a link:

```
(Local) In[23]:=   Begin["System`Dump`"];
                   ClearAttributes[ExternalCall, ReadProtected];
```

```
(Local) In[25]:=   ToString[Definition[ExternalCall]]
```

```
(Local) Out[25]=   ExternalCall[link_LinkObject, packet_CallPacket] := Block[
                       {ThisLink = link, $CurrentLink = link, $IterationLimit =
                       Infinity}, If[LinkWrite[link, packet] === $Failed,
                       $Failed, ExternalAnswer[link, LinkReadHeld[link]]]]
```

```
(Local) In[26]:=   SetAttributes[ExternalCall, ReadProtected];
                   End[];
```

ExternalCall[] sends the **CallPacket[0,{i,j}]** expression on a link using **LinkWrite[]**. If **LinkWrite[]** does not return **$Failed**, **ExternalCall[]** reads a value from the link using **LinkReadHeld[]**. This value becomes the return value of **AddTwo[]** using **ExternalAnswer**.

The list **{i,j}** in **CallPacket[0,{i,j}]** corresponds to :Arguments: {i,j} in the template. Here are the steps in the kernel evaluation:

[1] After evaluating the arguments, pattern-matching is applied to **AddTwo[2,3]**;

[2] **ExternalCall[link,CallPacket[0,{2,3}]]** is evaluated;

[3] Then **LinkWrite[link,CallPacket[0,{2,3}]]** is evaluated;

[4] Next, the expression **CallPacket[0,{2,3}]** will be sent on the link.

Next, we examine how **CallPacket[0,{2,3}]** is interpreted in the template file addtwo.tm.c. The program main() calls MLAnswer():

```c
int MLAnswer( MLINK mlp)
{
    int pkt = 0;

    while( !MLDone && !MLError(mlp) &&
               (pkt = MLNextPacket(mlp), pkt) && pkt == CALLPKT){
           MLAbort = 0;
           if( !MLDoCallPacket(mlp)) pkt = 0;
```

```
    }
    MLAbort = 0;
    return pkt;
} /* MLAnswer */
```

MLAnswer() is a while loop that checks expressions on the link using MLNextPacket(). If its type is CALLPKT, then MLDoCallPacket() is called.

```
int _MLDoCallPacket( MLINK mlp, struct func functable[], int nfuncs)
{
    long len;
    int n, res = 0;
    struct func* funcp;

    if( ! MLGetInteger( mlp, &n) || n < 0 || n >= nfuncs) goto L0;
    funcp = &functable[n];

    if( funcp->f_nargs >= 0
        && ( ! MLCheckFunction(mlp, "List", &len)
        || ( !funcp->manual && (len != funcp->f_nargs))
        || ( funcp->manual && (len < funcp->f_nargs))
            )
        ) goto L0;

    stdlink = mlp;
    res = (*funcp->f_func)( mlp);

L0: if( res == 0)
    res = MLClearError( mlp) && MLPutSymbol( mlp, "$Failed");
        return res && MLEndPacket( mlp) && MLNewPacket( mlp);
} /* _MLDoCallPacket */
```

MLDoCallPacket() gets an integer—in this case 0—from the link using MLGetInteger(), corresponding to the 0 in CallPacket[0,{1,2}].

```
static struct func {
    int    f_nargs;
    int    manual;
    int    (*f_func)P((MLINK));
    char   *f_name;
    } _tramps[1] = {
        { 2, 0, _tr0, "addtwo" }
        };
```

The 0 points to the zeroth element of the array _tramps[1], that is, {2,0,_tr0,"addtwo"}. Then _tr0() (examined in Section 3.8) is called by (*funcp->f_func)(mlp).

To summarize, here are the *MathLink* steps in the evaluation of **AddTwo[2,3]** (see Figure 3.16):

[1] MLNextPacket() checks the expression on a link. If it is CALLPKT, it calls MLDoCallPacket();

[2] MLDoCallPacket() reads the first argument, 0, of CallPacket[0,{2,3}] using MLGetInteger();

[3] the integer 0 is the array index of pointers to C functions, here _tr0();

[4] _tr0() retrieves its parameters, {2,3}, from the link using MLGetInteger() and then calls addtwo();

[5] _tr0() puts the return value of addtwo() onto the link using MLPutInteger();

[6] in the kernel, read the return value using **LinkReadHeld[]**.

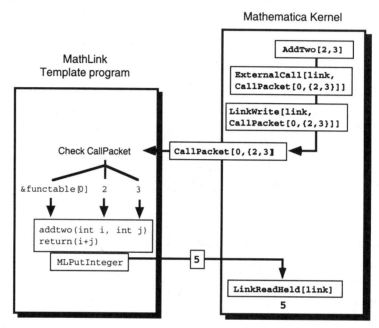

Figure 3.16. Steps in the process of **AddTwo[]** evaluation.

3.10. Summary

In this chapter, we compiled a sample program, AddTwo, modified it to handle real numbers and strings, and then we examined type conversion, an important feature of *MathLink*. When data are sent to a *MathLink* program, the data representation will be restricted by the inherent limitations of C. Also, we looked in detail at the steps in the evaluation process of **AddTwo[]**.

Chapter 4 — Transfer Time Using MathLink

The speed of data transfer on a network affects the performance of network programs. Knowing the evaluation time is important for *MathLink* programming but, in general, we cannot predict the evaluation time without making a measurement.

In this chapter, we:

[1] write a simple template for list transfer;

[2] learn the principles of memory allocation and deallocation of *MathLink*;

[3] build a *MathLink* tool for timing measurements;

[4] experimentally measure the transfer time of *MathLink* programs; and

[5] learn how to estimate the speed of data transfer in the users' environment.

4.1. Execution Time of AddTwo

In the `NetworkProgramming/Chapter4` directory there are two subdirectories — `Sources` and `addtwo.exe`. In the `Sources` directory (see Figure 4.1), there are four subdirectories — `PowerPC`, `Mac-FPU`, `Windows`, and `Linux` — and three common source codes — `addtwo.c`, `addtwo.tm`, and `main.c`. Each directory contains the source codes and project files for that platform.

We use `Install` to load `addtwo.exe`, which is located in the `NetworkProgramming/-Chapter4/addtwo.exe/$SystemID/` directory.

(Local) In[1]:= `prog = Install["NetworkProgramming`Chapter4`addtwo`", LinkMode → Launch];`

Note that, if *prog* is a directory then `Install[`*prog*`]` looks for a subdirectory of that directory whose name agrees with the current value of `$SystemID`, and will then try to execute a file named *prog* within that subdirectory. Using this approach, the appropriate executable is loaded automatically (see Section 2.12.5 of *The Mathematica Book* regarding the naming and automatic loading of executables).

Here we evaluate `AddTwo[1,2]` one thousand times and measure the execution time using `Timing[]`:

(Local) In[2]:= `First[Timing[Do[AddTwo[1, 2], {1000}]]]`

(Local) Out[2]= `1.73333 Second`

Let's compare this with the evaluation of a top-level *Mathematica* function `addtwo[]`:

(Local) In[3]:= `addtwo[x_Integer, y_Integer] := x + y`

(Local) In[4]:= `Do[addtwo[1, 2], {1000}] // Timing // First`

(Local) Out[4]= `0.0333333 Second`

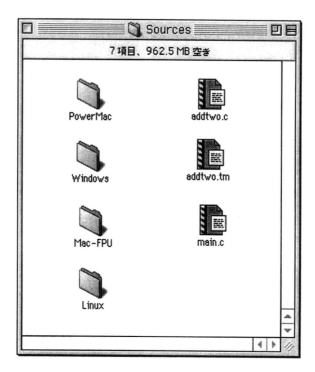

Figure 4.1. The Sources directory includes source codes for four platforms.

addtwo[] is much faster than **AddTwo[]** because evaluating **AddTwo[]** requires all the steps outlined in Section 3.9. Almost all of the evaluation time of **Do[AddTwo[1,2],{1000}]** involves data transfer and data conversions. Also, **Timing[]** only measures the kernel CPU time and hence does not show the correct time spent evaluating *MathLink* external functions. The overall execution time is considerably longer because data transfers over the link and the execution time of addtwo() are not measured.

There are several functions to measure timings in *Mathematica*: **Timing**, **TimeUsed**, **SessionTime**, and **AbsoluteTime**. For our purposes **SessionTime** is used:

```
(Local) In[5]:=   mlSessionTime[mlfun_, n__] :=
                      Module[{t0},
                          t0 = SessionTime[];
                          mlfun[n];
                          SessionTime[] - t0]
```

mlSessionTime[] computes the difference between the values of **SessionTime[]** before and after evaluation to obtain the *actual* execution time of **mlfun[n]**. To avoid counting the argument evaluation time, the function name **mlfun** and its argument(s) **n** are supplied separately as two arguments to **mlSessionTime[]** to be evaluated first. The definition of **mlSessionTime[]** may appear somewhat artificial, but later we will see why we have defined it this way.

For example, here we measure the execution time of **Do[AddTwo[1,2],{1000}]**:

    (Local) In[6]:= **mlSessionTime[Do[AddTwo[1, 2], {#}] &, 1000]**

    (Local) Out[6]= 2.

mlSessionTime[] returns the total execution time not just the CPU time. Note that, to use **mlSessionTime[]**, we rewrote **Do[AddTwo[1,2],{1000}]** as the pure function **Do[AddTwo[1,2],{#}]&** with the single argument **1000**.

4.2. Sending a List

In this section, we build a *MathLink* program that receives a one-dimensional list from the kernel. Using this program the list transfer time, which is proportional to the length of the list, is measured.

We add **SendList[]**, which takes a one-dimensional list and returns its length, to addtwo.tm and addtwo.c from the previous chapter. Here is the additional template:

```
:Begin:
:Function:    sendlist
:Pattern:     SendList[a_List]
:Arguments:   {a}
:ArgumentTypes: {IntegerList}
:ReturnType:  LongInteger
:End:
```

The corresponding sendlist() function reads

```
long sendlist(int *a, long alen)
{
    return(alen);
}
```

We have introduced the IntegerList argument type. The corresponding C function definition requires two arguments: the pointer, int *a, and the length, long alen.

When a list (or string) is sent to the *MathLink* program (see Figure 4.2), the storage is managed by *MathLink*. The pointer to the list and the length of the list are passed to the C function declared in the template.

When transferring lists, two points should be borne in mind:

[1] The C function needs two arguments: a pointer to the list, and the length of list;

[2] Since the data are managed by *MathLink*, the external program should not modify the data.

4.3. Execution of SendList

The following evaluation,

    (Local) In[7]:= **SendList[Range[20000]]**

    (Local) Out[7]= 20000

returns the length of the list, here 20000.

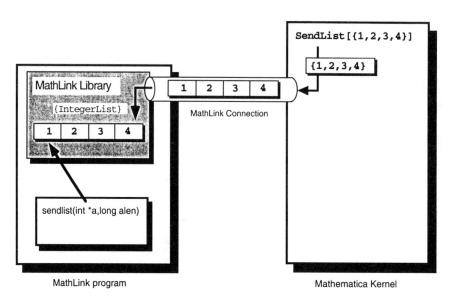

Figure 4.2. Sending a one-dimensional list to a *MathLink* program.

Unix or Microsoft Windows operating systems dynamically allocate memory for *MathLink* programs so users do not need to worry about the size of the list. In contrast, on a Macintosh, if the transferred list is too big to hold in memory, **$Failed** will be returned. In such cases, the user needs to select **Get Info** under the **File** menu and increase the program's Preferred Memory: setting to cope with longer lists.

4.4. Memory Deallocation in SendList

Whenever **SendList[]** is executed, memory is allocated to hold the list. This allocated memory should be deallocated after processing. Let's examine how memory is deallocated by looking at the relevant code in addtwo.tm.c:

```
static int _tr2( MLINK mlp)
{
    int res = 0;
    int _tp0;
    intp_nt _tp1;
    long _tp11;
    if ( ! MLGetIntegerList( mlp, &_tp1, &_tp11) ) goto L0;
    if ( ! MLNewPacket(mlp) ) goto L1;

    _tp0 = sendlist(_tp1, _tp11);

    res = MLAbort ?
        MLPutFunction( mlp, "Abort", 0) : MLPutLongInteger( mlp, _tp0);
L1: MLDisownIntegerList( mlp, _tp1, _tp11);

L0: return res;
} /* _tr2 */
```

The function _tr2 reads a list of integers using MLGetIntegerList(). Then sendlist() is called with a pointer to the list and its length. sendlist() returns a value, _tp0, and sends it to the link using MLPutLongInteger(). Then MLDisownIntegerList() is called to deallocate the memory allocated by MLGetIntegerList().

Now we create another *MathLink* function, **SendRealList[]**, that returns the length of a real list. As an example, we use Manual for the :ArgumentTypes: and :ReturnType: settings in the template file:

```
:Begin:
:Function:    sendreallist
:Pattern:     SendRealList[a_List]
:Arguments:   {a}
:ArgumentTypes: {Manual}
:ReturnType:    Manual
:End:
```

And here is the corresponding C function:

```
void sendreallist( )
{
    double *a; long alen;

    MLGetRealList(stdlink, &a, &alen);
    MLPutLongInteger(stdlink, alen);
    MLDisownRealList(stdlink, a, alen);
}
```

When Manual is used, the source code to transfer data is not automatically generated from the template. Instead, we need to write code for the data transfer. MLGetRealList() is explicitly used to read a list of reals from the link and MLPutLongInteger() is used to put a return value on the link. Notice that MLDisownRealList() is called to deallocate the memory that MLGetRealList() allocated.

4.5. Transfer Time in SendList

SendList[] sends a list from the kernel to the *MathLink* program, and a single value is returned. The execution time will be affected by the length of list sent from the kernel. Let's measure the transfer time of **SendList[]** (Figure 4.3). The result shows that execution time is approximately proportional to the length of the list. But the timings increase in a step-wise fashion because the SessionTime[] time unit, the second, is too coarse for this experiment.

```
(Local) In[8]:= ListPlot[Table[{i, mlSessionTime[SendList, Table[1234, {i}]]},
                {i, 5000, 600000, 10000}]];
```

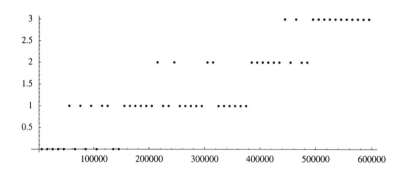

Figure 4.3. Transfer time of integer lists.

Now we measure the time to transfer real lists using **SendRealList[]** (Figure 4.4).

(Local) In[9]:= **ListPlot[Table[{i, mlSessionTime[SendRealList, Table[1.234, {i}]]},**
              {i, 5000, 600000, 10000}]];

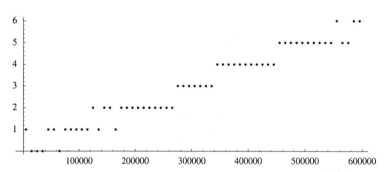

Figure 4.4. Transfer time of real lists.

These results show that transferring real lists is slower than transferring integer lists. Basically, data transfer involves three steps:

[1] data conversion from the kernel to the *MathLink* connection;

[2] data transfer through the link;

[3] data conversion from the link to the *MathLink* program.

Although transferring real lists is slower, we cannot identify which step causes the slowdown. In the next experiment, we send the same data to **SendList[]** and **SendRealList[]** and measure the transfer time to determine which step is responsible.

(Local) In[10]:= **data = Table[1234, {250000}];**

(Local) In[11]:= `{mlSessionTime[SendRealList, data], mlSessionTime[SendList, data]}`

(Local) Out[11]= `{1., 1.}`

Data sent to the *MathLink* program are wrapped with **CallPacket[]** (see Section 3.9), which means that **Send-List[]** and **SendRealList[]** send the *same* data to the program. Noting preceding points [1] and [2], we see that the timing difference between the two functions is entirely due to the data conversion, [3], in the *MathLink* program. Hence the data conversion time in MLGetRealList() and MLGetIntegerList() is similar.

The following experiment again shows that transferring real lists takes longer than transferring integer lists:

(Local) In[12]:= `data = Table[1.234, {250000}];`

(Local) In[13]:= `{mlSessionTime[ SendRealList, data], mlSessionTime[ SendList, data]}`

(Local) Out[13]= `{2., 2.}`

Comparing these timings with the previous experiment, we can conclude that the timing increase for the transfer of real lists results from the combination of [1] and [2]. However, we cannot separate the time taken by [1] and [2].

4.6. Time Measurement Function

In the previous section, graphs of the data transfer time increase in a step-wise fashion because the **Session-Time[]** time unit, the second, is too coarse. We need a timing function that has a finer time unit. However, *Mathematica* doesn't have such a function. In general, the best solution is to implement the required functionality using *MathLink*.

Every operating system provides a time measurement function. For example, the CodeWarrior ANSI C library provides the clock() function. Let's make a template that calls clock():

```
:Begin:
:Function:        clockcount
:Pattern:         Clock[]
:Arguments:       {  }
:ArgumentTypes:   {  }
:ReturnType:      Real
:End:
```

Clock[] has no parameters, and returns the time since the operating system started as a real value.

Now we define clockcount(). clock() returns the time in units of CLOCKS_PER_SEC and clockcount() divides by this value so as to return the time. The time.h header file is required by these functions.

```
#include <time.h>
double clockcount()
{
    return(((double)clock())/CLOCKS_PER_SEC);
}
```

Then we modify **mlSessionTime[]** to use **Clock[]** instead of **SessionTime[]**:

```
(Local) In[14]:=  mlSessionTime[mlfun_, n__]:=
                  Module[{t0},
                      t0 = Clock[];
                      mlfun[n];
                      Clock[]-t0]
```

We examine the evaluation time of **SendList[]** using **Clock[]** (Figure 4.5):

```
(Local) In[15]:=  data = Table[1234, {100000}];
```

```
(Local) In[16]:=  ListPlot[Table[mlSessionTime[SendList, data], {100}], PlotRange → {0, 1}];
```

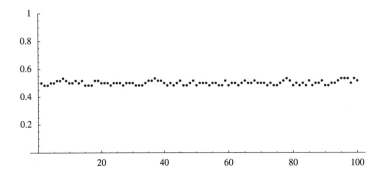

Figure 4.5. 100 time measurement trials using **Clock[]**.

The timings show finer granularity and small variance. Now we re-examine the first experiment in Section 4.5 using **Clock[]** (Figure 4.6):

```
(Local) In[17]:=  ListPlot[Table[{i, mlSessionTime[SendList, Table[1234, {i}]]},
                      {i, 5000, 600000, 10000}]];
```

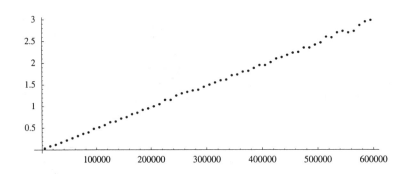

Figure 4.6. Transfer time of integer lists measured using **Clock[]**.

This result more clearly displays linearity. The slope of the line is the same as in the first experiment in Section 4.5, but the step-wise discontinuities have disappeared because **Clock[]** is finer-grained.

Next we repeat the second experiment in Section 4.5 (Figure 4.7):

(Local) In[18]:= `ListPlot[Table[{i, mlSessionTime[SendRealList, Table[1.234, {i}]]}, {i, 5000, 600000, 10000}]];`

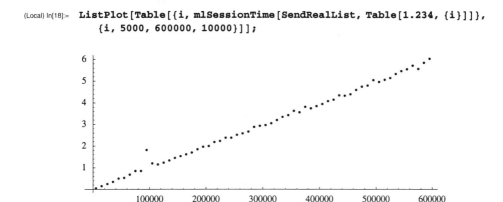

Figure 4.7. Transfer time of real lists measured using `Clock[]`.

Again, we obtain improved linearity.

`Clock[]` clearly displays the power of *MathLink*. *MathLink* extends *Mathematica* making it easy to implement functionality that is very difficult only using built-in functions. `Clock[]` is the first useful *MathLink* function in this book.

4.7. *MathLink* to Kernel Time Measurement

4.7.1 MakeList and MakeRealList

`SendList[]` sent lists from the kernel to a *MathLink* program. In this section, we will build two *MathLink* functions—`MakeList[]` and `MakeRealList[]`—which transfer lists from a *MathLink* program to the kernel. `MakeList[x, m]` (`MakeRealList[x, m]`) returns a list consisting of m copies of the integer (real) x, i.e., $\{x, x, x, \ldots, x\}$. These functions will be added into the previous template:

```
:Begin:
:Function:       makelist
:Pattern:        MakeList[x_Integer, len_Integer]
:Arguments:      { x, len }
:ArgumentTypes:  { Integer, LongInteger }
:ReturnType:     Manual
:End:
```

```
:Begin:
:Function:       makereallist
:Pattern:        MakeRealList[x_, i_Integer]
:Arguments:      { x, i }
:ArgumentTypes:  { Real, LongInteger }
:ReturnType:     Manual
:End:
```

The corresponding C functions are listed:

```
#include <stdlib.h>
```

```
void makelist( int x, long len )
{
    long i;
    int *p;

    if((p = (int *)malloc(sizeof(int)*len)) == NULL){
        MLPutSymbol(stdlink,"$Failed");
    }
    else {
        for(i=0;i<len; i++)
            p[i] = x;
        MLPutIntegerList(stdlink, p, len);
        free(p);
    }
}
```

```
void makereallist( double x, long len )
{
    long i;
    double *p;

    if((p = (double *)malloc(sizeof(double)*len)) == NULL){
        MLPutSymbol(stdlink,"$Failed");
    }
    else {
        for(i=0;i<len; i++)
            p[i] = x;
        MLPutRealList(stdlink, p, len);
        free(p);
    }
}
```

malloc(), an ANSI C standard function, is used to allocate the memory to hold the list. stdlib.h is included to enable the use of malloc(). Then MLPutIntegerList() or MLPutRealList() is used to send the list to the kernel. Finally, the allocated area is freed-up using free(). Here are two simple tests:

(Local) In[19]:= **MakeList[1234, 10]**

(Local) Out[19]= {1234, 1234, 1234, 1234, 1234, 1234, 1234, 1234, 1234, 1234}

(Local) In[20]:= **MakeRealList[1.234, 10]**

(Local) Out[20]= {1.234, 1.234, 1.234, 1.234, 1.234, 1.234, 1.234, 1.234, 1.234, 1.234}

Both functions work correctly. However, one concern is the size limitation of lists that can be generated using these functions. This is identical to the problem that we faced with **SendList[]** in Section 4.3.

4.7.2 Time Measurement of MakeList

Using **mlSessionTime[]**, we measure the execution time of **MakeList[]** (Figure 4.8):

(Local) In[21]:= **ListPlot[Table[**
                {i, mlSessionTime[MakeList[1234, #] &, i]}, {i, 5000, 600000, 10000}]];

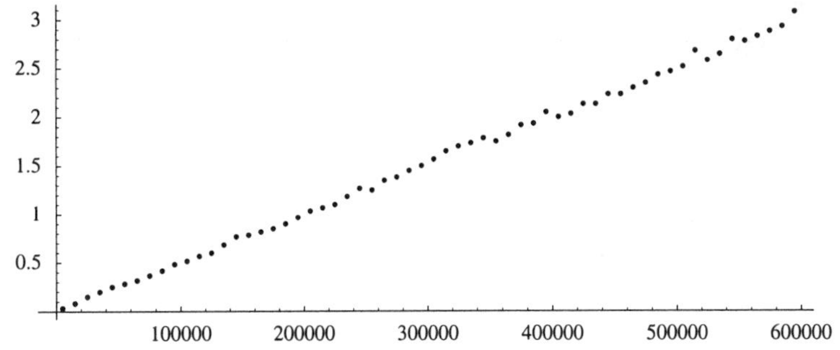

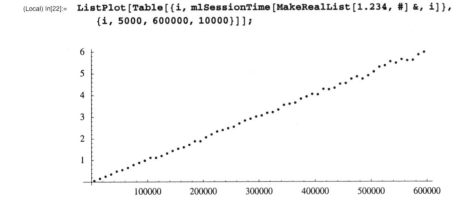

Figure 4.8. Integer list transfer time to the kernel.

We see that the execution time of **MakeList[]** is similar to **SendList[]**. Examining **MakeRealList[]** (Figure 4.9),

(Local) In[22]:= **ListPlot[Table[{i, mlSessionTime[MakeRealList[1.234, #] &, i]},**
                {i, 5000, 600000, 10000}]];

Figure 4.9. Real list transfer time to the kernel.

we observe that it is slower than **MakeList[]** for the reasons discussed in Section 4.5.

4.8. Improving MakeList

4.8.1 MakeList2

In **MakeList[]**, the size of lists is restricted to the memory that `malloc()` can allocate. However, *MathLink* can send not only numbers or lists but also expressions. Hence it is possible to send a list as an expression, e.g., **List**[*x*, *x*, …, *x*], instead of using `MLPutIntegerList()`. Using this, we can avoid calling `malloc()`. Here is the template:

```
:Begin:
:Function:       makelist2
:Pattern:        MakeList2[x_Integer, len_Integer]
:Arguments:      { x, len }
:ArgumentTypes:  { Integer, LongInteger }
:ReturnType:     Manual
:End:
```

Here is the C function `makelist2` that implements this idea:

```
void makelist2( int x, long len )
{
    long i;

    MLPutFunction(stdlink,"List",len);
    for(i=0;i<len; i++)
        MLPutInteger(stdlink, x);
}
```

`makelist2` sends the head `"List"` using `MLPutFunction()` to the link. The third argument to `MLPutFunction()` is the number of arguments corresponding to the head; here it is the length of the list.

Let us compare the data transfer time of sending the entire list in one step:

(Local) In[23]:= **mlSessionTime[MakeList[1234, #] &, 200000]**

(Local) Out[23]= `0.716667`

to sending the list elements one by one:

(Local) In[24]:= **mlSessionTime[MakeList2[1234, #] &, 200000]**

(Local) Out[24]= `1.98333`

MakeList2[] takes longer than **MakeList[]**. When list elements are transferred one by one, there is a large overhead and this slows down the data transfer. In general, the user should use higher level *MathLink* library functions whenever possible. Then your programs are likely to be optimal.

4.8.2 Buffered Transfer Using a *Mathematica* Function — MakeList3

So, how should we transfer large amounts of data to the kernel at high speed without size limitations? A general solution, called *buffered transfer*, is to:

[1] partition the data into smaller pieces;

[2] send each piece one by one;

[3] reconstruct the original data from the pieces.

Buffered transfer can be easily programmed using **Flatten[]** and the previous **MakeList[]**:

(Local) In[25]:=
```
MakeList3[x_, len_, size_] :=
    Flatten[
        If[Mod[len, size] == 0,
            Table[MakeList[x, size], {Quotient[len, size]}],
            {Table[MakeList[x, size], {Quotient[len, size]}],
            MakeList[x, Mod[len, size]]}]]
```

The third parameter of **MakeList3[]** is the buffer size.

Now we send an identical list using buffered transfer:

(Local) In[26]:= **mlSessionTime[MakeList3[1234, #, 1000] &, 200000]**

(Local) Out[26]= 1.83333

We see that buffered transfer is slower than sending the entire list in one step. The reasons why **MakeList3[]** is slower are the extra work required to:

[1] transfer the partitioned data; and

[2] reconstruct the original data from the partitioned data.

4.8.3 Buffered Transfer Using a *MathLink* Program — MakeList4

Another possibility is to implement buffered transfer in a *MathLink* program. Here is the template:

```
:Begin:
:Function:      makelist4
:Pattern:       MakeList4[x_Integer,len_Integer,size_Integer]
:Arguments:     {x,len,size}
:ArgumentTypes: {Integer,LongInteger,Integer}
:ReturnType:    Manual
:End:
```

Here is the C code for makelist4():

```
void makelist4(int x, long len, int size)
{
    int i, j, n, rem;
    int *buf;
```

```
    if((buf = (int *)malloc(sizeof(int)*size)) == NULL)
        MLPutSymbol(stdlink, "$Failed");
    else {
        n = len / size;
        rem = len % size;
        MLPutFunction(stdlink,"Flatten", 1L);
        MLPutFunction(stdlink,"List", n + (rem?1:0));
        for(i=0;i<n; i++){
            for(j = 0; j < size; ++j)
                buf[j] = x;
            MLPutIntegerList(stdlink, buf, size);
        }
        if(rem > 0){
            for(j = 0; j < rem; ++j)
                buf[j] = x;
            MLPutIntegerList(stdlink, buf, rem);
        }
        free(buf);
    }
}
```

makelist4() allocates memory and then sends **Flatten[List[List[*x*, *x*, ...],...,List[*x*, *x*, ...]]]** to the kernel. Using this, we examine how the buffer size affects the data transfer time (see Figure 4.10).

(Local) In[27]:= **ListPlot[Table[mlSessionTime[MakeList4[1234, 200000, #] &, 2^{i}], {i, 13}],**
　　　　　　PlotJoined → True, PlotRange → {0, Automatic}, Ticks →
　　　　　　{Table[{i, DisplayForm[SuperscriptBox[2, i]]}, {i, 13}], Automatic}];

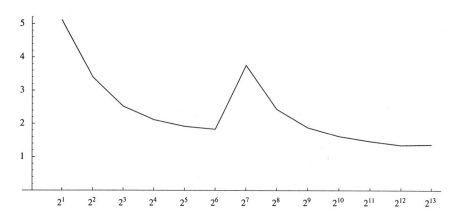

Figure 4.10. Data transfer time as a function of buffer size.

The transfer time is strongly size dependent for small buffer sizes. Hence one should choose an appropriate buffer size for data transfer. In our case, a buffer size of 2000 ($\approx 2^{11}$) appears reasonable:

(Local) In[28]:= **mlSessionTime[MakeList4[1234, #, 2000] &, 200000]**

(Local) Out[28]= 1.56667

`MakeList4[]` is still slower than transferring the entire data in one step, because we cannot avoid the extra partitioning and reconstruction operation for buffered transfer, but is slightly faster than buffered transfer using `MakeList3[]`. Although the speed increase is not dramatic, without making such measurements, we cannot evaluate the relative efficiency of each program.

4.9. Summary

We have shown that buffered transfer can be implemented using either a *MathLink* program or a *Mathematica* function. Which implementation should we choose? *Mathematica* functions are easy to write and modify. In comparison, C programming requires a cycle of writing, editing, saving, compiling, and debugging. In our experience, one should choose *Mathematica* in the prototyping phase. As the project proceeds, time-critical operations should be replaced with equivalent C functions.

The timings presented in this chapter should only be taken as an indication since they depend upon the machine-type and system configuration. Nevertheless it is important to know the actual data transfer time for your environment because you can use this information to estimate how long your *MathLink* program will take.

Chapter 5 — Debugging MathLink Programs

This chapter focuses on the practical aspects of using a debugger. A simple example of how to insert a print command is presented. Also, the template event-processing mechanism is described.

5.1. Using a Debugger

A debugger runs the target program and provides information during execution. In general, debuggers have the ability to:

[1] run a program;

[2] set break points to stop execution;

[3] run the program step by step; and

[4] inspect the value of variables.

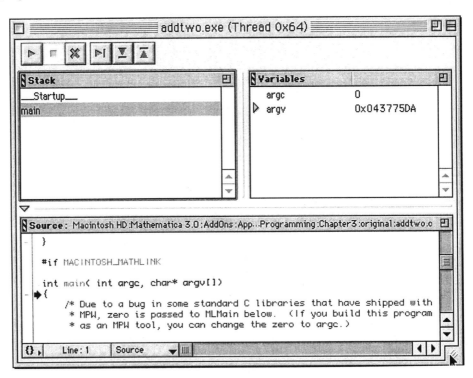

Figure 5.1. Debugging the addtwo.mcp project.

Commercial compilers include a debugger. In addition, there are several debuggers available under Unix, for example, adb, dbx, and gdb.

As an example, we debug the AddTwo program of Section 3.2 using the IDE CodeWarrior debugger. Double-click on the addtwo.mcp project (see Section 3.2.2) in the NetworkProgramming/Chapter3/original directory. From the **Project** menu choose **Debug**. If **Debug** does not appear in the **Project** menu, first choose **Enable Debugger** from the **Project** menu (see Figure 5.1).

The arrow indicates the current execution position. The **Debug** menu has **Step Over** (run a line of the program), **Step Into** (enter the function), and **Step Out** (exit the function) to control execution.

The **Project** menu has a **Run** item for continuous execution. Choosing **Run** causes the *MathLink* connection dialog to appear (refer to Figure 3.12). Click **OK** to complete the dialog and program execution starts, displaying a message as in Figure 5.2.

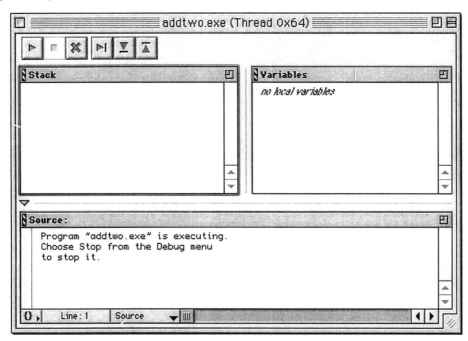

Figure 5.2. Program execution of the addtwo.mcp project.

Switch to *Mathematica*, and run **Install["addtwo.exe",LinkMode→Connect]** to establish the connection. The *MathLink* program is running. Now we set a break point in addtwo() (see Figure 5.3). Open addtwo.c in CodeWarrior IDE. Click on the left of the line to select the break point. A red dot will appear.

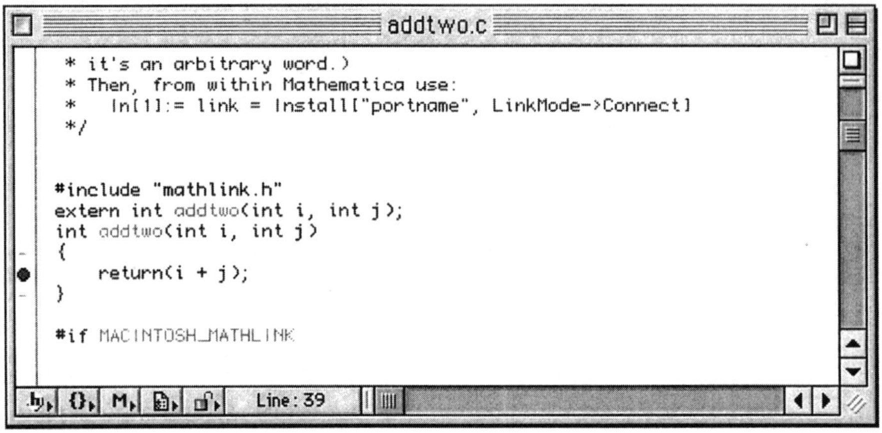

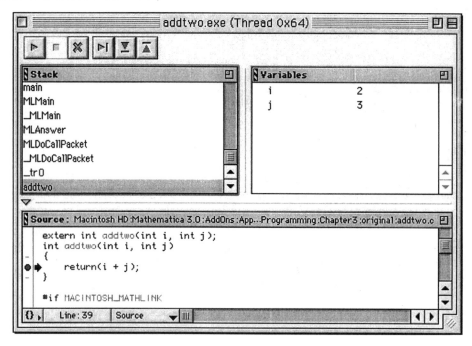

Figure 5.3. Setting a break point in addtwo().

After we call **Install** to connect to this program, when we evaluate **AddTwo[2,3]** the debugger will stop at this break point. In the Variables window (see Figure 5.4), we see the values of i and j. The Stack window (Figure 5.4) shows the function execution history.

Figure 5.4. Program execution stops at the break point.

One can continue execution using **Step Over** or **Run**. At any point, you can set a break point to stop execution, and examine the value of variables.

5.2. Event-processing Functions

What happens when the *MathLink* template program waits for the expression from the kernel? Choosing **Stop** from the **Debug** menu shows the current execution point. The program will stop at the WaitNextEvent() function in _handle_user_event() (see Figure 5.5).

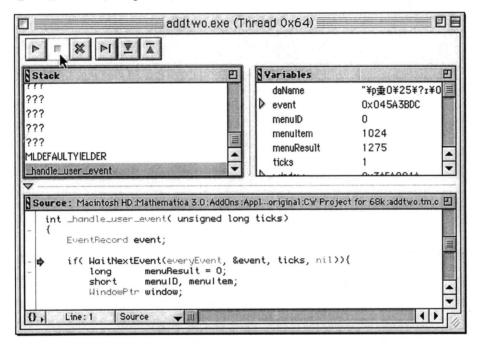

Figure 5.5. The result of choosing **Stop** from the **Debug** menu.

Expressions from the kernel are processed by MLNextPacket() in MLAnswer() as shown in Figure 5.6. At the same time, external events such as user input are processed by _handle_user_event() under MacOS and IconProcedure() under Microsoft Windows. These functions are automatically generated by mprep.

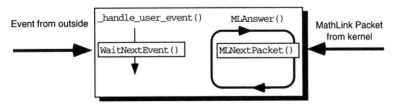

Figure 5.6. Schematic diagram showing kernel event processing and external events.

_handle_user_event() or IconProcedure() is invoked from the MLDefaultYielder function. Here is the definition of MLDefaultYielder under MacOS:

```
MLYDEFN( devyield_result, MLDefaultYielder, ( MLINK mlp, MLYieldParameters yp))
{
    mlp = mlp; /* suppress unused warning */
    return _handle_user_event( MLSleepYP(yp));
}
```

Under Windows the yielder function processes common event dispatching. And such dispatches call window procedures internally; in our case, IconProcedure():

```
MLYDEFN( devyield_result, MLDefaultYielder, ( MLINK mlp, MLYieldParameters yp))
{
    MSG msg;

#if !__BORLANDC__
    mlp = mlp; /* suppress unused warning */
    yp = (MLYieldParameters)0; /* suppress unused warning */
#endif

    if( PeekMessage( &msg, (HWND)0, 0, 0, PM_REMOVE)){
        TranslateMessage( &msg);
        DispatchMessage( &msg);
    }
    return MLDone;
}
```

The debugger window, Figure 5.5, shows that program execution goes to _handle_users_event() after entering MLNextPacket(). This means that _handle_users_event() is polled internally from MLNext-Packet() as shown in Figure 5.7. This is the role of the MLDefaultYielder function.

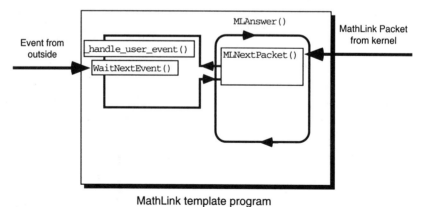

MathLink template program

Figure 5.7. Polling _handle_users_event() from MLNextPacket().

This polling enables the program to respond to two processes — expressions from the kernel and external events. If a process is blocked and waiting in MLNextPacket(), it is impossible to process the external events. Languages that use parallel processing would treat this as two threads instead.

Also MLDefaultYielder can be called in the tight loop to give processing time to other processes. In such cases, MLCallYieldFunction() is used.

```
...
while(condition){
    MLCallYieldFunction(MLYieldFunction(stdlink), stdlink,(MLYieldParameters)0);
    ...do some work in the loop...
}
```

5.3. Inserting Print Statements

Here we modify addtwo.c to use fprintf() to print the values of i and j when addtwo() is called.

```
int addtwo( int i, int j)
{
    fprintf(stderr,"i=%d j=%d\n", i, j);
    return i+j;
}
```

Console printout is the traditional input/output style for Unix. For MacOS or Microsoft Windows, there is no default console output because these systems use windows as output devices. To use printf() on such systems we need some wrapping environment that provides a window for console input/output. The CodeWarrior compiler provides SIOUX libraries for this purpose. To use SIOUX, we must first add the SIOUX libraries to the original addtwo.mcp project and modify addtwo.tm.c to match the SIOUX functions. The source code in AddOns/-Applications/NetworkProgramming/Chapter5/Sources includes these modifications.

After invoking the addtwo.exe program (in the Chapter5/Sources directory), we install it as follows.

(Local) In[1]:= **lnk = Install[LinkConnect["addtwo.exe"]];**

Now, executing

(Local) In[2]:= **AddTwo[2, 3]**

(Local) Out[2]= 5

causes the values of i and j to be printed out on the console window (Figure 5.8).

We disconnect addtwo.exe using **Uninstall[]**. The link is closed, and the application addtwo.exe is terminated.

(Local) In[3]:= **Uninstall[lnk]**

(Local) Out[3]= addtwo.exe

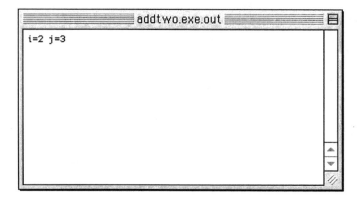

Figure 5.8. Output of `printf()` function.

5.4. Using MLAlert()

The method used in Section 5.3 is restricted to using a console window and is not portable for all platforms. `MLAlert()`, a *MathLink* library function that displays strings on the console or in a dialog, depending on the environment, can be used instead. Although `MLAlert()` is used in `.tm.c` files, `MLAlert()` is presently not documented in *The Mathematica Book*.

⚠   `MLAlert(MLEnvironment env, char *s)` displays the string in argument s.

Although `MLAlert()` is designed for displaying warning messages, it is also useful for printing out debugging messages. After inserting an `MLAlert()` instruction into `addtwo()`,

```
int addtwo( int i, int j)
{
    char s[256];

    sprintf(s, "i=%d j=%d\n", i, j);
    MLAlert(stdenv, s);
    return i+j;
}
```

recompiling the code, and then re-installing the *MathLink* application, running and executing

(Local) In[1]:= **lnk = Install[LinkConnect["addtwo.exe"]];**

(Local) In[2]:= **AddTwo[2, 3]**

(Local) Out[2]= 5

causes the values of i and j to be displayed in an `MLAlert()` dialog, as in Figure 5.9.

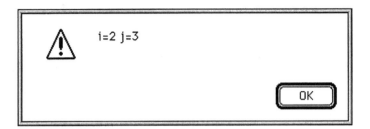

Figure 5.9. `MLAlert()` dialog.

The advantage of using `MLAlert()` is its portability.

We disconnect `addtwo.exe` using **Uninstall[]**. The link is closed, and the application `addtwo.exe` is terminated.

(Local) In[3]:= **Uninstall[lnk]**

(Local) Out[3]= addtwo.exe

5.5. Controlling Debugging Information

To better control the level of debugging information displayed, we add a template function to set a control flag.

```
:Begin:
:Function:       setprogramdebug
:Pattern:        SetProgramDebug[level_Integer]
:Arguments:      {level}
:ArgumentTypes:  {Integer}
:ReturnType:     Manual
:End:
```

The global variable `debuglevel` controls what debugging information is printed out.

```
#define NO_DEBUG 0
#define DEBUG_PRINT 1
#define DEBUG_ALERT 2
#define DEBUG_DEFAULT 3

int debuglevel=NO_DEBUG;
```

The *Mathematica* function **SetProgramDebug** sets the variable `debuglevel` using the `setprogramdebug` C function.

```
void setprogramdebug(int level)
{
    debuglevel=level;
    MLPutInteger(stdlink,level);
}
```

The C function debug_message(char *s) prints out the debugging information according to the value of debuglevel, and adds a time stamp to the output using the clockcount() function of Section 4.6. If debuglevel is set to DEBUG_PRINT, it sends the expression Print[message] to the kernel using MLEvaluateString. MLEvaluateString is generated automatically by mprep, and sends expressions to the kernel during template function processing. The variable in_template indicates whether or not the current execution is processing the template function. If debuglevel is DEBUG_PRINT, debug_message sends message to the kernel or stderr, according to the value of in_template. If debuglevel is DEBUG_ALERT, debug_message sends message to the MLAlert window, otherwise it sends message to stderr by default.

```
void debug_message(char *s)
{
    char str[256];

    switch(debuglevel){
        case DEBUG_PRINT:
            if(in_template){      // we are in the process of a template function.
                sprintf(str, "Print[\"%s(%8.4lfsec)\"]", s, clockcount());
                MLEvaluateString(stdlink, str);
            }
            else {
                fprintf(stderr, "%s(%8.4lfsec)\n", s, clockcount());
            }
            break;
        case DEBUG_ALERT:
            sprintf(str, "%s(%8.4lfsec)", s, clockcount());
            MLAlert(stdenv, str);
            break;
        default:
            fprintf(stderr, "%s(%8.4lfsec)\n", s, clockcount());
    }
}
```

Here is the modified version of addtwo. If the debuglevel is set, **AddTwo** will print out debugging messages.

```
int addtwo( int i, int j)
{
    if(debuglevel > 0){
        char s[256];
        sprintf(s, "addtwo:i=%d j=%d\n", i, j);
        debug_message(s);
    }

    return i+j;
}
```

Again, we recompile the program, run it, and connect to it from the kernel.

(Local) In[1]:= **Install[LinkConnect["addtwo.exe"]];**

(Local) In[2]:= **AddTwo[1, 2]**

(Local) Out[59]= 2

After setting `debuglevel` to 1,

    (Local) In[3]:=   **SetProgramDebug[1]**

    (Local) Out[3]=   1

AddTwo prints debugging messages during execution.

    (Local) In[4]:=   **Do[AddTwo[2, 3], {3}]**

               addtwo:i=2 j=3 (23.8500sec)

               addtwo:i=2 j=3 (23.9000sec)

               addtwo:i=2 j=3 (23.9667sec)

We will use this method in the following chapters to debug *MathLink* functions.

5.6. Summary

This chapter presents some debugging basics. Event-processing and polling mechanisms were examined using the debugger. These mechanisms are used intensively in later chapters. The insertion of `fprintf()` statements and the use of `MLAlert()` were described.

Chapter 6 — TurtleGraphics

In this book, we use the term real-time graphics to denote graphics drawn during the evaluation process. In this sense, *Mathematica*'s graphics are not real time since the front end draws graphics after the kernel evaluation is completed. There are many applications that require real-time graphics — *TurtleGraphics* and cellular automata simulation are two examples described in this book. In this chapter, we

[1] write a template program for real-time graphics;

[2] learn how to get user events; and

[3] learn how to make a package for a *MathLink* program.

6.1. Kernel Functions for *TurtleGraphics*

Turtle graphics are the graphics primitives of Logo (Papert, 1980). Commands to a turtle, like "Go forward 10 steps" or "Right turn 45 degrees", cause the turtle to move or change direction and the resulting trajectory creates a graphic. Although turtle graphics can be easily programmed using top-level *Mathematica* code, a better implementation is possible using real-time graphics that respond immediately to new commands. In this chapter, *MathLink* functions for performing real-time graphics are developed and *TurtleGraphics* is implemented using these functions.

For the drawing operation on window, the following eight *TurtleGraphics* (kernel) commands are defined:

[1] `RightTurn[θ]`:   turn right θ degrees.

[2] `LeftTurn[θ]`:   turn left θ degrees.

[3] `PenUp[]`:   lift turtle's pen up.

[4] `PenDown[]`:   lower turtle's pen down.

[5] `Home[]`:   return to home position.

[6] `Forward[n]`:   move n steps forward.

[7] `Backward[n]`:   move n steps backward.

[8] `ClearWindow[]`:   clear the window.

In addition, three global variables are used to hold the turtle's state:

[1] `curPos`:   turtle's current position.

[2] `curAng`:   turtle's current direction.

[3] `pen`:   current pen state. **Up** means pen is up, **Down** means pen is down.

This program's window coordinates differ from *Mathematica*: here (see Figure 6.1) the window's origin, O, is the top left corner; x increases to the right and y increases downwards.

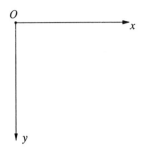

Figure 6.1. *TurtleGraphics* window coordinates.

We initialize the global variables to position the turtle in the middle of the window and set its direction to point upwards:

```
curPos = GetWindowSize[] / 2.0;
curAng = -90.0;
pen = Down;
```

All *TurtleGraphics* commands have simple and straightforward definitions. **RightTurn[deg]** increases **curAng** by **deg**:

```
RightTurn[deg_] := curAng += deg
```

LeftTurn[deg] is defined via **RightTurn[-deg]**:

```
LeftTurn[deg_] := RightTurn[-deg]
```

PenUp[] and **PenDown[]** change **pen**'s state:

```
PenUp[] := pen = Up;
PenDown[] := pen = Down;
```

Home[] moves the turtle to the middle of window, and resets its direction to point upwards:

```
Home[] :=
    (MoveTo[Round[curPos = GetWindowSize[] / 2.0]];
    curAng = -90.0)
```

Forward[n] draws a line of length **n** when **pen** is **Down**, or moves **n** steps when pen is **Up**:

```
Forward[n_] := If[pen === Down, lineto[n], moveto[n]]
```

lineto[n] and **moveto[n]** both move **n** steps. Each function converts **n** steps to **{x,y}** coordinates using **toPos[]** and then calls **LineTo[]** (respectively **MoveTo[]**), and changes the current position, **curPos**:

```
lineto[n_] := LineTo[curPos += toPos[n, curAng]];
moveto[n_] := MoveTo[curPos += toPos[n, curAng]];
```

`toPos[]` converts **n** steps from polar coordinates to cartesian coordinates:

```
toPos[n_, ang_] := n {Cos[ang Degree], Sin[ang Degree]}
```

`Backward[n]` calls `Forward[-n]`:

```
Backward[n_] := Forward[-n]
```

6.2. *MathLink* Template for *TurtleGraphics*

Our implementation of *TurtleGraphics* using *MathLink* will create a window in which the kernel can perform drawing operations. The overall design of this program is that each *MathLink* function corresponds to a primitive drawing operation. Only five general *MathLink* functions are required to implement all the *TurtleGraphics* commands of Section 6.1:

[1] **WOpen[]**:   open a window.

[2] **WClose[]**:   close a window.

[3] **MoveTo[{x,y}]**:   move pen to location **{x,y}**.

[4] **LineTo[{x,y}]**:   draw a line from current position to **{x,y}**.

[5] **ClearWindow[]**:   clear the window.

WOpen[] opens a window.

```
:Begin:
:Function:      wopen
:Pattern:       WOpen[
                {{x0_Integer,y0_Integer},{x1_Integer,y1_Integer}},
                    title_String]
:Arguments:     {x0,y0,x1,y1,title}
:ArgumentTypes: {Integer,Integer,Integer,Integer,String}
:ReturnType:    Integer
:End:
```

`{{x0,y0},{x1,y1}}` is the window position in global coordinates and `title` is the window's title as a string. **WOpen[]** returns 0 if the window was opened, otherwise it returns a negative value. **WClose[]** closes the open window.

```
:Begin:
:Function:        wclose
:Pattern:         WClose[]
:Arguments:       {}
:ArgumentTypes:   {}
:ReturnType:      Integer
:End:
```

The next three templates are for graphical primitives:

```
:Begin:
:Function:        moveto
:Pattern:         MoveTo[{x_, y_}]
:Arguments:       {x, y}
:ArgumentTypes:   {Integer, Integer}
:ReturnType:      Integer
:End:

:Begin:
:Function:        lineto
:Pattern:         LineTo[{x_, y_}]
:Arguments:       {x, y}
:ArgumentTypes:   {Integer, Integer}
:ReturnType:      Integer
:End:

:Begin:
:Function:        clearwindow
:Pattern:         ClearWindow[]
:Arguments:       { }
:ArgumentTypes:   { }
:ReturnType:      Integer
:End:
```

One extra utility function is required. **GetWindowSize[]** returns the window's width and height as a list:

```
:Begin:
:Function:        getwindowsize
:Pattern:         GetWindowSize[]
:Arguments:       {}
:ArgumentTypes:   {}
:ReturnType:      Manual
:End:
```

6.3. C Program

The C programs for MacOS are shown here. The Windows and Linux versions are included on the CD-ROM and the reader should be able to identify the corresponding functions on the CD-ROM. The main difference is the names of system functions, but the basic structure of the programs is similar.

gWindowPtr is a global variable to hold window structure.

```
WindowPtr gWindowPtr = nil;
```

wopen() opens a window. wopen() prepares arguments for the NewCWindow() toolbox function. If it success-
fully creates a new window, wopen() sets gWindowPtr and displays the window on the screen.

```
int wopen(int x0, int y0, int x1, int y1, char *title)
{
    Rect size;
    unsigned char ps[256];

    if(gWindowPtr != nil)    // window is already opened.
        return(-1);

    SetRect(&size, x0, y0, x1, y1);
    c2ps(title, ps);    // convert C string to Pascal string.

    gWindowPtr = NewCWindow(nil,&size,(unsigned char *)ps,true,
                            0,(WindowPtr)-1,true,(long)0);
    if(gWindowPtr == nil)
        return(-2);

    clearwindow();
    MacShowWindow(gWindowPtr);
    return(0);
}
```

wclose() closes the opened window using the DisposeWindow() toolbox function.

```
int wclose()
{
    if(gWindowPtr == nil)    // window is already closed.
        return(-1);
    DisposeWindow(gWindowPtr);
    gWindowPtr = nil;
    return(0);
}
```

clearwindow(), moveto(), and lineto() use a number of toolbox functions and have similar program
structures. Each checks gWindowPtr, saves the current port, sets the port to gWindowPtr and applies a toolbox
function and, finally, restores the current port.

clearwindow() gets the window size from the window structure, then uses the EraseRect() toolbox function
to clear the window.

```
int clearwindow()
{
    CGrafPtr curport;
    GDHandle curdev;

    if(gWindowPtr == nil){ // window is not opened.
        return(-1);
    }
    GetGWorld(&curport,&curdev);    // save the current port.
```

```
        MacSetPort(gWindowPtr);      // set to window port.
        EraseRect(&gWindowPtr->portRect);   // call toolbox function.
        SetGWorld(curport,curdev);  // restore the current port.
        return(0);  // return 0 for success.
}
```

`moveto()` and `lineto()` are almost identical.

```
int moveto(int x, int y)
{
    CGrafPtr curport;
    GDHandle curdev;

    if(gWindowPtr == nil)    // window is not opened.
        return(-1);
    GetGWorld(&curport,&curdev);    //save the curent port.
    MacSetPort(gWindowPtr);      // set to window port.
    MoveTo(x,y);            // call toolbox function.
    SetGWorld(curport,curdev);  // restore the current port.
    return(0);// return 0 for sccess.
}
```

```
int lineto(int x, int y)
{
    CGrafPtr curport;
    GDHandle curdev;

    if(gWindowPtr == nil)    // window is not opened.
        return(-1);
    GetGWorld(&curport,&curdev);    // save the current port.
    MacSetPort(gWindowPtr);      // set to window port.
    MacLineTo(x,y);       // call toolbox function.
    SetGWorld(curport,curdev);  // restore the current port.
    return(0);        // return 0 for sccess.
}
```

getwindowsize() obtains the window's width and height from its window structure and returns them as an integer list using MLPutIntegerList().

```
void getwindowsize(void)
{
    int x[2];

    if(gWindowPtr == nil){
        MLPutInteger(stdlink, -1);
        return;
    }
    x[0] = (gWindowPtr->portRect).right-(gWindowPtr->portRect).left;
    x[1] = (gWindowPtr->portRect).bottom-(gWindowPtr->portRect).top;
    MLPutIntegerList(stdlink,x,2);
}
```

6.4. Updating

After compilation, we run the program and use **WOpen[]** to create a new window. Then, using the **LineTo[]** command,

```
Do[(MoveTo[{i, i}];
    LineTo[{100 + i, 100 - i}]),
    {i, 0, 100, 5}]
```

we draw lines on the window (Figure 6.2).

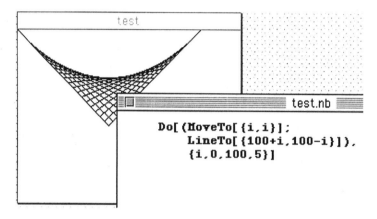

Figure 6.2. Running some graphics commands.

So far, so good. However, when the test.nb window is moved, the lines that were covered by the window are not updated (see Figure 6.3).

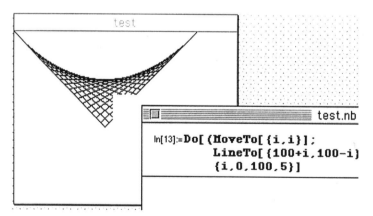

Figure 6.3. Background window is not updated.

This problem arises because our program does no redraw processing. When some hidden area becomes exposed, the program should receive an update event from the system and redraw the exposed window content.

Window redrawing in our program is achieved via an offscreen buffer which exists in memory. When hidden areas are exposed, the system sends an update event to the program. According to the event, the program copies the offscreen content to the window so that we can see the hidden area, as shown in Figure 6.4.

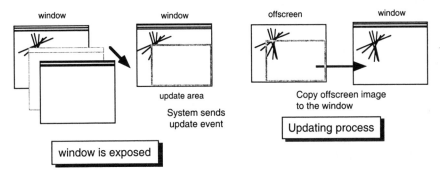

Figure 6.4. Process of redrawing hidden areas.

There is another situation requiring window updating. When the kernel sends a drawing command, the program draws on the offscreen buffer, not on the window. The window must reflect the new offscreen content so the program sends an update request to the system. Using the window updating mechanism, the new drawing appears on the window as shown in Figure 6.5.

We summarize the window drawing strategy:

[1] The kernel drawing command draws on the offscreen buffer.Then an update request is sent to the system for that area;

[2] When the program receives an update event from the system, the program redraws the offscreen image to the window.

6.5. Offscreen Buffer

We modify our program to add an offscreen buffer and update processing. The modifications are summarized as follows:

[1] When the window is opened, an offscreen buffer is created;

[2] When the window is closed, dispose of the offscreen buffer;

[3] Drawing commands draw on the offscreen buffer and send update request to the system;

[4] To update the window, copy the offscreen content to the window.

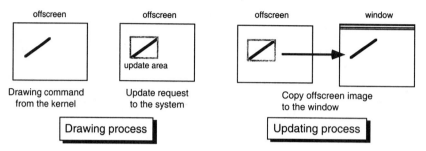

Figure 6.5. Process of displaying drawing commands.

All offscreen information is accessed through the (global) pointer `gOffscreenWptr`.

```
GWorldPtr gOffscreenWptr;
```

The `wopen()` function is redefined, creating an offscreen buffer immediately after the window is opened. The size of the offscreen buffer is the same as the screen display size. After creating the window, the `NewGWorld()` toolbox function creates an offscreen buffer. Here are the code modifications for `wopen()`:

```
...
    CGrafPtr curport;
    GDHandle curdev;
...


...
    GetGWorld(&curport, &curdev);
    er = NewGWorld(&gOffscreenWptr,32,&qd.screenBits.bounds,
            0,0,useTempMem); // toolbox call to create offscreen
    if(er != noErr){
        DisposeWindow(gWindowPtr);
        return(-3);
    }
...
```

`wclose()` disposes of the window and offscreen buffer:

```
int wclose()
{
    if(gWindowPtr == nil)
        return(-1);
    DisposeWindow(gWindowPtr);
    DisposeGWorld(gOffscreenWptr);
    gWindowPtr = nil;
    gOffscreenWptr = nil;
    return(0);
}
```

To update the window under MacOS, `flushoffscreen()` is used between `BeginUpdate()` and `EndUpdate()` toolbox functions:

```
void doupdate(WindowPtr window)
{
    BeginUpdate(window);
    flushoffscreen();
    EndUpdate(window);
}
```

doupdate() is called in _handle_user_event():

```
    case updateEvt:
        doupdate((WindowPtr)event.message);
        break;
```

PixMap is the area in memory that holds the window's pixel image. flushoffscreen() copies the offscreen window's PixMap to the window's PixMap using the CopyBit() toolbox function.

```
void flushoffscreen(void)
{
    PixMapHandle offpix;
    GrafPtr cp;

    if(gWindowPtr==nil)
        return;

    GetPort(&cp);
    MacSetPort(gWindowPtr);
    offpix = GetGWorldPixMap(gOffscreenWptr);
    LockPixels(offpix);
    CopyBits((BitMap *)*offpix,
        (BitMap *)*(((CGrafPtr)gWindowPtr)->portPixMap),
        &(gWindowPtr->portRect),&(gWindowPtr->portRect),srcCopy,0);
    UnlockPixels(offpix);
    MacSetPort(cp);
}
```

We now modify the drawing functions. Here is the modified lineto().

```
int lineto(int x, int y)
{
    CGrafPtr curport;
    GDHandle curdev;
    Rect rec;

    if(gWindowPtr == nil)
        return(-1);

    GetGWorld(&curport,&curdev);    // save the current port.
    LockPixels(GetGWorldPixMap(gOffscreenWptr));    // lock pixel
    SetGWorld(gOffscreenWptr,0);        // set to offscreen
    MacLineTo(x,y);        // draw it using toolbox function.
    UnlockPixels(GetGWorldPixMap(gOffscreenWptr)); // unlock pixel
    mySetRect(&rec,pt.h,pt.v,x,y);
    MacSetPort(gWindowPtr);        // set to window port
```

```
    InsetRect(&rec,-1,-1);  // enlarge rectangle to cover the line.
    InvalRect(&rec);        // sends update request using toolbox function.
    SetGWorld(curport,curdev); // restore the current port.
    return(0);
}
```

lineto() draws offscreen the update request sent to the system. Before sending an update request, the rectangle requiring updating is calculated, then InvalRect() sends an update request to the system. Modifications to the other drawing functions are similar.

6.6. Handling User Events

The machine-specific functions for processing external events were discussed in Section 5.2. In this section, we modify the function turtleProc() in win_turtle.c (Windows) and _handle_users_event() (MacOS) that processes external events for the window.

Here is the Windows function turtleProc().

```
LRESULT CALLBACK MLEXPORT
turtleProc( HWND hWnd, UINT msg, WPARAM wParam, LPARAM lParam)
{
    PAINTSTRUCT ps;

    switch( msg){
    case WM_CLOSE:
        wclose();
        break;
    case WM_PAINT:
        BeginPaint(hWnd, &ps);
        flushoffscreen(hWnd, &ps);
        EndPaint(hWnd, &ps);
        break;
    }
    return DefWindowProc( hWnd, msg, wParam, lParam);
}
```

WM_PAINT catches window update events and calls the flushoffscreen() function. WM_CLOSE calls wclose() to close the window.

For the MacOS we modify _handle_users_event() to process the following events:

[1] close event (when window's close button is pressed);

[2] drag event (when window's title bar is dragged);

[3] resize event (when window is resized).

When the user pushes the window's close button, _handle_user_event() calls TrackGoAway(). If TrackGo-Away() returns True, wclose() is called to close the window:

```
case inGoAway:
    if(TrackGoAway(window, event.where))
        wclose();
```

When the title bar is dragged, `DragWindow()` traces the mouse-dragging and moves the window:

```
case inDrag:
    DragWindow(window,event.where, &qd.screenBits.bounds);
    break;
```

When the window's right bottom corner is dragged, `GrowWindow()` is called to trace dragging and, if it returns true, `SizeWindow()` resizes the window:

```
case inGrow:
    grow=GrowWindow(window,event.where,qd.screenBits.bounds);
    if(grow)
        SizeWindow(window,LoWord(grow),HiWord(grow),true);
    break;
```

To summarize, the project file for *TurtleGraphics* is indicated in Figure 6.6. `turtle.c` contains the functions that were described in Sections 6.3, 6.4, and 6.5. `turtle.tm.c` is the file generated by SAmprep. `mac-turtle.c` and `win-turtle.c` contain the MacOS- and Windows-specific code respectively.

6.7. OpenWindow — A Better Interface to WOpen

As written, **WOpen[]** returns the integer 0 if there is no error and negative values to indicate specific errors. These numeric values are not much help to the user so we embed **WOpen[]** in **OpenWindow[]** and process error messages and options using this function.

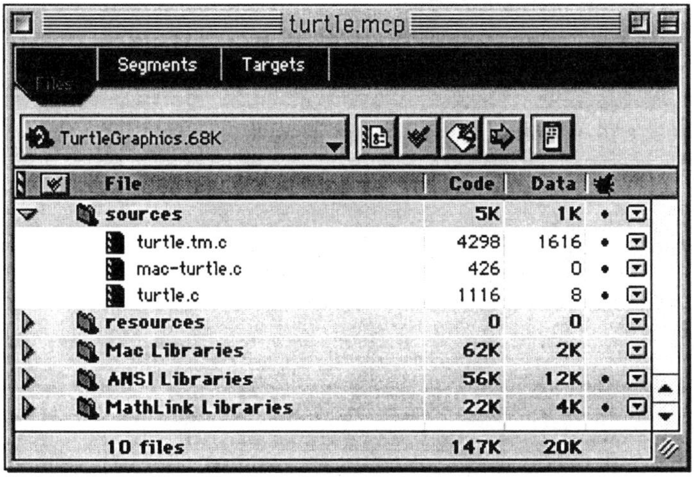

Figure 6.6. Project file for *TurtleGraphics* under MacOS.

```
OpenWindow[opt___Rule] :=
    Switch[
        WOpen[WindowSize /. {opt} /. Options[OpenWindow],
            WindowTitle /. {opt} /. Options[OpenWindow]], 0, 0,
        -1, Message[OpenWindow::reopen]; $Failed,
        -2, Message[OpenWindow::noopen, title]; $Failed,
        -3, Message[OpenWindow::ofscrn, title]; $Failed,
        $Failed, $Failed,
        _, Message[OpenWindow::unknown]; $Failed]
```

We use the built-in Message mechanism for processing error messages. Five tagged message strings are defined:

```
OpenWindow::reopen = "file already opened.";
OpenWindow::noopen = "can't open file `1`.";
OpenWindow::ofscrn = "can't create offscreen for file `1`.";
OpenWindow::unknown = "unknown error.";
OpenWindow::nowin = "window is not opened.";
```

For example, if **OpenWindow[]** is evaluated while the window is already open, the OpenWindow::reopen message is printed out.

    (Local) In[4]:= **OpenWindow[]**

        OpenWindow::reopen : file already opened.

    (Local) Out[4]= $Failed

Note that it is also possible to access this messaging mechanism directly from a *MathLink* program. For example, we can modify ClearWindow[] to return (Message[OpenWindow::nowin];$Failed) to the kernel instead of -1 as follows:

```
void clearwindow()
{
    // fail to clear window...
        MLPutFunction(stdlink,"CompoundExpression",2);
            MLPutFunction(stdlink,"Message", 1);
                MLPutFunction(stdlink,"MessageName", 2);
                    MLPutSymbol(stdlink,"OpenWindow");
                    MLPutString(stdlink,"nowin");
            MLPutSymbol(stdlink,"$Failed");
        MLEndPacket(stdlink);
    }
    else
        MLPutInteger(stdlink, 0);
}
```

We see that there are two ways of returning **Message[]** functions to the kernel: one uses *Mathematica* functions, and the other uses C functions from the *MathLink* library. The advantage of using *Mathematica* functions — which are much easier to write and modify — should be clear.

6.8. *TurtleGraphics* **Package**

Packages can be used to hide local variables and provide a suitable user interface. Our *TurtleGraphics* program — which is a combination of *Mathematica* functions and template functions — is easier to access from a package. Its functionality can be separated into two categories: *TurtleGraphics* commands and template functions. Accordingly, we create two packages: TurtleCommands.m and Templates.m. The complete TurtleGraphics package is installed into the AddOns`Applications`NetworkProgramming` directory, and the file structure is as follows.

```
(Local) In[1]:=  SetDirectory[ToFileName[{$TopDirectory, "AddOns",
                   "Applications", "NetworkProgramming", "TurtleGraphics"}]];

(Local) In[2]:=  FileNames["*"] // ColumnForm

(Local) Out[2]=  :Kernel
                 :Sources
                 :Templates.m
                 :TurtleCommands.m
                 :turtle.exe
                 :turtle-test.nb
```

Invoking **<<NetworkProgramming`TurtleGraphics`** causes init.m (in the Kernel subdirectory) to be loaded first, by default. This executes the following code.

```
BeginPackage["NetworkProgramming`TurtleGraphics`",
    "NetworkProgramming`TurtleGraphics`Templates`"]

$TTLink::usage="$TTLink is a LinkObject of the Turtle executable."
$TTLink::load="Install Turtle executable."

EndPackage[]

(* Declarations *)

DeclarePackage["NetworkProgramming`TurtleGraphics`TurtleCommands`",
    {"Forward","Backward","RightTurn","LeftTurn","PenUp","PenDown","Home"}]

(* Install Turtle executable *)

(* Install "turtle.exe" MathLink program *)
If[Head[$CurrentLink] =!= LinkObject,
    If[Head[$TTLink] =!= LinkObject || LinkDieQ[$TTLink] === True,
    $TTLink = Install["NetworkProgramming`TurtleGraphics`turtle`", LinkMode-
>Launch]]]
```

$TTLink is declared and then the TurtleCommands.m package is loaded using **DeclarePackage[]**. The last **If** command permits launching TurtleGraphics` using either **<<NetworkProgramming`TurtleGraphics`** or directly via an **Install[]** command. Both Windows and PowerPC executables are included and the appropriate executable is loaded automatically as explained in Section 4.1.

(Local) In[3]:= **FileNames["*", "turtle.exe", 2] // ColumnForm**

(Local) Out[3]= :turtle.exe:PowerMac

　　　　　::turtle.exe:PowerMac:turtle.exe

　　　　　:turtle.exe:Windows

　　　　　::turtle.exe:Windows:turtle.exe

Here are the first four lines of the template file Turtle.m.

```
:Evaluate:NetworkProgramming`TurtleGraphics`$TTLink = $CurrentLink
:Evaluate:Needs["NetworkProgramming`TurtleGraphics`"]
:Evaluate:BeginPackage["NetworkProgramming`TurtleGraphics`Templates`"]
:Evaluate:Begin["`Private`"]
```

Mathematica commands can be inserted into a template using :Evaluate:. These commands are evaluated when **Install[]** loads the template program. The variable **$TTLink** is defined at the top of the template followed by commands to load the packages.

　　$CurrentLink is a global variable automatically set to the **LinkObject** of the template program when it is loaded. If **<<NetworkProgramming`TurtleGraphics`** is executed, init.m is read first. At this point, **$CurrentLink** and **$TTLink** are not defined so the **Install[]** command is executed. Alternately, using **Install[]** directly causes **$CurrentLink** and **$TTLink** to be defined. Then the **Needs[]** command loads the TurtleGraphics` package, but this time **Install[]** is not executed again.

　　Here is Templates.m.

```
BeginPackage["NetworkProgramming`TurtleGraphics`Templates`"]

OpenWindow::usage = "OpenWindow[opt] open an window."
WindowSize::usage = "WindowSize is a option for OpenWindow. Default is
{{100,100},{300,300}}."
WindowTitle::usage = "WindowTitle is a option for OpenWindow. Default is
\"untitled\"."
CloseWindow::usage = "CloseWindow[] close the window."
MoveTo::usage = "MoveTo[{x,y}] move current point to {x,y}."
LineTo::usage = "LineTo[{x,y}] draw line from current point to {x,y}."
GetWindowSize::usage = "GetWindowSize[] return the window size {width,height}."
ClearWindow::usage = "ClearWindow[] clear the current window content."

Begin["`Private`"]

OpenWindow::reopen = "file already opened.";
OpenWindow::noopen = "can't open file `1`.";
OpenWindow::ofscrn = "can't create offscreen for file `1`. nieces program's memory
size";
OpenWindow::unknown =  "unknown error.";
OpenWindow::nowin = "window is not opened.";
CloseWindow::nowin = "file already closed.";

Options[OpenWindow] = {WindowSize->{{100,100},{300,300}}, WindowTitle->"untitled"};

OpenWindow[opt___Rule] :=
    Switch[WOpen[WindowSize /.{opt} /. Options[OpenWindow],
        WindowTitle/.{opt}/.Options[OpenWindow]],
        0,0,
```

```
            -1,Message[OpenWindow::reopen];$Failed,
            -2,Message[OpenWindow::noopen,title];$Failed,
            -3,Message[OpenWindow::ofscrn,title];$Failed,
            $Failed,$Failed,
            _,Message[OpenWindow::unknown];$Failed]

CloseWindow[] :=
    Switch[WClose[],
        0,0,
        -1,Message[CloseWindow::nowin];$Failed,
        $Failed,$Failed,
        _,Message[CloseWindow::unknown];$Failed]

End[]
EndPackage[]
```

`TurtleCommands.m` is the package to construct turtle commands from functions in `Templates.m`.

```
BeginPackage["NetworkProgramming`TurtleGraphics`TurtleCommands`",
"NetworkProgramming`TurtleGraphics`Templates`"]

Forward::usage = "Forward[n] moves turtle n steps forward."
Backward::usage = "Backward[n] moves turtle n steps backward."
RightTurn::usage = "RightTurn[n] turns turtle n degrees to the right."
LeftTurn::usage = "LeftTurn[n] turns turtle n degrees to the left."
PenUp::usage ="PenUp[] lifts turtle's pen up."
PenDown::usage ="PenDown[] lowers turtle's pen down."
Home::usage ="Home[] re-sets turtle to its home position."

Begin["`Private`"]

curPos = GetWindowSize[]/2.0;
curAng = -90.0;
pen = Up;
RightTurn[deg_] := curAng += deg;
LeftTurn[deg_] := RightTurn[-deg];
PenUp[] := pen = Up;
PenDown[] := pen = Down;
Home[] := (TMoveTo[Round[curPos = GetWindowSize[]/2.0]];curAng=-90.0;);
Forward[n_] := If[pen===Down, lineto[n], moveto[n]];
moveto[n_] := MoveTo[Round[curPos += toPos[n,curAng]]];
lineto[n_] := LineTo[Round[curPos += toPos[n,curAng]]];
toPos[n_,ang_] := n {Cos[ang Degree],Sin[ang Degree]};
Backward[n_] := Forward[-n];

End[]
EndPackage[]
```

6.9. Examples of *TurtleGraphics*

After loading the package,

(Local) In[4]:= **<< NetworkProgramming`TurtleGraphics`**

we open a window using **OpenWindow[]**,

(Local) In[5]:= **OpenWindow[]**

(Local) Out[5]= 0

and draw a simple turtle graphic.

(Local) In[6]:= **ClearWindow[]; Home[]; PenUp[]; RightTurn[135]; Forward[80 / Sqrt[2]];
LeftTurn[135]; PenDown[]; Do[Forward[80]; LeftTurn[90], {4}]**

These commands clear the window and draw a square (see Figure 6.7).

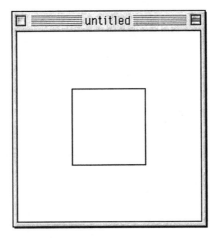

Figure 6.7. A square drawn using `TurtleGraphics`` commands.

Now we draw some more complicated graphics.

(Local) In[9]:= **ClearWindow[]; Home[]; PenUp[]; RightTurn[135]; Forward[80 / Sqrt[2]];
LeftTurn[135]; PenDown[]; Do[Forward[80]; LeftTurn[91], {90}]**

This is Logo's archetypal "sun flower" example. A simple combination of *Mathematica* functions and Turtle-
Graphics` commands can easily be used to create some rather complicated graphics, as in Figure 6.8.

An approximation to the Hilbert curve can be generated using the following recursive definition.

(Local) In[12]:= **hilbert[1, s_, size_] := (Forward[size];
LeftTurn[s 90]; Forward[size]; LeftTurn[s 90]; Forward[size];)**

```
(Local) In[13]:=  hilbert[n_, s_, size_] := (LeftTurn[s 90]; hilbert[n - 1, -s, size];
                   LeftTurn[s 90]; Forward[size]; hilbert[n - 1, s, size]; RightTurn[s 90];
                   Forward[size]; RightTurn[s 90]; hilbert[n - 1, s, size]; Forward[size];
                   LeftTurn[s 90]; hilbert[n - 1, -s, size]; LeftTurn[s 90];)

(Local) In[14]:=  ClearWindow[]; Home[]; PenUp[]; RightTurn[135];
                   Forward[80 / Sqrt[2]]; LeftTurn[135]; PenDown[]; hilbert[5, 1, 3]
```

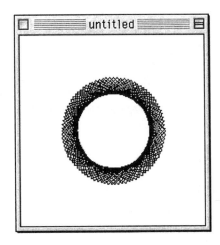

Figure 6.8. Drawing a "sun flower" using `TurtleGraphics`` commands.

Real-time graphics let us watch the drawing process and help our understanding of the recursive nature of Hilbert's curve (Figure 6.9).

Figure 6.9. Hilbert's space-filling curve.

`CloseWindow[]` closes the window and `Uninstall[]` terminates the program.

(Local) In[17]:= `CloseWindow[];`

(Local) In[18]:= `Uninstall[$TTLink]`

(Local) Out[18]= turtle.exe

6.10. Summary

In this chapter, a real-time graphics program, which enables us to see the drawing process during evaluation, was implemented via a *MathLink* template program.

TurtleGraphics was defined using template functions. Once these external graphics primitives were implemented, the other parts were defined as *Mathematica* functions. *Mathematica*'s flexibility and power greatly enhance the *MathLink* program, making it very easy to draw recursive pictures using this implementation of *TurtleGraphics*.

6.11. References

[1] Dave Mark and Scott Knaster, *Macintosh C Programming Primer: Mastering the Toolbox Using Think C*, Addison-Wesley, Reading, MA, 1990.

[2] David Mark and Cartwright Reed, *Macintosh C Programming Primer: Inside the Toolbox Using Think C*, Second Edition, Addison-Wesley, Reading, MA, 1992.

[3] Seymour Papert, *Mindstorms: Children, Computers, and Powerful Ideas*, Basic Books Inc., NewYork, 1980.

[4] Charles Petzold, *Programming Windows 95*, Microsoft Press, Redmond, Washington, 1996.

Chapter 7—Cellular Automata

Cellular automata were suggested by Stanislaw Ulam in the 1940s and first formalized by John von Neumann (see also Wolfram, 1994). Several interesting cellular automata models and corresponding *Mathematica* programs are presented in the book, *Modeling Nature: Cellular Automata Simulations with Mathematica* (Gaylord and Nishidate, 1996).

In this chapter, the *TurtleGraphics* program from Chapter 6 is extended to draw cellular automata graphics in real time. The purposes of this chapter are to:

[1] implement the *Forest Fire* and *Game of Life* cellular automata models (see Gaylord and Nishidate, 1996) in real time;

[2] improve data transfer times for faster animation.

7.1. Introduction

The real-time graphics of Chapter 6 are also useful for displaying cellular automata simulations. Direct animation of the *Game of Life* using the current notebook front end is impractical because of the large amount of memory required to display each *life state* during computation. However, using real-time graphics it is easy to display and update the *life state* during computation (Figure 7.1).

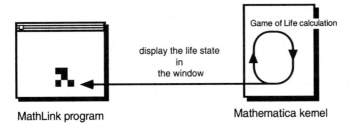

Figure 7.1. Displaying the *life state* during computation.

7.2. Displaying in *MathLink* Program Window

To display cellular automata, a region is divided into small *cells* that are colored according to the cellular automata state. Our *MathLink* program colors the cells, by processing **Raster[]** or **RasterArray[]** graphics primitives (see Section 2.9.2 of *The Mathematica Book*), and then displays them in its window using the template function, **PutGraphicsObject**[*graphics* [, *options*]]. The template for **RasterArray[]** graphics primitives follows.

```
PutGraphicsObject[RasterArray[ras_], opt___Rule] :=
        Module[{bounds, mymode, myframe},
        bounds = Dimensions[ras][[{2, 1}]];
        mymode = TransferMode /. {opt} /. Options[PutGraphicsObject];
```

```
    myframe = FrameSize /. {opt} /. Options[PutGraphicsObject];
    PutPixRect[setupcpix[Flatten[ras /. RGBColor -> List]],
        bounds, myframe, mymode /. TransferModeName]]
```

The default options for **PutGraphicsObject[]** are as follows.

```
Options[PutGraphicsObject] =
  {FrameSize :→ {{0, 0}, GetWindowSize[]}, TransferMode → SourceCopy };
```

```
TransferModeName = {SourceCopy → 0, SourceOr → 1, SourceXor → 2};
```

The **FrameSize** option indicates the rectangular area in which to draw the object with default value being the full window. **TransferMode** indicates the graphics overlay mode.

   PutPixRect[] is the template function for transferring the data.

```
:Begin:
:Function:      putpixrect
:Pattern:       PutPixRect[data_List,{w_Integer,h_Integer},
                {{dx0_Integer,dy0_Integer},{dx1_Integer,dy1_Integer}},
                mode_Integer,wnum_Integer]
:Arguments:     {data, w, h, dx0, dy0, dx1, dy1, mode, wnum}
:ArgumentTypes: {IntegerList,Integer,Integer,Integer,Integer,Integer,
                Integer,Integer,Integer}
:ReturnType:    Manual
:End:
```

The list of **RGBColor[**r, g, b**]** values is converted to a one-dimensional array of integers using the *Mathematica* function **setupcpix**, which converts a list of real values, each in the range 0 to 1, to integer values in the range 0 to 255. **setupcpix** is defined as a compiled function in the template file using :Evaluate: (see Section 6.8).

```
setupcpix = Compile[{{x, _Real, 1}}, Round[255 x]]
```

putpixrect() is the external function called from **PutPixRect[]**.

```
void putpixrect(int *data, long len, int width, int height,
    int dx0,int dy0,int dx1,int dy1,int mode, int wnum)
```

wnum is the identification number of the window. If the window is open, the window information is stored in win, otherwise the if statement causes putpixrect() to return -1.

```
win = getWindowSlotPtr(wnum);
if(win == NULL){
    MLPutInteger(stdlink,-1);
    return;
}
```

The window information WindowIndex is a structure that contains window and offscreen.

```
typedef struct WindowIndex{
    WindowPtr window;
```

```
    GWorldPtr offscreen;
} WindowIndex;
```

First, we create a temporary offscreen buffer to hold the pixel data.

```
MacSetRect(&bounds,0,0,width,height);
er = NewGWorld(&tmp,32,&bounds,0,0,0);
if(er != noErr){
    MLPutInteger(stdlink,-2);
    return;
}
```

The data structure of color pixels in the offscreen buffer is indicated in Figure 7.2.

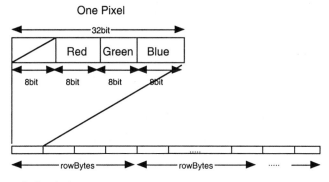

Figure 7.2. Data structure of color pixels.

Next we set the pointers `base` and `rowbytes`. `base` is a pointer to the pixel data, and `rowbytes` is the size of the temporary offsceen buffer (see Figure 7.2).

```
MacSetRect(&dest, dx0, dy0, dx1, dy1);
GetGWorld(&curport,&curdev);
tmppix = GetGWorldPixMap(tmp);
LockPixels(tmppix);
base = (unsigned char *)(**tmppix).baseAddr;
rowbytes = (**tmppix).rowBytes & 0x3fff;
```

Then we copy the data to the temporary offscreen pixels. `p` is the pointer to the pixel row.

```
SetGWorld(tmp,0);
for(j=0;j < height; ++j){
    p = base + rowbytes * j;
    for(i=0;i < width; ++i){
        p++;
        m = 3*(width*j+i);
        *p++ = data[m];
        *p++ = data[m+1];
        *p++ = data[m+2];
    }
}
```

After that, we copy the temporary offscreen buffer to the real destination—in this case, `offscreen`—using `CopyBits`, and then `InvalRect()` sends a rectangle update request to the system as described in Section 6.5.

```
CopyBits((BitMap *)*tmppix,
    (BitMap *)*(((CGrafPtr)(win->offscreen))->portPixMap),
        &bounds,&dest,mode,nil);
UnlockPixels(tmppix);
MacSetPort(win->window);
InvalRect(&dest);
```

Finally, the temporary offscreen is removed.

```
SetGWorld(curport,curdev);
DisposeGWorld(tmp);
```

7.3. Forest Fire Simulation

Let's demonstrate one popular cellular automata model—a *Forest Fire* simulation. First we launch the *MathLink* program.

(Local) In[1]:= **<< NetworkProgramming`CellularAutomata`**

This uses the same method to load the package and install the executable as described in Section 6.8.

7.3.1 Definitions

Assign constants using values from Gaylord and Nishidate (1996).

```
(Local) In[2]:=  n = 100;
                 s = 0.3;
                 k = 0;
                 p = 0.05;
                 f = 0.00025;
                 g = 0;
                 t = 100;
                 sprout = (1 + p);
                 catch = (2 - g);
                 spont = 1 + (1 - g) f;
```

n=100 indicates 100×100 cells. Now we set up the initial (random) state of the forest (see Figure 7.3).

```
(Local) In[12]:=  forestPreserve =
                    Table[Floor[1 + s - Random[]], {n}, {n}] /. 1 :> Floor[1 + k + Random[]];
```

spread[*n*, __] defines how the fire spreads using rule-based (pattern-matching) programming.

```
(Local) In[13]:=  spread[0, _, _, _, _] := Floor[sprout - Random[]];
                  spread[2, _, _, _, _] = 0;
                  spread[1, a_, b_, c_, d_] :=
                    1 + Floor[catch - Random[]] /; MatchQ[2, a | b | c | d];
                  spread[1, a_, b_, c_, d_] := 1 + Floor[spont - Random[]];
```

This model has three cell states, indicated by the argument, *n*. The relationship, ▪▪▪, between the four nearest neighbors, ▪, of a specified cell, , is implemented as **VonNeumann[]** using list operations.

```
(Local) In[17]:=   VonNeumann[func_, lat_] :=
                     MapThread[func, Map[RotateRight[lat, #] &,
                       {{0, 0}, {1, 0}, {0, -1}, {-1, 0}, {0, 1}}]], 2];
```

7.3.2 Display

To display these three cell states in a window, a **RasterArray[]** of corresponding **RGBColor[]** values is created using pattern-matching and **PutGraphicsObject[]** reads the resulting **RasterArray[]** object.

```
(Local) In[18]:=   ShowForest[lat_] :=
                     (PutGraphicsObject[RasterArray[lat /.
                       {0 → RGBColor[0.380, 0.210, 0.050],
                        1 → RGBColor[0.240, 0.580, 0.110],
                        2 → RGBColor[1.000, 1.000, 0.170]}]]; lat)
```

After opening a new window called Forest Fire,

```
(Local) In[19]:=   OpenWindow[WindowTitle → "Forest Fire"]
```

```
(Local) Out[19]=   0
```

we use **ShowForest[]** to display the state of the forest in the program's window (Figure 7.3).

```
(Local) In[20]:=   ShowForest[forestPreserve];
```

Figure 7.3. Initial state of the forest.

7.3.3 Animation

We can animate the evolution using **Nest**.

(Local) In[21]:= **forestPreserve =**
                  Nest[VonNeumann[spread, ShowForest[#1]] &, forestPreserve, 20];

After 20 time-steps several fires are visible in the forest (Figure 7.4).

Figure 7.4. State of the forest after 20 time-steps.

7.4. Execution Time of PutGraphicsObject

To measure the execution time of **PutGraphicsObject[]**, we first compute the execution time of **ShowForest[]** by taking the difference between the time taken for one time-step of the forest fire simulation with and without **ShowForest[]**.

(Local) In[22]:= **mlSessionTime[VonNeumann[spread, ShowForest[#]] &, forestPreserve] -**
                  mlSessionTime[VonNeumann[spread, #] &, forestPreserve]

(Local) Out[22]= 1.75

One time-consuming part of **ShowForest[]** is its transfer format. The original matrix consists of integer data values, 0, 1, and 2. This matrix is converted to a **RasterArray[]** of **RGBColor** values for **PutGraphicsObject[]**, which converts **RGBColor** values to a **List**. It should be apparent that these transformations are unnecessary and time consuming. The other time-consuming part is the actual data transfer. Sending a 100×100 matrix involves the transfer of 30000 integers.

(Local) In[23]:= **mlSessionTime[SendList, Range[30000]]**

(Local) Out[23]= 1.13333

For cellular automata applications, the number of colors is usually not large: *Forest Fire* only uses three colors. Instead of sending **RGBColor** values, sending a color index number will reduce data transfer. Using a *color index table*, the integers 0, 1, and 2 are interpreted by the program as colors.

7.5. Color Index Table

We now implement a color index table that pairs up each index entry with a color. The user can set the color for each table item. The following structure, myRGBcolor, is used to represent colors.

```
typedef struct myRGBColor{
    double red;
    double green;
    double blue;
} myRGBColor;
```

We set the size of our color table to 256.

```
static myRGBColor colortable[256];
```

The templates to set up the color index table follow. **SetColor[**n→**RGBColor[**r,g,b**]]** maps the nth color to **RGBColor[**r,g,b**]**.

```
:Begin:
:Function:        setcolor
:Pattern:         SetColor[Rule[n_Integer/;0<=n<256,RGBColor[r_,g_,b_]]]
:Arguments:       {n, r, g, b}
:ArgumentTypes:   {Integer,Real,Real,Real}
:ReturnType:      Manual
:End:
```

The range of each color value is from 0 to 1, that is, $0 \le r, g, b \le 1$.

```
void setcolor(int num, double r, double g, double b)
{
    if(num < 256){
        colortable[num].red = r;
        colortable[num].green = g;
        colortable[num].blue = b;
        MLPutInteger(stdlink,0);
    }
    else
        MLPutInteger(stdlink,-1);
}
```

GetColor[n**]** returns the nth color.

```
:Begin:
:Function:        getcolor
:Pattern:         GetColor[n_Integer]
:Arguments:       {n}
:ArgumentTypes:   {Integer}
:ReturnType:      Manual
:End:
```

```
void getcolor(int num)
{
    if(num < 256){
        MLPutFunction(stdlink,"RGBColor",3);
        MLPutReal(stdlink, colortable[num].red);
        MLPutReal(stdlink, colortable[num].green);
        MLPutReal(stdlink, colortable[num].blue);
        MLEndPacket(stdlink);
    }
    else
        MLPutInteger(stdlink,-1);
}
```

SetColorList[] sets the color list {$n \to$ **RGBColor**$[r, g, b]$**,** ...**}** of a color table.

```
SetColorList[colorlist_] := Map[SetColor, colorlist]
```

GetColorList[{2,4,5,...}] returns a list of numbered colors in a color table.

```
GetColorList[nl_] := Map[GetColor, nl]
```

We extend **PutGraphicsObject[]** to handle index color objects of the form **IndexColor[{{n,...},...}]**.

```
PutGraphicsObject[IndexColor[ctm_], opt___Rule] :=
    Module[{bounds, mymode, myframe},
        bounds = Dimensions[ctm][[{2, 1}]];
        mymode = TransferMode /. {opt} /. Options[PutGraphicsObject];
        myframe = FrameSize /. {opt} /. Options[PutGraphicsObject];
    PutPixTable[Flatten[ctm], bounds, myframe, mymode /. TranferModeName]]
```

PutGraphicsObject[] calls the template function **PutPixTable[]**.

```
:Begin:
:Function:       putpixtable
:Pattern:        PutPixTable[data_List, {w_Integer,h_Integer},
                 {{dx0_Integer,dy0_Integer},{dx1_Integer,dy1_Integer}},
                 mode_Integer,wnum_Integer]
:Arguments:      {data, w, h, dx0, dy0, dx1, dy1, mode, wnum}
:ArgumentTypes:  {IntegerList,Integer,Integer,
                 Integer,Integer,Integer,Integer,Integer,Integer}
:ReturnType:     Manual
:End:
```

The loop structure of `putpixtable()` is similar to `putpixrect()` but, instead, gets values from `colortable`.

```
void putpixtable(int data[], long len, int width, int height,
    int dx0,int dy0,int dx1,int dy1,int mode, int wnum)
{
    ...
    for(j=0;j < height; ++j){
        p = base + rowbytes * j;
        for(i=0;i < width; ++i){
```

```
            p++;
            m = width*j+i;
            *p++ = 255 * colortable[data[m]].red;
            *p++ = 255 * colortable[data[m]].green;
            *p++ = 255 * colortable[data[m]].blue;
        }
    }
    ...
}
```

To test the operation of our color index table, three states are paired up with colors using **SetColorList[]**.

(Local) In[24]:= **SetColorList[**
                  {0 → RGBColor[0.380, 0.210, 0.050],
                   1 → RGBColor[0.240, 0.580, 0.110],
                   2 → RGBColor[1.000, 1.000, 0.170]}]

(Local) Out[24]= {0, 0, 0}

ShowForest2[] uses **IndexColor[]** instead of **RasterArray[]** used by **ShowForest[]**.

(Local) In[25]:= **ShowForest2[lat_] := (PutGraphicsObject[IndexColor[lat]]; lat)**

We now measure the ratio of evaluation times using **mlSessionTime[]**.

(Local) In[26]:= $\dfrac{\text{mlSessionTime[ShowForest, forestPreserve]}}{\text{mlSessionTime[ShowForest2, forestPreserve]}}$

(Local) Out[26]= 2.36585

From this result, the evaluation using a color table is more than three times faster. This approach is faster because:

[1] data transfer is decreased by 2/3;

[2] there is no data conversion from real numbers to integers.

We conclude this section by closing the open window.

(Local) In[27]:= **CloseWindow[]**

(Local) Out[27]= 0

7.6. The *Game of Life*

Conway's *Game of Life* was popularized in Martin Gardner's mathematical games column in the October 1970 and February 1971 issues of *Scientific American*. The game board consists of a rectangular $m \times n$ array of cells, with each cell either empty or filled. At each time-step, the next generation is produced by the following rules:

[1] if a cell is empty, fill it if exactly 3 of its neighbors are filled. Otherwise leave it empty.

[2] if a cell is filled, it continues to live if it has 2 or 3 neighbors. Otherwise the cell dies.

Neighbors include the cells on the diagonals.

Even with such a simple set of rules, the evolution is amazingly varied. The principles and applications of the *Game of Life* are described in more detail in Poundstone (1987).

Several *Mathematica* packages for the *Game of Life* exist. In this section, we re-implement the *Game of Life* program following Gaylord and Nishidate (1996).

7.6.1 Program

The initial state, **initConfig**, is created using **Table[]**. We start with a 10×10 configuration.

```
(Local) In[28]:=  n = 10;
```

```
(Local) In[29]:=  initConfig = Table[Random[Integer], {n}, {n}];
```

Here are the function definitions.

```
(Local) In[30]:=  LiveConfigs = Join[
                      Map[Join[{0}, #] &, Permutations[{1, 1, 1, 0, 0, 0, 0, 0}]],
                      Map[Join[{1}, #] &, Permutations[{1, 1, 1, 0, 0, 0, 0, 0}]],
                      Map[Join[{1}, #] &, Permutations[{1, 1, 0, 0, 0, 0, 0, 0}]]];
```

```
(Local) In[31]:=  DieConfigs = Complement[Flatten[
                      Map[Permutations,
                        Map[Join[Table[1, {#}], Table[0, {(9 - #)}]] &,
                        Range[0, 9]]], 1], LiveConfigs];
```

```
(Local) In[32]:=  Apply[(update[##] = 1) &, LiveConfigs, 1];
```

```
(Local) In[33]:=  Apply[(update[##] = 0) &, DieConfigs, 1];
```

The relationship, ▦, between the eight neighbors, ▪, of a specified cell, , is implemented as **Moore[]** using list operations.

```
(Local) In[34]:=  Moore[func__, lat_] := MapThread[func,
                      Map[RotateRight[lat, #] &,
                      {{0, 0}, {1, 0}, {0, -1}, {-1, 0}, {0, 1},
                       {1, -1}, {-1, -1}, {-1, 1}, {1, 1}}], 2];
```

7.6.2 Display

It is very simple to display stages in the evolution of the *Game of Life*. First we open a new blank window.

```
(Local) In[35]:=  OpenWindow[WindowTitle → "Life Game"]
```

```
(Local) Out[35]=  0
```

After defining a color table,

```
(Local) In[36]:=  SetColorList[{0 → RGBColor[1, 1, 1], 1 → RGBColor[0, 0, 0]}]
```

```
(Local) Out[36]=  {0, 0}
```

we can display the state using **showLife[]**, which calls **PutIndexColor[]** (Figure 7.5).

```
(Local) In[37]:=  showLife[lat_] := (PutGraphicsObject[IndexColor[lat]]; lat)
```

(Local) In[38]:= **showLife[initConfig];**

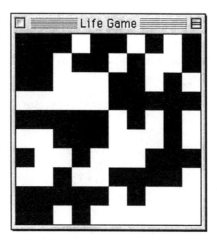

Figure 7.5. Displaying a state in the *Game of Life*.

The initial configuration,

(Local) In[39]:= **MatrixForm[showLife[initConfig]]**

(Local) Out[39]=
$$
\begin{pmatrix}
1 & 1 & 1 & 0 & 1 & 1 & 0 & 1 & 0 & 1 \\
1 & 1 & 0 & 1 & 1 & 0 & 1 & 0 & 0 & 1 \\
1 & 1 & 0 & 0 & 0 & 1 & 1 & 0 & 1 & 0 \\
0 & 0 & 0 & 0 & 0 & 1 & 1 & 1 & 1 & 1 \\
1 & 1 & 1 & 1 & 1 & 0 & 1 & 0 & 1 & 0 \\
0 & 0 & 1 & 1 & 1 & 0 & 0 & 0 & 1 & 0 \\
1 & 0 & 0 & 1 & 0 & 0 & 0 & 1 & 1 & 1 \\
0 & 0 & 1 & 0 & 0 & 1 & 1 & 1 & 1 & 0 \\
1 & 1 & 1 & 1 & 1 & 0 & 1 & 0 & 0 & 0 \\
1 & 1 & 0 & 1 & 0 & 0 & 0 & 0 & 0 & 0
\end{pmatrix}
$$

is displayed in the *MathLink* program window. State 0 is white (**RGBColor[1,1,1]**), and state 1 is black (**RGBColor[0,0,0]**). Time-steps in the evolution are computed using **update**.

(Local) In[40]:= **MatrixForm[Moore[update, initConfig]]**

(Local) Out[40]=
$$
\begin{pmatrix}
0 & 0 & 0 & 0 & 0 & 1 & 1 & 0 & 1 & 0 \\
0 & 0 & 0 & 1 & 0 & 0 & 0 & 0 & 0 & 0 \\
0 & 1 & 1 & 0 & 0 & 0 & 0 & 0 & 0 & 0 \\
0 & 0 & 0 & 1 & 0 & 0 & 0 & 0 & 0 & 0 \\
1 & 1 & 0 & 0 & 0 & 0 & 1 & 0 & 0 & 0 \\
0 & 0 & 0 & 0 & 0 & 1 & 0 & 0 & 0 & 0 \\
0 & 1 & 0 & 0 & 0 & 1 & 0 & 0 & 0 & 0 \\
0 & 0 & 0 & 0 & 0 & 1 & 0 & 0 & 0 & 0 \\
1 & 0 & 0 & 0 & 1 & 0 & 1 & 0 & 0 & 1 \\
0 & 0 & 0 & 0 & 0 & 0 & 1 & 0 & 0 & 0
\end{pmatrix}
$$

Successive time-steps are easily computed using **Nest[]**.

7.6.3 Processing Time

We now examine a 100×100 configuration (Figure 7.6).

(Local) In[41]:= **n = 100;**

(Local) In[42]:= **initConfig = Table[Random[Integer], {n}, {n}];**

We then animate the evolution of 20 generations.

(Local) In[43]:= **initConfig = Nest[Moore[update, showLife[#]] &, initConfig, 20];**

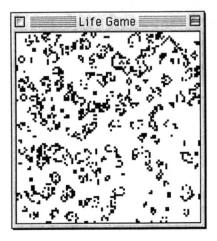

Figure 7.6. Displaying the state of 100×100 cells in the *Game of Life*.

To improve our *Game of Life* program, we need to know which part of the program takes the most time — computation or data transfer. We now measure the time fractions due to computation (excluding display) and transfer using **mlSessionTime[]**. **t0** is the total evaluation time for one time-step, including display. Of course, this timing will vary from system to system.

(Local) In[44]:= **t0 = mlSessionTime[Moore[update, showLife[#]] &, initConfig]**

(Local) Out[44]= 1.71667

To estimate the transfer time via *MathLink*, we make a **dummy[]** function that contains the same code as **PutGraphicsObject[]** except that it does no data transfer.

(Local) In[45]:= **dummy[ctm_List, opt___Rule] := Module[{bounds, myframe, mymode},**
bounds = Dimensions[ctm][[{2, 1}]];
mymode = TransferMode /. {opt} /. Options[PutGraphicsObject];
myframe = FrameSize /. {opt} /. Options[PutGraphicsObject];
{Flatten[ctm], bounds, x0, y0, x1, y1, mode}]

(Local) In[46]:= **showLife2[lat_] := (dummy[lat]; lat)**

(Local) In[47]:= **t1 = mlSessionTime[Moore[update, showLife2[#]] &, initConfig] / t0**

(Local) Out[47]= 0.456311

t1 is the *computation fraction* of the total time. Although it measures a *timing ratio*, it will still vary from system to system because of differences in system configuration.

t2 is the *transfer fraction*, computed as the time taken to transfer 10000 integers using **SendList** divided by **t0**.

(Local) In[48]:= **t2 = mlSessionTime[SendList, Range[10000]] / t0**

(Local) Out[48]= 0.52

The sum of **t1** and **t2** is close to 1 because the computation time plus the data transfer time equals the total evaluation time.

(Local) In[49]:= **t1 + t2**

(Local) Out[49]= 1.

There are several possible ways of improving the evaluation time, for example, transfer compressed data or use a different computational algorithm. In any case, it is worth measuring the fractional transfer times so we can optimize our programming effort. For example, if data transfer takes less than 20% of the total evaluation time, one should focus on improving the computational algorithm instead of speeding up data transfer.

We conclude this section by uninstalling CellularAutomata.exe.

(Local) In[50]:= **Uninstall[$CALink]**

(Local) Out[50]= CellularAutomata.exe

7.7. Summary

As another application of real-time graphics, we extended the *Turtle Graphics* program to display cellular automata states. Data transfer is an important consideration when writing *MathLink* programs and, using a color table, transfer times were greatly reduced.

The essential programming concept used here is to create an interface between toolbox functions and *Mathematica*. Using this approach makes it very easy to add new functionality.

The final version of the *Turtle Graphics* program (included on the CD) has additional functions and options:

[1] **PutGraphicsObject[]** also accepts **Raster[]** objects.

[2] Multiple windows are supported.

7.8. References

[1] Richard J. Gaylord, Samuel N. Kamin, and Paul R. Wellin, *An Introduction to Programming with Mathematica*, TELOS/Springer-Verlag, Second Edition, New York, 1996. URL: http://store.wolfram.com/view/ISBN0387944346.

[2] Richard J. Gaylord and Kazume Nishidate, *Modeling Nature: Cellular Automata Simulations with Mathematica*, TELOS/Springer-Verlag, New York, 1996. URL: http://store.wolfram.com/view/ISBN0387946209.

[3] William Poundstone, *The Recursive Universe*, Oxford University Press, 1987.

[4] Stephen Wolfram, *Cellular Automata and Complexity: Collected Papers*, Addison-Wesley, Reading, MA, 1994. URL: http://store.wolfram.com/view/ISBN0201626640.

7.9. Command Summary

In the following, a gray font is used to indicate optional arguments, for example, *opts*.

OpenWindow[*opts*]

OpenWindow[] opens an "untitled" window. If a window is opened a window number, n, in the range 0-19 is returned. If an error occurs -1 is returned. The current window is the last opened window. The option Window-Title→"title" specifies the window's title, WindowSize→{{x0,y0},{x1,y1}} specifies the size of the window in global coordinates.

CloseWindow[*n*]

CloseWindow[] clears the current window. CloseWindow[n] closes window number n. If the window does not exist, -1 is returned.

GetWindowSize[*n*]

GetWindowSize[] returns the width and height of the current window as a list. If the window does not exist, -1 is returned.

SetCurrentWindow[*n*]

SetCurrentWindow[n] sets the current window to window n. All drawing commands are drawn on the current window.

GetCurrentWindow[]

GetCurrentWindow[] returns the window number of the current window.

MoveTo [{*x*,*y*}, *n*]

MoveTo [{*x*,*y*}] moves the location of the pen to {*x*, *y*} in the current window. 0 is returned for normal operation. If the window does not exist, -1 is returned.

LineTo [{*x*,*y*}, *n*]

LineTo [{*x*,*y*}] draws a line from current pen position to {*x*, *y*} in the current window. 0 is returned for normal operation. If the window does not exist, -1 is returned.

ClearWindow [*n*]

ClearWindow [*n*] clears window *n*. ClearWindow [] clears the current window. 0 is returned for normal operation. If the window does not exist, -1 is returned.

PutGraphicsObject [*g, dest, n, opts*]

PutGraphicsObject [*g,dest*] copies **Raster []**, **IndexColor []**, or **RasterArray []** graphics objects, *g*, into the destination rectangle, dest, in the current window. 0 is returned for normal operation. If the window does not exist, -1 is returned.

Chapter 8 — MovieDigitizer

In this chapter, we make a *MathLink* program that imports information from QuickTime movies into *Mathematica*. Using this program one can:

[1] obtain the location of a mouse click in a window;

[2] get the image data from the window's area;

[3] step through a QuickTime movie frame by frame; and

[4] write a kernel program for automatically digitizing QuickTime movies.

The original motivation behind this program was for analysis of human movement captured on video using *Mathematica* (Miyaji, 1995). This program demonstrates the power of network programming and the ease with which sophisticated applications can be developed using the synergy of *Mathematica* and *MathLink* programs.

8.1. Running MovieDigitizer

Let's run the MovieDigitizer program. First, we load the **MovieDigitizer`** package.

(Serializer) In[1]:=   **<< NetworkProgramming`MovieDigitizer`**

The MovieDigitizer executable, MovieDigitizer.exe, is launched and a *MathLink* connection is established using the same method as described in Section 6.8. Now switch to MovieDigitizer and use **Open** in the **File** menu to open a QuickTime movie file (sample.mov, shown in Figure 8.1, is included on the CD-ROM that comes with this book). At the bottom of the QuickTime movie window, below the movie control buttons, is a text field with a list, {x, y}, which shows the mouse location in local coordinates whose origin is the top left corner. Moving the mouse changes these coordinate values.

Evaluating **GetMovieMouse[]** causes the status area at the bottom of the MovieDigitizer window to become GetMovieMouse:{x, y} where {x, y} are the current coordinates (see Figure 8.2).
Clicking the mouse in the window returns the coordinates.

(Serializer) In[2]:=   **GetMovieMouse[]**

(Serializer) Out[2]=   {124, 125}

StepMovie[*n*] advances the movie *n* steps, for example,

(Serializer) In[3]:=   **StepMovie[3]**

Evaluating **GetMovieGraphicsObject[]** returns a -Graphics- object in **Raster** or **RasterArray** format as shown in Figure 8.3.

Figure 8.1. Opening a QuickTime movie `sample.mov` using `MovieDigitizer`.

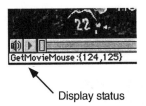

Display status

Figure 8.2. `MovieDigitizer` displays the **GetMovieMouse[]** status.

(Serializer) In[4]:= **Show[GetMovieGraphicsObject[**
    {{120, 200}, {140, 210}}, MovieReverseOrder → True]];

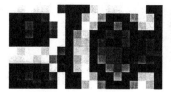

Figure 8.3. **GetMovieGraphicsObject[]** returns a -Graphics- object to the front end.

A combination of **GetMovieMouse[]** and **GetMovieGraphicsObject[]** can be used to load specified image areas, selected by the mouse, into the kernel (see Figure 8.4).

(Serializer) In[5]:= `Show[rast = GetMovieGraphicsObject[`
`{GetMovieMouse[], GetMovieMouse[]}, MovieReverseOrder → True]];`

Figure 8.4. Importing an image area specified by two `GetMovieMouse[]` calls.

We can easily apply filters to **Raster** objects (see Figure 8.5). For example,

(Serializer) In[6]:= `filter[Graphics[Raster[im_], op___Rule]] := Graphics[`
`Raster[Apply[Plus,`
`Map[RotateRight[im, #] &,`
`{{0, 0}, {-1, 0}, {0, -1}, {1, 0}, {0, 1}}]] / 5.0], op]`

(Serializer) In[7]:= `Show[filter[rast]];`

Figure 8.5. Applying a smoothing filter to the grayscale values returned by `GetMovieGraphicsObject[]`.

Once the image is imported into *Mathematica*, image processing involves simple list operations. With the utilities provided by `MovieDigitizer` it is not difficult to read off color values, calculate the center of an area, and use this information in a program for tracing the motion of an object in a movie.

The rest of this chapter describes our `MovieDigitizer` program. Five template functions are implemented:

[1] **OpenMovie[]** opens a file;

[2] **CloseMovie[]** closes a file;

[3] **StepMovie[]** steps through;

[4] **GetMovieMouse[]** obtains the mouse coordinates; and

[5] **GetMovieGraphicsObject[]** returns a graphics object from the selected area.

8.2. About QuickTime

QuickTime (URL: http://www.apple.com/quicktime/download/index.html) is a standard format for movie and sound media produced by Apple Computer Inc. QuickTime — and its developer's kit — is available for MacOS and Windows 95/NT, and `MovieDigitizer` uses QuickTime to access movie files.

Programs can access QuickTime files through toolbox functions. With these toolbox functions it is possible to open movie files, play movies, and do various operations on movies. All toolbox functions are described in *Inside Macintosh QuickTime* (Apple Computer, 1993a) and *QuickTime Components* (Apple Computer, 1993b).

Usually window manipulation relies on system primitives and varies from system to system. In this chapter, we use QuickTime 4.0 for Windows and MacOS (see Figure 8.6). It enables the use of MacOS-style toolbox calls in the Windows environment, apart from a small number of system dependencies. Here we focus on the common part of these programs. All source files are included on the CD-ROM. For more detail on system-specific programming see Mark (1990) and Mark (1992) for the MacOS and Petzold (1996) for Microsoft Windows.

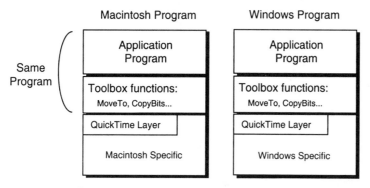

Figure 8.6. Using QuickTime 4 layer for window manipulation functions.

For more information about QuickTime programming, have a look at the sample program `VerySimple-Player.c` in *Macworld Ultimate Mac Programming* (Mark, 1994). This program is the basis of `MovieDigitizer`.

8.3. OpenMovie and CloseMovie

The implementation of `MovieDigitizer` has system-dependent and system-independent parts:

[1] `common-movie.c` contains system-independent functions such as `openmovie()` and `closemovie()`;

[2] `movie.tm.c` file is created from the template file `movie.tm` using `mprep` (**SAmprep**);

[3] System-dependent functions are defined in `mac-main.c` and `win-main.c`.

In the template file, `movie.tm`, the kernel functions **OpenMovie[]** and **CloseMovie[]**, which call `openmovie()` and `closemovie()`, respectively, are defined. This template is successively modified and extended in the following sections.

```
:Begin:
:Function:       openmovie
:Pattern:        OpenMovie[]
:Arguments:      {  }
:ArgumentTypes:  {  }
:ReturnType:     Integer
:End:
```

```
:Begin:
:Function:       closemovie
:Pattern:        CloseMovie[]
:Arguments:      {  }
:ArgumentTypes:  {  }
:ReturnType:     Integer
:End:
```

`openmovie()` creates a window and an offscreen buffer to which the movie frame is copied. `openmovie()` has conditional macros to switch between source codes for MacOS and Windows95/NT.

```
int openmovie(const char *fname)
{
    OSErr err;
    ...
    // find the file to open using dialog.
    ...
    err = loadMovie(&reply.sfFile, &theMovie);
    if (err) {
        return(-4);
    }

#if TARGET_OS_WIN32
    FSSpecToNativePathName(&reply.sfFile, cpathname, 256, kFileNameOnly);
    myhwnd = CreateWindow( "MovieWindowClass", cpathname,
            0, 75, 75, 200, 200,
            (HWND)MLIconWindow, (HMENU)0, MLInstance, (void FAR*)0);
    if(myhwnd == nil){
        DisposeMovie(theMovie);
        return(-5);
    }
    theWindow = GetHWNDPort(myhwnd);
#elif TARGET_OS_MAC
    theWindow = NewCWindow(nil, &tmpbounds, reply.sfFile.name,
                      false, 0, (WindowPtr)-1, true, 0);
```

```
#endif
    ...
    // then, set Movie to the Window.
    SetMovieGWorld(theMovie, (CGrafPtr)theWindow, nil);
    ...
    // set MovieController to it.
    theController = NewMovieController(theMovie, &bounds, mcTopLeftMovie);
    ...
    MacSetPort((GrafPtr)theWindow);
    MacShowWindow(theWindow);
    ...
    // open offscreen and set the Movie to the offscreen.
    ...
    return(0);
}
```

closemovie() closes all resources: MovieController, Movie, and Window.

```
int closemovie()
{
    if(theWindow != nil){
        DisposeMovieController(theController);
        DisposeMovie(theMovie);
        DisposeWindow(theWindow);
        theWindow = nil;
        theMovie = nil;
        return(0);
    }
    return(-1);
}
```

8.4. Initialization and Event Handling

There are initialization routines for both operating systems. EnterMovies() and ExitMovies() are common QuickTime routines for initialization and termination. Here is the Macintosh main() function:

```
int main( int argc, char* argv[])
{
    int ret;

    argc = argc; /* suppress warning */
    if(IsQuickTime4Later() != true)
        return(1);
    EnterMovies();
    GetCurrentProcess(&current);

    ret = MLMain( 0, argv);

    ExitMovies();
    return(ret);
}
```

The Windows Winmain() function uses InitializeQTML() (TerminateQTML()) to initialize (terminate) the QuickTime Media Layer.

```
int WINAPI WinMain( HINSTANCE hinstCurrent,        /*Win32 entry-point routine */
                    HINSTANCE hinstPrevious,
                    LPSTR lpszCmdLine,
                    int nCmdShow )
{
    char  buff[512];
    char FAR * buff_start = buff;
    char FAR * argv[32];
    char FAR * FAR * argv_end = argv + 32;
    int ret;

    if( !MLInitializeIcon( hinstCurrent, nCmdShow)) return 1;
    MLScanString( argv, &argv_end, &lpszCmdLine, &buff_start);

    if(InitializeQTML(0) != noErr) {
        MessageBox(MLIconWindow,"Can't initialize QuickTime 4.0.","",MB_OK);
        return(1);
    }
    EnterMovies();

    InstallMovieWindow( hinstCurrent, nCmdShow);
    ret = MLMain( argv_end - argv, argv);
    closemovie();

    ExitMovies();
    TerminateQTML();
    return(ret);
}
```

The next modifications involve adding QuickTime event processing to the main event loop: _handle_user_event() for Macintosh, and movieProc() for Windows. QuickTime's event processing is done in MCIsPlayerEvent(). Here is the Macintosh version.

```
int _handle_user_event( unsigned long ticks)
{
    EventRecord event;
    ...
    WaitNextEvent(everyEvent, &event, ticks, nil);
    if((window = FrontWindow()) != 0)
        mc = MCIsPlayerEvent(theController, &event);
    if(event.what != nullEvent){
        switch ( event.what ) {
    ...
```

For Windows, there are extra lines to convert Windows events to Macintosh-style events. Then, these events are sent to MCIsPlayerEvent().

```
MovieProc( HWND hWnd, UINT message, WPARAM wParam, LPARAM lParam)
{
    ...
    if(GetHWNDPort(hWnd)){
```

```
        MSG msg;
        LONG thePoints = GetMessagePos();

        msg.hwnd = hWnd;
        msg.message = message;
        msg.wParam = wParam;
        msg.lParam = lParam;
        msg.time = GetMessageTime();
        msg.pt.x = LOWORD(thePoints);
        msg.pt.y = HIWORD(thePoints);
        NativeEventToMacEvent(&msg, &macEvent); // convert event

        MCIsPlayerEvent(theController,&macEvent);
    ...
```

Processing for **Open**, **Close**, and **Quit** is added to the **File** menu, as shown in Figure 8.7, and openmovie() and closemovie() are inserted in the event-handling function.

```
    case mFile:
        switch( menuItem ){
            case mOpen:
                openmovie();
                break;
            case mClose:
                closemovie();
                break;
            case mQuit:
                MLDone = MLAbort = 1;
                closemovie();
                break;
        }
```

Figure 8.7. **File** menu in MovieDigitizer.

8.5. GetMovieMouse Function

It is often useful to obtain the coordinates of a point or object in an image, selected using a mouse click. For example, in the analysis of human movement, to calculate the angle of the knee, it is necessary to get the coordinates of the waist, knee, and ankle.

We now add a template function, **GetMovieMouse[]**, which returns the coordinates of the selected point.

```
:Begin:
:Function:          getmouse
```

```
:Pattern:          GetMovieMouse[s_String:"GetMovieMouse"]
:Arguments:        { s }
:ArgumentTypes:    { String }
:ReturnType:       Manual
:End:
```

getmouse() checks if a window is open and then waits for a mouse click event in a while loop.

```
void getmouse(char *s)
{
    GrafPtr cptr;

    if(theWindow != nil){
        strcpy(mouse_message, s);
        sprintf(status,"%s:{%3d,%3d}", mouse_message, previousPoint.h,previous-
Point.v);
        showstatus(status);
        notifyToFront();      // bring to front
        GetPort(&cptr);
        MacSetPort(theWindow);
        sendclick = true;
        while(sendclick)
            MLCallYieldFunction(MLYieldFunction(stdlink), stdlink, (MLYield-
Parameters)0);
        MacSetPort(cptr);
        sprintf(status,"{%3d,%3d}",previousPoint.h,previousPoint.v);
        showstatus(status);
    }
    else
        MLPutSymbol(stdlink,"$Failed");
}
```

The while loop calls the default event-handling function via MLCallYieldFunction(), as explained in Section 5.2. A case statement is added to the event-handling function to handle a mouse click event. Here is the Macintosh version:

```
    ...
    case inContent:
        pt = event.where;
        GlobalToLocal(&pt);
        if(sendclick && PtInRect(pt,&moviebox)){
            pbuf[0] = (int)pt.h;
            pbuf[1] = (int)pt.v;
            MLPutIntegerList(stdlink,pbuf,2);
            sendclick = false;
        }
    break;
```

Here is the Windows version:

```
    case WM_LBUTTONDOWN:
        pt = macEvent.where;
        GlobalToLocal(&pt);
        if(sendclick && MacPtInRect(pt,&moviebox)){
```

```
                    pbuf[0] = (int)pt.h;
                    pbuf[1] = (int)pt.v;
                    MLPutIntegerList(stdlink,pbuf,2);
                    sendclick = false;
              }
          break;
```

The mouse location is converted to local window coordinates using `GlobalToLocal()`. If `sendclick` is `true` and the mouse click is in the window content (not in the movie controller), the coordinates are returned using `MLPutIntegerList()` and then `sendclick` is set to `false`.

It is convenient to create a status field that displays the current location of the mouse at the bottom of the movie window, as shown in Figure 8.2. The function `trackmouse()` is polled by `_handle_user_event()`.

```
int _handle_user_event( unsigned long ticks)
{
    WaitNextEvent(everyEvent, &event, ticks, nil);
    trackmouse(event.where);
    //Event process...
```

If `MovieDigitizer` is in the foreground, and if the mouse is in the window, `trackmouse()` sets the cursor to be a cross.

```
void trackmouse(Point pt, char *message)
{
    if(theWindow == nil)
        return;
    GlobalToLocal(&pt);
    if(isfront()){
        if(MacPtInRect(pt, &moviebox)){
            if(!MacPtInRect(previousPoint,&moviebox)){
                SetCrossCursor();
            }
            if(!EqualPt(pt, previousPoint)){
                sprintf(status,"%s:{%3d,%3d}",message, pt.h, pt.v);
                showstatus(status);
            }
        }
         else if(MacPtInRect(previousPoint,&moviebox))
            SetArrowCursor();
    }
    previousPoint = pt;
}
```

If the mouse has moved from its previous location, the new location is displayed using `showstatus()`.

```
void showstatus(char *s)
{
    GrafPtr cptr;
    unsigned char ps[255];

    if(theWindow != nil){
        GetPort(&cptr);
        MacSetPort(theWindow);
```

```
        ctopstr(s, ps);
        TextSize(9);
        MoveTo(statusPt.h,statusPt.v);
        EraseRect(&statusRect);
        DrawString(ps);
        MacSetPort(cptr);
    }
}
```

The following global variables are used for the status field.

```
#define EXTRASPACE  10
Rect         statusRect;
Point        statusPt;
char         status[40];
Point        previousPoint = {-1,-1};
```

These variables are set when the window is opened using openmovie().

```
openmovie()
{
    //Open Movie...
    SetRect(&statusRect,0,0,bounds.right,EXTRASPACE);
    OffsetRect(&statusRect,2,bounds.bottom);
    SetPt(&statusPt,2,bounds.bottom+EXTRASPACE-2);
    //
}
```

statusRect is a rectangle on which the text is drawn as indicated in Figure 8.8. statusPt is the location of the top of the text, and status[] is a text string.

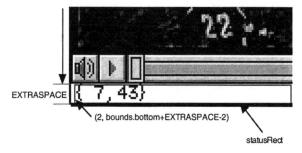

Figure 8.8. Parameters for displaying the status.

8.6. Stepping through a Movie

It is useful to be able to step forwards and backwards through a movie so that we can process images frame by frame. dostep() uses the Toolbox function MCDoAction() for this purpose.

```
:Begin:
:Function:       dostep
:Pattern:        StepMovie[n_Integer]
:Arguments:      { n }
:ArgumentTypes:  {Integer}
:ReturnType:     Manual
:End:
```

```
void dostep(int n)
{
    if(theWindow == nil){
        MLPutSymbol(stdlink,"$Failed");
    }
    MCDoAction(theController, mcActionStep, (Ptr)n);
    MLPutSymbol(stdlink,"Null");
}
```

theController is a handle to the movie controller. mcActionStep is a constant whose value indicates that we want to step through the movie. (Ptr)n moves n frames forward.

dostep() first checks if the window is open. If the window is not open, $Failed is returned. Otherwise the frame of the movie is set using MCDoAction(). Finally, Null is returned because no return value is required.

8.7. Reading Pixel Images

We would like to be able to import pixel information from a rectangular area of the image. One practical application of such pixel information is for locating and tracking objects of a specified color in a movie. Two template functions are implemented.

```
:Begin:
:Function:       getmoviepixrect
:Pattern:        GetMoviePixRect[{{x_Integer,y_Integer},{h_Integer,v_Integer}},rev_-
Integer]
:Arguments:      {x, y, h, v, rev}
:ArgumentTypes:  {Integer,Integer,Integer,Integer,Integer}
:ReturnType:     Manual
:End:
```

```
:Begin:
:Function:       getgraymoviepixrect
:Pattern:        GetMovieGrayPixRect[{{x_Integer,y_Integer},{h_Integer,v_Integer}},
                    RGBColor[r_,g_,b_],rev_Integer]
:Arguments:      {x, y, h, v, r, g, b, rev}
:ArgumentTypes:  {Integer,Integer,Integer,Integer,Real,Real,Real,Integer}
:ReturnType:     Manual
:End:
```

getmoviepixrect() calls getpixrect(). getgraymoviepixrect() is similar to getmoviepixrect() but returns the graphics object as a grayscale image.

```
void getmoviepixrect(int x, int y, int h, int v, int rev)
{
    TimeValue ctimevalue;
    TimeRecord timerecord;
    double t0;

    if(theWindow == nil){
        MLPutInteger(stdlink, -1);
        return;
    }
    t0 = clock();
    ctimevalue = GetMovieTime(theMovie, &timerecord);
    sprintf(status,"Transfer...");
    showstatus(status);
    GetGWorld(&curport,&curdev);
    SetGWorld(offport,0);
    SetMovieTimeValue(offMovie, ctimevalue);
    MoviesTask(offMovie, 0L);
    SetGWorld(curport,curdev);

    getpixrect(x, y, h, v, rev);

    sprintf(status,"Transfer done in %3.2f seconds",(double)((clock()-t0)/CLOCKS_-
PER_SEC));
    showstatus(status);
}
```

```
void getpixrect(int x, int y, int h, int v, int rev)
{
    PixMapHandle offpix;
    int *buf, *bp;
    unsigned char *p, *base;
    long size;
    long rowbytes;
    long i, j;

    if(theWindow == nil){
        MLPutInteger(stdlink, -1);
        return;
    }
    size = 3 * h;
    if((buf = (int *)NewPtr(sizeof(int) * size)) == nil){
        MLPutInteger(stdlink, -2);
        return;
    }

    offpix = GetGWorldPixMap(offport);
    LockPixels(offpix);

    base = (unsigned char *)(**offpix).baseAddr;
    rowbytes = (**offpix).rowBytes & 0x3fff;
    MLPutFunction(stdlink,"List", v);
    if(rev > 0){    // ReverseOrder->True
        for(i=v-1; i >= 0; --i){
```

```
                bp = buf;
                p = base + (4 * x + rowbytes * (y + i));
                for(j=0; j < h; ++j){
                    ++p;
                    *bp++ = *p++;
                    *bp++ = *p++;
                    *bp++ = *p++;
                }
                MLPutIntegerList(stdlink, buf, size);
            }
        }
        else {
            for(i=0; i < v; ++i){
                bp = buf;
                p = base + (4 * x + rowbytes * (y + i));
                for(j=0; j < h; ++j){
                    ++p;
                    *bp++ = *p++;
                    *bp++ = *p++;
                    *bp++ = *p++;
                }
                MLPutIntegerList(stdlink, buf, size);
            }
        }
        UnlockPixels(offpix);
        DisposePtr((Ptr)buf);
}
```

8.8. MovieDigitizer Command Summary

MovieDigitizer is a *MathLink* program that enables *Mathematica* interaction with QuickTime movie files. MovieDigitizer includes functions for opening and closing movies, exchanging graphical information — such as mouse click positions and color or grayscale values of selected movie areas — and movie frame control. These functions can be used as building blocks in programs for movie image processing, automatic digitizing, and object tracing.

<<NetworkProgramming`MovieDigitizer`

MovieDigitizer can be launched using **<<NetworkProgramming`MovieDigitizer`** which loads the package and connects to the *MathLink* executable.

(Serializer) In[1]:= **<< NetworkProgramming`MovieDigitizer`**

To uninstall MovieDigitizer we use **Uninstall[$MDLink]**.

(Serializer) In[2]:= **Uninstall[$MDLink]**

(Serializer) Out[2]= MovieDigitizer.exe

Alternatively, MovieDigitizer can be launched manually. We start MovieDigitizer.exe by double-clicking on it and then use **Install[]** to connect MovieDigitizer.exe with the kernel.

(Serializer) In[3]:= **Install["MovieDigitizer.exe", LinkMode → Connect]**

(Serializer) Out[3]= LinkObject[MovieDigitizer.exe, 4, 3]

$MDLink is the **LinkObject** of MovieDigitizer.exe.

(Serializer) In[4]:= **$MDLink**

(Serializer) Out[4]= LinkObject[MovieDigitizer.exe, 4, 3]

OpenMovie[]

To open a QuickTime movie file, you can use **Open** in the **File** menu of MovieDigitizer, or invoke the **OpenMovie[]** command from the kernel. **OpenMovie**[*file*] attempts to open the QuickTime movie named *file*.

One can use **ToFileName** to construct the full, machine-specific, file name in a machine-independent fashion. In the notebook front end, one can also use **Get File Path...** under the **Input** menu to obtain full, machine-specific, file names.

(Serializer) In[5]:= **fname = ToFileName[{$TopDirectory, "AddOns", "Applications",
                "NetworkProgramming", "MovieDigitizer", "sample.mov"}]**

(Serializer) Out[5]= Tigger:Applications:Mathematica 4.0:AddOns:
                Applications:NetworkProgramming:MovieDigitizer:sample.mov:

(Serializer) In[6]:= **OpenMovie[fname]**

(Serializer) Out[6]= 0

The output 0 indicates that **fname** has been opened. If no argument is supplied to **OpenMovie[]**, the Open File dialog appears in MovieDigitizer, and the user is notified to switch to the MovieDigitizer application.

CloseMovie[]

CloseMovie[] closes the current movie window.

(Serializer) In[7]:= **CloseMovie[]**

(Serializer) Out[7]= 0

The output 0 indicates that the movie window has been closed.

GetMovieMouse[]

GetMovieMouse[] returns the coordinates of the mouse click point. The required steps follow:

[1] invoke **GetMovieMouse[]** in the kernel;

[2] after notification, switch to the MovieDigitizer application;

[3] the MovieDigitizer mouse cursor changes to a cross-hair and the {*x*, *y*} coordinates are indicated in the status field;

[4] the {*x*, *y*} coordinates of the point where you click the mouse are returned to the kernel as a list. The origin of the coordinate system is the top left corner of the window.

(Serializer) In[8]:= **OpenMovie[fname]**

(Serializer) Out[8]= 0

(Serializer) In[9]:= **GetMovieMouse[]**

(Serializer) Out[9]= {66, 66}

GetMovieGraphicsObject[]

GetMovieGraphicsObject[{{x_1, y_1}, {x_2, y_2}}] returns pixels from the rectangular area specified by vertices {x_1, y_1} and {x_2, y_2} in **Raster[]** format. Setting **GetGraphicsFormat→RasterArray** returns the pixels as a **RasterArray**. Here are the default options for **GetMovieGraphicsObject[]**.

(Serializer) In[10]:= **Options[GetMovieGraphicsObject]**

(Serializer) Out[10]= {GetGraphicsFormat → Raster,
MovieReverseOrder → True, DefaultColor → RGBColor[0, 0, 0]}

StepMovie[]

StepMovie[n] advances the movie n frames. One can step backwards through a movie using negative n. **StepMovie[]** returns **Null**.

(Serializer) In[11]:= **Table[StepMovie[1], {i, 13}]**

(Serializer) Out[11]= {Null, Null, Null, Null, Null, Null, Null, Null, Null, Null, Null, Null, Null}

Uninstall[]

To uninstall MovieDigitizer, we use **Uninstall[$MDLink]**.

(Serializer) In[12]:= **Uninstall[$MDLink]**

(Serializer) Out[12]= MovieDigitizer.exe

8.9. References

[1] Chikara Miyaji and Harutoshi Yukawa, "Automatic Human Movement Analysis using QuickTime and MathLink Program" in *Mathematics with Vision — Proceedings of the First International Mathematica Symposium*, Computational Mechanics Pub., Southanpton, 103-110, 1995.

[2] Apple Computer, *INSIDE MACINTOSH:QuickTime*, Addison-Wesley, Reading, MA, 1993.
URL:http://www.apple.com/quicktime/developers/devsupport.html#tech

[3] Apple Computer, *INSIDE MACINTOSH:QuickTime Components*, Addison-Wesley, Reading, MA, 1993.
URL:http://www.apple.com/quicktime/developers/devsupport.html#tech

[4] Dave Mark, *Macworld Ultimate Mac Programming*, IDG Books, San Mateo, CA, 1994.

Chapter 9 — Object-oriented Programming

The real-time graphics introduced in Chapters 6 and 7 can be easily extended to become interactive graphics. Before designing interactive graphics we show that it is quite simple to implement object-oriented programming (OOP) in *Mathematica*. Much use of these OOP concepts will be made in the following chapters.

9.1. Introduction

Turtle Graphics, described in Section 6.1, sends graphics commands such as **Forward[n]** to a "turtle object". Sending commands or messages to an object is a basic idea of object-oriented programming. In this paradigm, program execution is modeled by "objects" and "messages". An "object" includes descriptions on how to react to certain messages and data to represent their internal state. These data cannot be accessed from outside the "object" except by sending a specific "message" to it. These concepts are known as *message passing* and *information hiding*.

Other objects can be derived from a given "object". By way of analogy, a turtle is a kind of animal. The definition of the "turtle object" will be an extension of the definition of the "animal object". When defining the "turtle object", it is convenient to reuse the definition of the "animal object". This is called *inheritance*.

9.2. Creating a Dog Object

Let's define a "dog object" using top-level *Mathematica* code. This object has a local variable, **weight**, representing its weight, and it accepts two messages, **setweight** and **getweight**, to access its weight. A "dog object" is created using **New[dog]**:

```
(Local) In[1]:=   New[dog] :=
                    Module[{weight = 60, self},
                      self[setweight, w_] := weight = w;
                      self[getweight] := weight;
                      self]
```

taro and **jiro** are "dog objects", sometimes called *instances*:

```
(Local) In[2]:=   taro = New[dog];
```

```
(Local) In[3]:=   jiro = New[dog];
```

These objects will be treated like a function name when we send messages to them.

⚠   An instance is a created object that is implemented as a *Mathematica* function name.

After sending **setweight** messages to **taro**,

```
(Local) In[4]:=   taro[setweight, 100]
```

```
(Local) Out[4]=   100
```

and **jiro**,

(Local) In[5]:= **jiro[setweight, 50]**

(Local) Out[5]= 50

we check their **weight** values (see Figure 9.1)

(Local) In[6]:= **{taro[getweight], jiro[getweight]}**

(Local) Out[6]= {100, 50}

Their **weight** values are as expected.

> ⚠ Messages are sent to objects as function arguments.

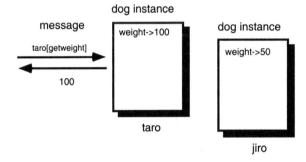

Figure 9.1. Two dog instances — **taro** and **jiro** — and a **getweight** message.

self is defined inside, and returned by, **New[dog]**. There are two definitions of **self**: one for **getweight** and the other for **setweight**, and which definition applies is determined by pattern-matching. But, how do the two instances, **taro** and **jiro**, differ? The answer is due to **Module[]**. When local variables are evaluated in a **Module[]**, *Mathematica* adds *unique* numbers to the variable names (see Section 2.6.3 of *The Mathematica Book*). For example,

(Local) In[7]:= **taro**

(Local) Out[7]= self$5

(Local) In[8]:= **jiro**

(Local) Out[8]= self$6

As you can see, each time **New[dog]** is evaluated it returns a different and unique value for **self**.

The definitions of **taro** and **jiro** can be checked using the **Definition[]** function. Note that, because **Definition** has the **HoldAll** attribute,

(Local) In[9]:= **Attributes[Definition]**

(Local) Out[9]= {HoldAll, Protected}

we need to **Evaluate** its argument first.

```
(Local) In[10]:=  Definition[Evaluate[taro]]
```

```
(Local) Out[10]=  Attributes[self$5] = {Temporary}
                  self$5[getweight] := weight$5
                  self$5[setweight, w$_] := weight$5 = w$
```

```
(Local) In[11]:=  Definition[Evaluate[jiro]]
```

```
(Local) Out[11]=  Attributes[self$6] = {Temporary}
                  self$6[getweight] := weight$6
                  self$6[setweight, w$_] := weight$6 = w$
```

You can also see that **taro** and **jiro** have different **weight** variables. This is because **weight** is a local variable in the **New[dog]** module.

In essence, the OOP style introduced here is achieved by:

[1] the use of **Module[]**, which generates unique functions (here **self**) and variables (**weight**) for each instance;

[2] using the function overloading capability of *Mathematica* to accept multiple messages (**getweight** and **setweight**);

[3] returning the function definition itself (here **self**). This is known as *function closure*.

9.3. Instance Method and Class Method

New[dog] is a function for creating "dog" objects. Such a function is generally known as a *class*. Invoking **New[dog]** creates an *instance* of the **dog** class. The message patterns that can be received by given classes are called *methods*. For example, the **dog** class has **getweight** and **setweight** methods.

> ⚠ A *method* is a message pattern that a given object can receive.
> A *class* is a template to create objects and consists of a collection of methods.

Let's extend the **dog** class so as to be able to accept a **hello** message:

```
(Local) In[12]:=  New[dog] :=
                   Module[{weight = 60, self},
                     self[hello] := "bow,wow!";
                     self[setweight, w_] := weight = w;
                     self[getweight] := weight;
                     self]
```

Our new dog, **goro**, can receive the message **hello**:

```
(Local) In[13]:=  goro = New[dog];
```

```
(Local) In[14]:=  goro[hello]
```

```
(Local) Out[14]=  bow, wow !
```

The old dog, **taro**, created from the previous definition of **New[dog]**, cannot:

(Local) In[15]:= **taro[hello]**

(Local) Out[15]= self$5[hello]

After adding the following definition to **taro** (this delayed assignment works because the left-hand side, **taro[hello]**, is evaluated *before* the assignment to the right-hand side takes place):

(Local) In[16]:= **taro[hello] := "bow,wow!"**

taro can receive the **hello** message:

(Local) In[17]:= **taro[hello]**

(Local) Out[17]= bow, wow!

Because the method definitions (initially **setweight** and **getweight**) belong to an instance (here **taro**, **jiro**, and **goro**), once an instance is created, it is difficult to change methods or add a new method (such as **hello**) in all instances.

> ⚠ The collection of definitions (here **self**) that make up the class (here **New[dog]**) is called the *instance method*.

Instead of modifying all instances, we introduce the *class method*. Consider the following implementation of **New[dog]**:

(Local) In[18]:=
```
New[dog] :=
  Module[{weight = 60, self},
    self[hello] := "bow,wow!";
    self[setweight, w_] := weight = w;
    self[getweight] := weight;
    self[selector_, args___] := dog[self, selector, args];
    self]
```

The "catch-all" pattern, **self[selector_,args___]**, is only matched if the instance method fails. For example, after creating a new instance,

(Local) In[19]:= **koro = New[dog];**

and entering an associated function definition,

(Local) In[20]:=
```
dog[self_, food, m_] := self[setweight, self[getweight] + m]
```

if we send the message matched by the "catch-all" pattern, for example,

(Local) In[21]:= **koro[food, 10]**

(Local) Out[21]= 70

then, effectively, **dog[koro,food,10]** is evaluated.

⚠ This idea, known as the *class method*, makes it possible to change methods or add a new method for *all* instances.

9.4. Improvement of the Class Method

In the class method implementation of Section 9.3, if there is no applicable class method, *Mathematica* will return an unevaluated result, for example,

```
(Local) In[22]:=  koro[water]
```

```
(Local) Out[22]=  dog[self$8, water]
```

because there is no method that matches the **water** message. It is better to return something like **$MethodNot-Found** to indicate that no method was found. Here is an implementation of a test, **findmethod**, which checks whether there is an applicable class method (see Figure 9.2):

```
(Local) In[23]:=    SetAttributes[findmethod, HoldAll];
                    findmethod[f_[m___], next_] := sub[f[m], f[m], next]
```

```
(Local) In[25]:=    SetAttributes[sub, HoldRest];
                    sub[f1_, f2_, next_] :=
                     If[Hold[f1] === Hold[f2] || f1 === $MethodNotFound, next, f1]
```

This implementation of **findmethod** is rather subtle. We set the attributes of **findmethod** to be **HoldAll** so that *none* of its arguments are evaluated. **findmethod[]** calls **sub[f[m],f[m],next]**. The attributes of **sub** are **HoldRest** so that only its *first* argument, **f1**, is evaluated. This construct allows us to compare the evaluated (**f1**) and unevaluated (**f2**) forms of **f[m]**. We make this comparison in an **If[]** statement. Since **If[]** evaluates its first argument,

```
(Local) In[27]:=  Attributes[If]
```

```
(Local) Out[27]=  {HoldRest, Protected}
```

we wrap the **f1** and **f2** with **Hold[]** to prevent undesired evaluation during comparison using **SameQ** (===). If this comparison returns **True**, or **f1** matches **$MethodNotFound** (i.e., no applicable class method exists), then the *evaluated* form of **next** is returned. Otherwise **f1** is returned. This second **SameQ** test is required in Section 9.5.

We redefine **New[dog]** using **findmethod**:

```
(Local) In[28]:=    New[dog] := Module[{weight = 60, self},
                      self[hello] := "bow,wow!";
                      self[setweight, w_] := weight = w;
                      self[getweight] := weight;
                      self[selector_, args___] :=
                       findmethod[dog[self, selector, args], $MethodNotFound];
                      self]
```

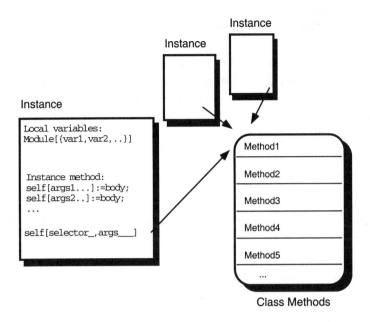

Figure 9.2. **findmethod[]** searches class methods that are shared among instances.

After redefining **koro**,

(Local) In[29]:= **koro = New[dog];**

there is still no applicable class method:

(Local) In[30]:= **koro[water]**

(Local) Out[30]= $MethodNotFound

However, now **$MethodNotFound** is returned.

9.5. Inheritance

9.5.1 Single Inheritance

Let's create a new class, **cat**. Of course, a **cat** does not bark, but many characteristics of **cat** will be similar to that of **dog**:

(Local) In[31]:=
```
New[cat] :=
  Module[{weight = 30, self},
    self[hello] := "meow,meow!";
    self[setweight, w_] := weight = w;
    self[getweight] := weight;
```

```
            self[selector_, args___] :=
             findmethod[cat[self, selector, args], $MethodNotFound];
            self]
```

(Local) In[32]:=
```
cat[self_, food, m_] := self[setweight, self[getweight] + m]
```

tama is an instance of **cat**:

(Local) In[33]:= **tama = New[cat];**

tama can receive the message **hello**:

(Local) In[34]:= **tama[hello]**

(Local) Out[34]= meow,meow!

The **dog** and **cat** classes use very similar definitions so we should not need to write the common code twice. Instead, we create a new **animal** class that defines the common methods in **dog** and **cat**:

(Local) In[35]:=
```
New[animal] :=
 Module[{weight = 60, self},
  self[setweight, w_] := weight = w;
  self[getweight] := weight;
  self[selector_, args___] :=
   findmethod[animal[self, selector, args], $MethodNotFound];
  self]
```

(Local) In[36]:=
```
animal[self_, food, m_] := self[setweight, self[getweight] + m]
```

Using the **animal** class, we can define **dog** and **cat** more easily:

(Local) In[37]:=
```
New[dog] :=
 Module[{self, super = New[animal]},
  self[hello] := "bow,wow!";
  self[selector_, args___] :=
   findmethod[dog[self, selector, args], super[selector, args]];
  self]
```

(Local) In[38]:=
```
New[cat] :=
 Module[{self, super = New[animal]},
  self[hello] := "meow,meow!";
  self[selector_, args___] :=
   findmethod[cat[self, selector, args], super[selector, args]];
  self]
```

In both classes, there is a **super** variable, which is an instance of **animal**. Messages for which there is no applicable class method are sent to the **super** instance. This is an implementation of *single inheritance*.

> ⚠   *Inheritance* occurs when a class uses another class's methods. For example, the **dog** and **cat** classes inherit the **animal** class.

For example, **hachikou** is a new instance of **dog**:

(Local) In[39]:=   **hachikou = New[dog];**

hachikou can receive the message **hello** (processed by the **dog** method):

(Local) In[40]:=   **hachikou[hello]**

(Local) Out[40]=   bow, wow!

and the message **food** (processed by the **animal** method):

(Local) In[41]:=   **hachikou[food, 3]**

(Local) Out[41]=   63

9.5.2 Multiple Inheritance

It is possible to list a number of instances, the "super list", which will be searched to find a matching method. We call this *multiple inheritance* and implement this idea by overloading **findmethod**:

(Local) In[42]:=
```
findmethod[super_List, m___] := findmethod[
  Evaluate[First[super]][m], findmethod[Evaluate[Rest[super]], m]]
```

(Local) In[43]:=
```
findmethod[{}, m___] := $MethodNotFound
```

When supplied with a list, **findmethod[]** checks the first element for a match. If this fails, **findmethod[]** is called recursively on to the rest of the list. If we reach the empty list, **{}**, the search will fail and **$MethodNot-Found** is returned. **Evaluate** is required because **findmethod** has the **HoldAll** attribute. For example, consider **New[pet]**:

(Local) In[44]:=
```
New[pet] :=
 Module[{self, price},
  self[setprice, p_] := price = p;
  self[getprice] := price;
  self[selector_, args___] :=
   findmethod[pet[self, selector, args], $MethodNotFound];
  self]
```

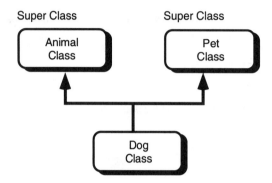

Figure 9.3. Class hierarchy of dog class.

Now, we redefine **dog** as a class that has **animal** and **pet** as its super classes (Figure 9.3). **Evaluate[super]** is required because **findmethod** has the **HoldAll** attribute.

(Local) In[45]:=
```
New[dog] :=
  Module[{self, super = {New[animal], New[pet]}},
    self[hello] := "bow,wow!";
    self[selector_, args___] := findmethod[dog[self, selector, args],
      findmethod[Evaluate[super], selector, args]];
    self]
```

For example, **rover** is a new instance of **dog**:

(Local) In[46]:= **rover = New[dog];**

rover can receive the message **hello** (processed by the **dog** method):

(Local) In[47]:= **rover[hello]**

(Local) Out[47]= bow,wow!

and the message **food** (processed by the **animal** method):

(Local) In[48]:= **rover[food,30]**

(Local) Out[48]= 90

Moreover, **rover** understands the message **setprice** (processed by the **pet** method):

(Local) In[49]:= **rover[setprice, 100]**

(Local) Out[49]= 100

However, **rover** cannot understand the message **goodbye**:

(Local) In[50]:= **rover[goodbye]**

(Local) Out[50]= $MethodNotFound

A schematic of the way methods are searched is shown in Figure 9.4. First the **dog** instance and class method are searched. If this fails, the **animal** instance and class method are searched, then the pet instance and class method and, finally, if the method has not been found, **$MethodNotFound** is returned.

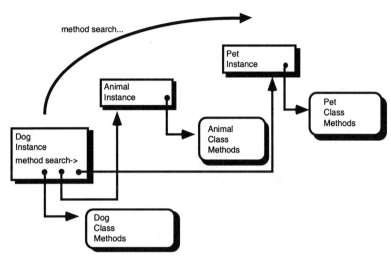

Figure 9.4. The search sequence of the super method.

9.6. Summary

In this chapter, a *Mathematica* object-oriented programming style has been outlined. The instance method and class method were introduced and the class method was then enhanced to allow single inheritance and then further extended to permit multiple inheritance.

We summarize inheritance, as described in this chapter:

[1] For classes that do not have a super class see Section 9.4.

[2] For classes that have a single super class see Section 9.5.1.

[3] For classes that have multiple super classes see Section 9.5.2.

Chapter 10—Creating an Event-driven Mechanism

The purpose of this chapter is to establish an environment that can run an event-driven interactive program by combining real-time graphics with object-oriented programming. The core functionality required is the ability to handle user events and to send messages to the kernel. We achieve this by writing a `Serializer` program which relays expressions between the front end and kernel. Using `Serializer` we can send events from *multiple MathLink* programs to one kernel.

10.1. Getting an Event

In Chapter 7, we created a general real-time graphic program, `CellularAutomata`, in which we displayed a *Forest Fire* (Section 7.3) and the *Game of Life* (Section 7.6). It is natural to extend this program so that we can use the mouse to edit cells or select an area of an image. Once we get a position by clicking the mouse, it will be easy to immediately draw a point at that location using our extended real-time graphics program.

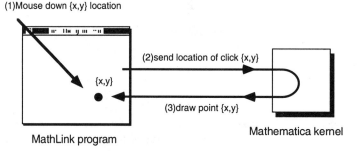

Figure 10.1. The kernel receives a mouse-down event and draws a point at that location.

To get a mouse click, for example, means that the *MathLink* program has to be able to get user events. Returning a mouse-click event to the kernel using **GetMovieMouse[]** was implemented in Section 8.1. But this event-driven mechanism cannot handle various asynchronous events which the user will generate. Here we implement getting user events, not using a template function, but in a user-event loop (see Section 5.2 and Figure 10.1).

> ⚠   User events are handled in the template program's user-event loop and sent to the kernel.

10.2. Event Format

The format of the event depends on the kind of event and what information needs to be sent. For example, `get-mouse()` returns a mouse-down event as a list of {*x, y*} coordinates. *MathLink* can send not only a numerical value or a list, but also arbitrary expressions. Sending events as expressions—the most flexible and versatile format—enables us to send *any* kind of complicated information structure. Such expressions will be evaluated by the kernel in the same way as front end expressions.

What expressions do we need to send? Suppose the user clicks on an object in a window. If we define objects in a window as OOP objects, using the ideas of Chapter 9, then it is natural to send the message, "I clicked at the point (x, y)" to such objects.

> ⚠ Event format: Messages are sent as *Mathematica* expressions to objects defined in the kernel. The message format is *object* [*selector*, *arguments*, ...].

10.3. Sending Events

Normally, the kernel only evaluates expressions from one *MathLink* connection and returns a value to that link. This link is called **$ParentLink**. If we send events to **$ParentLink**, they will be evaluated automatically by the kernel. In this chapter, we will build a general relay program called `Serializer`. The steps in the operation of `Serializer` are indicated in Figures 10.2, 10.3, and 10.4.

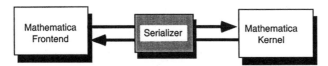

Figure 10.2. `Serializer` relays expressions between front end and kernel.

Front end and template program events are sent to `Serializer`, which serializes the events and relays them to the kernel for evaluation, as indicated in Figure 10.3.

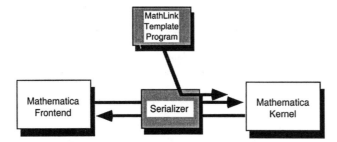

Figure 10.3. Template program sends events to `Serializer`.

Generally, template programs just execute C functions, which are invoked by the kernel as external calls. This is indicated in Figure 10.4 by the template link. Using `Serializer`, the template program can send events at *any* time using the **$ParentLink** in Figure 10.4. There are now *two* links, and each can send expressions asynchronously. This is the key that enables interaction between template programs and the kernel.

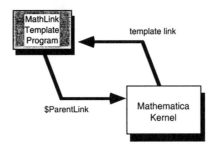

Figure 10.4. Interaction is provided between the template program and the kernel.

10.4. Serializer as a Template Program

Template programs wait for expressions from the kernel as shown in Figure 10.5.

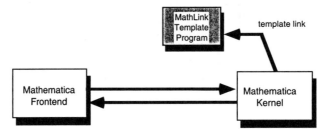

Figure 10.5. Normal relationship between the front end, kernel, and template program.

Consider moving the template program *in between* the front end and the kernel and making it relay front end ⟺ kernel expressions in its event loop as indicated in Figure 10.6.

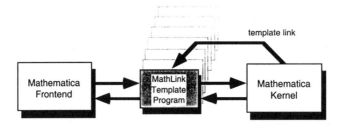

Figure 10.6. The template program is put in between the front end and kernel.

The advantages of this approach are that:

[1] the template link can be used to control the template program (in this case, `Serializer`);

[2] the programming is easier;

[3] the program is more portable.

The template program has a user-event loop, as discussed in Section 5.2. In this loop, we will add do_packet(), a function which relays expressions between the front end and the kernel in both directions using MLTransferExpression():

```
void do_packet()
{
    while(true){
        if(MLReady(flp))
            MLTransferExpression(klp, flp);
        else if(MLReady(klp))
            MLTransferExpression(flp, klp);
        else
            break;
    }
    MLFlush(klp);
    MLFlush(flp);
}
```

This code simply relays expressions between the front end and the kernel.

Two links, to the kernel (klp) and the front end (flp), are declared as global variables:

```
MLINK klp = (MLINK)0;
MLINK flp = (MLINK)0;
```

The _MLMain() function is the entry point of the template program, which is where we establish these links using MLOpenString(). The connection to the kernel is established with the -linkmode Launch option:

```
klp = MLOpenString(stdenv,"-linkname MathKernel -linkmode Launch", &err);
if(klp == (MLINK)0)
    goto R1;
MLActivate(klp); // Activate it
skip_LinkObject = true;
```

We then connect to the front end:

```
flp = commandline
    ? MLOpenString( stdenv, commandline, &err)
    : MLOpenArgv( stdenv, argv, argv_end, &err);

if(flp == (MLINK)0)
    goto R2;
```

Next, the template function link (mlp) is opened, using the -linkcreate option, and waits for connection:

```
mlp = MLOpenString(stdenv, "-linkcreate -linkoptions MLDontInteract", &err);
if( mlp == (MLINK)0){
    MLAlert( stdenv, MLErrorString( stdenv, err));
    goto R3;
}
strcpy(str,"Install[\"");
strcat(str, MLName(mlp));
strcat(str,"\", LinkMode->Connect]");
```

```
     MLEvaluate(klp, str);
     MLFlush(klp);
     MLActivate(mlp);
```

Then `Serializer` sends an `Install[]` command to the kernel with the `LinkMode->Connect` option. The kernel connects to `mlp` using this command. The `Install[]` command needs to know the link name of `mlp` before connection. The *MathLink* library function `MLName()` is used for this purpose.

⚠ char* MLName(MLINK *link*) returns a pointer to a name of *link*.

Here is the full code we insert into the event loop:

```
int _handle_user_event( unsigned long ticks)
{
    EventRecord event;

    ...
    if(skip_LinkObject && (MLReady(klp) || MLReady(flp))){
        if(MLError(flp)==MLECLOSED || MLError(klp)==MLECLOSED){
            MLDone = MLAbort = 1;
            return(MLDone);
        }
        do_init_packet();
    }
    else if(MLReady(klp)||MLReady(flp)){
        if(MLError(flp)==MLECLOSED || MLError(klp)==MLECLOSED){
            MLDone = MLAbort = 1;
            return(MLDone);
        }
        do_packet();
    }
    ...
```

`do_init_packet()` is only used at installation time to filter out the output of `Install[]` because the front end does not need to receive this packet. The *MathLink* library function `MLError()` is used to detect if the front end closes `flp` or if the kernel closes `klp` and, in either case, we quit `Serializer`.

10.5. Sending an Abort Message

Sometimes you want to abort an evaluation while the kernel is executing it. Selecting **Abort Evaluation** under the **Kernel** menu causes the kernel to abort the current evaluation and return **$Aborted**. How does the front end send the kernel an abort message over the link? Expressions on the link are processed in FIFO (first in, first out) order, as shown in Figure 10.7.

Figure 10.7. Expressions on the link are evaluated in FIFO order.

However, if there were an abort message on this link, it would not be evaluated until all expressions ahead of it on the link were evaluated. How does *MathLink* treat such emergency messages? A separate internal link, shown in Figure 10.8, is used for emergency messages.

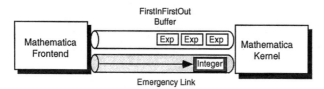

Figure 10.8. Internal link for sending emergency messages.

The existence of this link was demonstrated in Section 2.3. When a link is established, a second internal link is created automatically. However, this internal link is invisible to the user. The programmer can access this link using the message handler or `MLMessageReady()`, `MLGetMessage()`, and `MLPutMessage()`.

If the message handler function is registered, incoming messages can be captured by this function. Here is the registration of the handler function in `MLMain()`:

```
MLMessageHandlerObject flphandler = 0;
MLMain()
{
    ...
    flphandler = MLCreateMessageHandler( stdenv,
            NewMLHandlerProc( MLFrontHandler), 0);
    ...
```

`MLCreateMessageHandler()` registers `MLFrontHandler` as the handler function. Here is the definition of `MLFrontHandler()`:

```
MLMDEFN( void, MLFrontHandler, ( MLINK mlp, unsigned long message, unsigned long
n))
{
    n = 0; /* suppress unused warning */
    mlp = (MLINK)0; // suppress unused warning
    MLPutMessage(klp, message);
}
```

This function simply sends the message to the kernel, as shown in Figure 10.9.

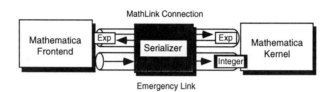

Figure 10.9. Emergency message transfer in `Serializer`.

Instead of handling the message internally, `MLGetMessage()` explicitly processes the message. For this purpose, three API functions are provided for message handling.

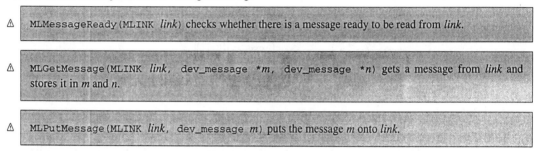

⚠ `MLMessageReady(MLINK` *link*`)` checks whether there is a message ready to be read from *link*.

⚠ `MLGetMessage(MLINK` *link*`,` `dev_message *m,` `dev_message *n)` gets a message from *link* and stores it in *m* and *n*.

⚠ `MLPutMessage(MLINK` *link*`,` `dev_message m)` puts the message *m* onto *link*.

10.6. Testing Serializer

10.6.1 Installation

[1] Move the `serializer.exe` application into your **$LaunchDirectory**, and install the **Serializer`** package following the instructions in Setting Up New Add-ons.

[2] Add **Serializer** to the **Kernel** submenus by following the steps outlined in the on-line Kernel Configuration Options documentation. Choose **Serializer** as the Kernel Name.

10.6.2 Basic Tests

Now we run `Serializer`. Because this Notebook's kernel is set to be `Serializer`, evaluating any expression in this Notebook automatically launches `Serializer` *and* `MathKernel`.

(Serializer) In[1]:= **1 - 2**

(Serializer) Out[1]= −1

Setting **PacketMonitor[]** will show packets as **Print** messages:

(Serializer) In[2]:=   **PacketMonitor[]**

> < -k : FrontEnd`NotebookClose[NotebookObject[
>   FrontEndObject[LinkObject[serializer.exe, 1, 1]], 43] Rule[Interactive, False]]

> < -k : OutputNamePacket[Out[2] =]

(Serializer) Out[2]=   1

> < -k : ReturnExpressionPacket[BoxData[1, StandardForm]]

This is what we did in Section 2.7.

Now we test aborting an evaluation. Enter **100000!** and select **Abort Evaluation** under the **Kernel** menu.

(Serializer) In[3]:=   **100000 !**

> < -k : InputNamePacket[In[3] :=]

> f0 -> : EnterExpressionPacket[
>   MakeExpression[BoxData[RowBox[List[100000, !]]], StandardForm]]

> < -k : OutputNamePacket[Out[3] =]

(Serializer) Out[3]= $Aborted

> < -k : ReturnExpressionPacket[BoxData[$Aborted, StandardForm]]

Choosing **Serializer** under the **Quit Kernel** submenu will quit Serializer *and* MathKernel.

10.7. Linking Serializer and a Template Program

Next, we make functions to establish a link between a template program and Serializer. Both routines are implemented as template functions. One function forces Serializer to create a link. The other function forces the template program to connect to that link. This is indicated in Figure 10.10.

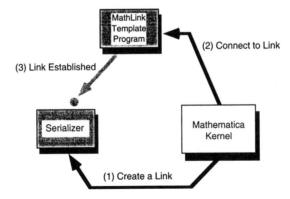

Figure 10.10. Kernel instructs Serializer and the template program to establish a link.

10.7.1 Making a Link on Serializer—Step 1

We define the structure EVENTLINK—which contains the link (link), connection type (type), and mode variable (mode)—and store the information about the links between Serializer and template programs in the array eventlinks[MAXLINK]:

```
typedef struct EVENTLINK {
    MLINK link;
    int type;
    int mode;
} EVENTLINK;

struct EVENTLINK eventlinks[MAXLINK];
```

The size of the eventlinks array determines the maximum number of connections. Then we define the connection types and modes:

```
// eventlink type
#define NotUsed     0
#define MLProg      1
#define FrontEnd    2

//eventlink mode
#define NoMode      0
#define EnterMode   1
#define EvalMode    2
```

initlinks() initializes the eventlinks array:

```
void initlinks(void)
{
    int i;

    for(i=0; i < MAXLINK; ++i){
        eventlinks[i].link = (MLINK)0;
        eventlinks[i].type = NotUsed;
        eventlinks[i].mode = NoMode;
    }
}
```

appendlink() appends a new link and its type to the array:

```
int appendlink(MLINK lp, int t)
{
    int i;

    for(i=0; i < MAXLINK; ++i)
        if(eventlinks[i].type == NotUsed){
            eventlinks[i].link = lp;
            eventlinks[i].type = t;
            eventlinks[i].mode = NoMode;
            return(i);
        }
```

```
        return(-1);
    }
```

and `removelink()` removes a link:

```
:Begin:
:Function:        removelink
:Pattern:         RemoveLink[n_Integer]
:Arguments:       { n }
:ArgumentTypes:   { Integer }
:ReturnType:      Integer
:End:
```

```
int removelink(int n)
{
    if(0 <= n && n < MAXLINK){
        if(eventlinks[n].link != (MLINK)0)
            MLClose(eventlinks[n].link);
        eventlinks[n].link = (MLINK)0;
        eventlinks[n].type = NotUsed;
        eventlinks[n].mode = NoMode;
        return(0);
    }
    return(-1);
}
```

The `eventlinks` array is first used when the connection is established between the front end and `Serializer`. `eventlinkcreate()` creates a link and appends the information using `appendlink()`:

```
:Begin:
:Function:        eventlinkcreate
:Pattern:         SerializerEventLinkCreate[lproto_String]
:Arguments:       { lproto }
:ArgumentTypes:   { String }
:ReturnType:      Manual
:End:
```

```
void eventlinkcreate(const char *protocol)
{
    long err;
    char *av[7];
    MLINK lp;
    int n0;

    av[0] = "-linkmode";
    av[1] = "listen";
    av[2] = "-linkprotocol";
    av[3] = (char *)protocol;
    av[4] = "-linkoptions";
    av[5] = "MLDontInteract";
    av[6] = '\0';
```

```
    lp = MLOpenArgv(stdenv, av, av + 6, &err);
    if(lp == (MLINK)0){
        MLPutSymbol(stdlink, "$Failed");
        return;
    }
    if((n0 = appendlink(lp, MLProg)) < 1){
        MLPutSymbol(stdlink, "$Failed");
        return;
    }
    MLPutFunction(stdlink, "List", 2);
        MLPutInteger(stdlink, n0);
        MLPutString(stdlink, MLName(lp));
    MLEndPacket(stdlink);
    MLFlush(stdlink);

    MLActivate(lp);
    MLFlush(lp);
}
```

The type of link is MLProg. A two-element list consisting of the link name and index number is returned to the kernel. Then eventlinkcreate() waits for a connection from the template program.

10.7.2 Making a Link on Template Program — Step 2

In the template program, the global variables, eventlink and linksymbol, are defined:

```
MLINK eventlink;
char * linksymbol;
```

All template programs that connect with Serializer need the two templates and associated routines given as follows: **EventLinkConnect[]** connects to Serializer:

```
:Begin:
:Function:          eventlinkconnect
:Pattern:           EventLinkConnect[lname_String, lproto_String, obj_Symbol]
:Arguments:         { lname, lproto, obj }
:ArgumentTypes:     { String, String, Manual }
:ReturnType:        Manual
:End:
```

```
void eventlinkconnect(const char *lname, const char *lproto)
{
    long err;
    char *argv[7], *s;

    MLGetSymbol(stdlink, &s);
    linksymbol = s;

    argv[0] = "-linkname";
    argv[1] = (char *)lname;
    argv[2] = "-linkmode";
    argv[3] = "connect";
    argv[4] = "-linkprotocol";
```

```
    argv[5] = (char *)lproto;
    argv[6] = nil;
    eventlink = MLOpenArgv(stdenv, argv, argv+6, &err);
    if( eventlink == (MLINK)0){
        MLDisownSymbol(stdlink, linksymbol);
        MLPutSymbol(stdlink, "$Failed");
    }
    else {
        while(MLReady(eventlink)==0){
            MLCallYieldFunction(MLYieldFunction(stdlink), stdlink,(MLYield-
Parameters)0);
            if(MLAbort){      // if kernel send abort to me,
                MLClose(eventlink);
                MLDisownSymbol(stdlink, linksymbol);
                MLPutFunction(stdlink, "Abort", 0L);     // Return[Abort[]]
                MLFlush(stdlink);
                break;
            }
        }
        MLActivate(eventlink);
        MLFlush(eventlink);
        MLPutInteger(stdlink, 0);    // return 0 to the kernel.
        MLFlush(stdlink);
    }
}
```

eventlinkconnect() connects to the link opened by Serializer. The object name sent by **EventLinkConnect[]** is saved as linksymbol for later use.

   EventLinkClose[] calls eventlinkclose() to close the link to Serializer and dispose of the memory area associated with linksymbol:

```
:Begin:
:Function:        eventlinkclose
:Pattern:         EventLinkClose[]
:Arguments:       {  }
:ArgumentTypes:   {  }
:ReturnType:      Integer
:End:
```

```
int eventlinkclose()
{
    if(eventlink != (MLINK)0){
        MLClose(eventlink);
        eventlink = (MLINK)0;
        MLDisownSymbol(stdlink, linksymbol);
        return(0);
    }
    else {
        return(-1);
    }
}
```

10.7.3 Linking the Template Program and Serializer—Step 3

Now we can link the template program and `Serializer` using the following command:

```
If[({mlid, elname} = SerializerEventLinkCreate[lproto]) =!= $Failed,
 EventLinkConnect[elname, lproto, self]]
```

The steps in this connection process are as follows:

[1] **SerializerEventLinkCreate[]** forces `Serializer` to create a link, and it returns the name of the link;

[2] Using that name, **EventLinkConnect[]** forces the template program to connect to it.

10.8. More on Serializer

In the previous section, we connected `Serializer` and a template program. The template program will send packets to `Serializer`, and these will be relayed to the kernel. The front end will also send packets. For each packet, the `Serializer` must manage the return packet. The variable `currentlink`, which is the index of the `eventlinks` array, is used to indicate the packet-processing status. If `currentlink` is `-1`, there is no packet waiting to be processed and `Serializer` waits for a new input packet. A `currentlink` greater than `-1` means that a link, indexed by `currentlink`, is being processed.

When waiting for input, `process_idle()` is called. In other cases, `process_front_packet()` processes front end packets or `process_mathprog_packet()` processes packets from a template program. The following is the relevant part of the event-processing loop:

```
_handle_user_event()
{   ...
    if(currentlink >= 0){   // processing a link is already started
        if(eventlinks[currentlink].type == FrontEnd)
            process_front_packet(currentlink);
        else if(eventlinks[currentlink].type == MLProg)
            process_mathprog_packet(currentlink);
        else if(eventlinks[currentlink].type == 0)
            process_cleanup(currentlink);
    }
    else if(initialize)
        do_initialize();
    else
        process_idle(); // check new input and link closed
    ...
}
```

`process_idle()` checks for new input packets using `MLReady()`, and calls `do_newinput()` if a packet exists:

```
static void process_idle()
{
    int i;
    char s[MAXLINK];

    for(i=0; i <= maxlinkp; ++i){
        if(eventlinks[i].type > 0){
            if(MLReady(eventlinks[i].link)&&(MLError(eventlinks[i].link) == 0)){
```

```
                    do_newinput(i);
                    break;
            }
            else if(MLError(eventlinks[i].link)==MLECLOSED){
                removelink(i);
                if(i == 0){        // front end is closed
                    MLDone = MLAbort = 1;
                    break;
                }
                sprintf(s,"Serializer:port %d closed.", i);
                MLAlert(stdenv, s);
            }
        }
    }
}
```

do_newinput(int i) sets currentlink to i, checks the expression type, and sets eventlinks[i].mode depending on the type. Then the expression is transferred to the kernel:

```
static void do_newinput(int i)
{
    char *s, buf[MAXLINK];
    long len;
    int j;

    currentlink = i;
    MLGetFunction(eventlinks[i].link, &s, &len);
    if(strcmp(s, "EvaluatePacket")==0)
        eventlinks[i].mode = EvalMode;
    else
        eventlinks[i].mode = EnterMode;
    MLPutFunction(klp, s, len);
    for(j=0; j < len; ++j)
        MLTransferExpression(klp, eventlinks[i].link);
    MLDisownSymbol(eventlinks[i].link, s);
    MLEndPacket(klp);
    MLFlush(klp);
}
```

process_front_packet() processes expressions transferred between the front end and the kernel. Expressions from the front end are relayed to the kernel using front_to_kernel(). Expressions from the kernel are relayed to the front end using kernel_to_front():

```
void process_front_packet(int n)
{
    while(currentlink >= 0 && (MLReady(klp) || MLReady(eventlinks[n].link))){
        if(MLReady(klp))
            kernel_to_front(n);
        else
            front_to_kernel(n);
    }
    MLFlush(eventlinks[n].link);
    MLFlush(klp);
}
```

`process_mathprog_packet()` processes packets between the template program and the kernel. `process_cleanup()` cleans up expressions remaining from a disconnected link. These functions are not described in the book but can be found on the CD-ROM.

10.9. Template Program Object

Using our OOP style, we create a *Mathematica object* which connects a template program with `Serializer`. Each new *instance* of this *object* makes a new connection.

```
New[MLProgram, lname_String, opts___Rule] :=
 Module[{self, mylink, lmode, lproto, elproto, elname},
   self[dispose] := (Map[#[dispose] &, ListAllWindowObjects[mylink]];
     EventLinkClose[mylink];
     RemoveLink[elname[[1]]];
     Uninstall[mylink];
     Remove[self, mylink, lmode, lproto, elproto, elname]);
   self[link] := mylink;
   self[elink] := elname;
   self[selector_, args___] :=
     findmethod[MLProgram[self, selector, args], $MethodNotFound];
   lmode = LinkMode /. {opts} /. Options[MLProgram];
   lproto = LinkProtocol /. {opts} /. Options[MLProgram];
   elproto = EventLinkProtocol /. {opts} /. Options[MLProgram];
   If[$MSGLink === Null, MessageLinkCreate[]];      (*check MessageLink*)
   mylink = Install[lname, LinkMode -> lmode, LinkProtocol -> lproto];
   If[LinkConnectedQ[mylink] =!= True,
     Message[MLProgram::install, lname]; Return[$Failed]];
   If[(elname = SerializerEventLinkCreate[elproto]) === $Failed,
     Message[MLProgram::eventlink1]; Return[$Failed]];
   If[EventLinkConnect[mylink, elname[[2]], elproto,
       FilterObject /. {opts} /. {FilterObject -> self}] === $Failed,
     Message[MLProgram::eventlink2, lname]; $Failed, self]]
```

```
Options[MLProgram] = {LinkMode -> Launch, LinkProtocol -> PPC};
```

The following methods are available for this program object:

Method	Action
self[dispose]	quits a link between the object and `Serializer` and disposes of the object.
self[link]	returns a link between the object and the template program.
self[elink]	returns the link name and index number of the object – `Serializer` link.

10.10. Summary

In this chapter, the `Serializer` program for sending events from template programs to the kernel was described. `Serializer` was first demonstrated at the Second International *Mathematica* Symposium (Miyaji, 1997), and similar ideas can be found in `Interceptor` (Schreiner, 1997). `Serializer`, itself, is a template program that relays expressions between the front end and kernel and, moreover, it transfers expressions from the template program. `Serializer` also demonstrates how to create various kinds of links and how to send interrupts. `Serializer` is the most complicated template program described in this book, but it is portable between MacOS, Microsoft Windows, and Unix with only a few minor modifications. Applications of `Serializer` are demonstrated in Chapters 11-15.

10.11. References

[1] Chikara Miyaji and Hiroshi Kimura, *Writing a Graphical User Interface Using Mathematica and MathLink*, Innovation in Mathematics—Proceedings of Second International *Mathematica* Symposium, 307-314, Computational Mechanics Pub., Southampton, 1997.

[2] Wolfgang Schreiner, *A Distributed Education Environment Based on Mathematica*. IDIMT'97—5th Interdisciplinary Information Management Talks, Zadov, Czech Republic, October 15-17, 1997, pp. 287-301, Volume 102 of the Austrian Computer Society Series, Oldenbourg Verlag, Vienna.
URL: http://www.risc.uni-linz.ac.at/people/schreine/papers/idimt97/.

Chapter 11 — Creating a Window Object

In this chapter, we implement an event-driven mechanism and, using object-oriented programming, a window object is created. After creating this object it is possible to define its response to events as a new instance method. In this chapter, we learn:

[1] how to construct and send event expressions to the kernel;

[2] how to define a window object;

[3] the general concept of event processing by the kernel;

[4] how to add a new instance method to an object.

Using these ideas it is easy to create a program for drawing lines or points in a window under the control of *Mathematica*. These applications are discussed in Chapter 12.

11.1. What Events Will Be Sent?

Event expressions are constructed using *MathLink* library functions and sent to the kernel through `Serializer` using `eventlink`. For example, we can send an event expression, say `EvaluatePacket[self$123[dispose]]`, to the kernel, as follows.

```
MLPutFunction(eventlink,"EvaluatePacket",1L);
MLPutFunction(eventlink,self$123,1L);
MLPutSymbol(eventlink,"dispose");
MLEndPacket(eventlink);
MLFlush(eventlink);
```

`MLPutFunction()` creates the `EvaluatePacket[]` packet. `MLPutFunction()` and `MLPutSymbol()` create `self$123[dispose]`, and `MLEndPacket()` terminates the expression which `MLFlush()` flushes to `Serializer`.

Here is a summary of the events described and implemented in this chapter:

- Clicking on a close box sends a `dispose` event to the window object.

- Clicking sends a `click` event and dragging sends a `drag` event to the window object.

11.1.1 Closing a Window

When a window close box is selected, the case of `inGoAway` in `_handle_user_event()` is executed and a `dispose` event is sent using `sendwclose()`.

```
case inGoAway:
    if(TrackGoAway(window, event.where))
        sendwclose(getWindowSymbol(window));
    break;
```

`sendwclose()` needs to know the name of the target window object to send the `dispose` message. `getWindow-Symbol()` returns the object's name. This object name is passed from the kernel to the template program when `WOpen()` is invoked. `sendwclose()` sends a `dispose` message to the window object.

```
void sendwclose(char *name)
{
    MLPutFunction(eventlink,"EvaluatePacket",1L);
    MLPutFunction(eventlink,name,1L);
    MLPutSymbol(eventlink,"dispose");
    MLEndPacket(eventlink);
    MLFlush(eventlink);
}
```

Let's examine the window close event sequence. Clicking the close box of a window object, say `self$123`, creates the following event expression, which is sent to the kernel.

```
EvaluatePacket[self$123[dispose]]
```

The kernel evaluates **`self$123[dispose]`**, which invokes **`CloseWindow[]`**. **`CloseWindow[]`** calls the external function `wclose()`, which closes the window and disposes of the window data structures (see Figure 11.1).

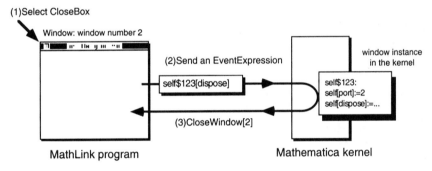

Figure 11.1. Expression flow when a window is closed.

11.1.2 Clicking and Dragging

Mouse click and drag events are detected in `_handle_user_event()`, and `doMouseDown()` handles these events. If a mouse-down event is detected within a background window, the window is first brought to the front. Otherwise, the location of the mouse in local coordinates is calculated and `doMouseDown()` is called.

```
                case inContent:
                    if(window != FrontWindow()){
                        SelectWindow(window);
                        SetPort(window);
                    }
                    else {
                        SetPort(window);
                        point = event.where;
                        GlobalToLocal(&point);
```

```
                    doMouseDown(window, point, &event);
            }
        break;
```

doMouseDown() gets the object name of the clicked window and waits 1/6 second (using `Delay()`). Then, if the mouse is still down, it calls `senddrag()`; otherwise, it calls `sendclick()`.

```
void doMouseDown(WindowPtr window, Point point, EventRecord *event)
{
    char *name;
    unsigned long dummy;

    name = getWindowSymbol(window);

    Delay(10, &dummy);  // wait 1/6 sec and check...
    if(StillDown())
        senddrag(name, point.h, point.v, modifier(event));
    else
        sendclick(name, point.h, point.v, modifier(event));
}
```

`sendclick()` and `senddrag()` are defined next. `modifier(event)` checks the status of the modifier key.

```
void sendclick(char *name, int x, int y, int mod)
{
    int v[2];

    v[0] = x;
    v[1] = y;
    MLPutFunction(eventlink, "EvaluatePacket",1);
    MLPutFunction(eventlink, name, mod?3:2);
    MLPutSymbol(eventlink,"click");
    MLPutIntegerList(eventlink, v, 2);
    if(mod)MLPutInteger(eventlink, mod);
    MLEndPacket(eventlink);
    MLFlush(eventlink);
}
```

```
void senddrag(char *name, int x, int y, int mod)
{
    int v[2];

    v[0] = x;
    v[1] = y;
    MLPutFunction(eventlink, "EvaluatePacket",1);
    MLPutFunction(eventlink, name, mod?3:2);
    MLPutSymbol(eventlink,"drag");
    MLPutIntegerList(eventlink, v, 2);
    if(mod)MLPutInteger(eventlink, mod);
    MLEndPacket(eventlink);
    MLFlush(eventlink);
}
```

Here is a typical `click` event expression,

```
EvaluatePacket[self$123[click, {x, y}]]
```

and a `drag` event expression.

```
EvaluatePacket[self$123[drag, {x, y}]]
```

11.2. Modifying the Window Template

Here is the `WindowIndex` structure for holding window information that includes `wSymbol` to record the window object name and `pensize` for the window.

```
typedef struct WindowIndex{
    WindowPtr window;
    GWorldPtr offscreen;
    char * wSymbol; // remember the window's symbol.
    int pensize;    // remember pensize for the window.
} WindowIndex;
```

A new item, `obj`, is added to the `wopen()` template.

```
:Begin:
:Function:       wopen
:Pattern:        WOpen[{{x0_Integer,y0_Integer},{x1_Integer,y1_Integer}},
                     title_String, obj_Symbol]
:Arguments:      {x0,y0,x1,y1,title,obj}
:ArgumentTypes:  {Integer,Integer,Integer,Integer,String,Manual}
:ReturnType:     Integer
:End:
```

Note that the `obj` is the last argument and is declared as `Manual` in the `ArgumentTypes` field. For this reason, `wopen()` does not have the argument for `obj`; instead the window name must be obtained manually in `wopen()` using `MLGetSymbol()`, which allocates memory for the string, reads the symbol from the link, and returns a pointer to `wopen()`. This memory area must be disposed of using `MLDisownSymbol()`. We postpone this disposal until `wclose()` is called, and keep this name string while the window is open. Next is the modified `wopen()` (c.f. Sections 6.3 and 6.5).

```
int wopen(int x0, int y0, int x1, int y1, const char *title)
{
    OSErr er;
    Rect bounds;
    int slot;
    WindowPtr window;
    GWorldPtr offscreen;
    unsigned char ps[256];
    Rect size;
    const char *obj;
    WindowIndexPtr win;
```

```
    MLGetSymbol(stdlink, &obj);      // read window symbol

    if((slot = newWindowSlot()) == -1){
        MLDisownSymbol(stdlink, obj);
        return(-1);
    }

    SetRect(&size, x0, y0, x1, y1);
    c2ps((char *)title, ps);
    window = NewCWindow(nil,&size,(unsigned char *)ps,true,
                        0,(WindowPtr)-1,true,(long)slot);
    if(window == nil){
        MLDisownSymbol(stdlink, obj);
        return(-2);
    }

    getScreenBounds(&bounds);
    er = NewGWorld(&offscreen,32,&bounds,0,0,0);
    if(er != noErr){
        MLDisownSymbol(stdlink, obj);
        DisposeWindow(window);
        clearWindowSlot(slot);
        return(-3);
    }
    if((win = (WindowIndexPtr)NewPtr(sizeof(WindowIndex))) == nil){
        MLDisownSymbol(stdlink, obj);
        DisposeWindow(window);
        clearWindowSlot(slot);
        return(-4);
    }
    win->window = window;
    win->offscreen = offscreen;
    win->wSymbol = (char *)obj; // save the symbol name.
    win->pensize = 1;   // set pensize.
    putWindowSlot(slot, win);

    clearwindow(slot);
    MacShowWindow(window);
    return(slot);
}
```

The `wclose()` function gets a pointer to the name of the window, `win`, and disposes of it using `MLDisownSymbol()` (c.f. Sections 6.3 and 6.5).

```
int wclose(int windex)
{
    WindowIndexPtr win;

    win = getWindowSlotPtr(windex);
    if(win == NULL)
        return(-1);
    MLDisownSymbol(stdlink, win->wSymbol);
    DisposeGWorld(win->offscreen);
    DisposeWindow(win->window);
    DisposePtr((Ptr)win);   // we use NewPtr instead of malloc in wopen on Mac, so
we use DisposePtr.
```

```
        clearWindowSlot(windex);
        return(0);
}
```

`putWindowSlot()` saves the window index pointer,

```
Boolean putWindowSlot(int slot, WindowIndexPtr win)
{
    if(mywindowlist[slot] == NULL){
        mywindowlist[slot] = win;
        return(true);
    }
    return(false);
}
```

and `getwindowSlotPtr()` returns `WindowInterPtr` for the slot number.

```
WindowIndexPtr getWindowSlotPtr(int slot)
{
    if(-1< slot && slot < MAX_WINDOW)
        return(mywindowlist[slot]);
    return(NULL);
}
```

11.3. Defining a Window Object

Now we define a window object.

```
New[Window, super_Symbol, opts___Rule] :=
  Module[{wport, self, mylink = super[link]},
    self[port] := wport;
    self[receiver, s_] := SetWindowReceiver[mylink, s, wport];
    self[dispose] := (CloseWindow[mylink, wport]; Remove[wport, self, mylink]);
    self[selector_, args___] :=
      findmethod[Window[self, selector, args], super[selector, args]];
    wport = OpenWindow[mylink, ReceiverObject /. {opts} /. {ReceiverObject -> self},
      opts]; If[wport === $Failed, Remove[wport, self, mylink]; $Failed, self]]
```

`OpenWindow[]` is called to open a window. If successful, the window instance is saved as **wport** and a window object is returned. The parent of the window object is the program object specified by **prog**. Our window object has two instance methods:

[1] **self[receiver, s]**   sets window instance to s;

[2] **self[dispose]**   disposes of the window object.

The name of the object that will receive events is assigned using **ReceiverObject/.{opts}/.{ReceiverObject → self}**. Normally it will be the window object name (**self**). However, sometimes we need to assign a different object to receive events. If the **ReceiverObject** option exists, it is assigned to be the object that will receive events (see Figure 11.2).

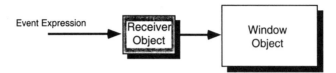

Figure 11.2. An event for a window object is sent to the **ReceiverObject** object.

Also, **ReceiverObject** can be assigned by receiving a message. **SetWindowReceiver** is a template function to set **ReceiverObject**.

```
self[receiver, s_] := SetWindowReceiver[mylink, s, wport];
```

Here is the overall framework (see Figure 11.3):

[1] User sends an event to the *MathLink* program;

[2] Event is sent to the kernel as an event expression that is a message to an object;

[3] Message invokes the object's method and, in the method, a template function is called;

[4] Template function calls external function such as wopen() or wclose();

[5] External function modifies the window data structure, which results in a reaction to the user's event.

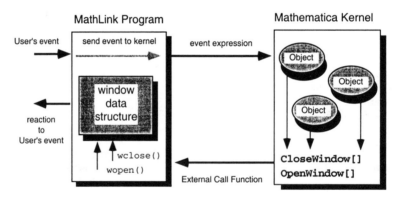

Figure 11.3. The relationship between event expressions, objects, and template functions.

The relationship between an object and its method can be summarized as follows:

- Creation, handling, and disposal of the data structure of objects in a *MathLink* program are defined as template functions.

- Kernel objects wrap these template functions and are defined as methods.

11.4. Testing the Window Object

In the `WindowObjects` directory there are two *Mathematica* files: `Templates.m` and `WindowObjectsClass.m`. `Templates.m` contains functions that wrap template functions, and `WindowObjectsClass.m` defines the window objects class.

The executable program—`wobjects.exe`—is located in the appropriate subfolder of the `Window-Objects/wobjects.exe` directory. `wobjects.exe` is loaded using **Install[]** when **New[MLProgram,...]** is invoked, and an **MLProgram** instance, **prog**, is created.

```
(Serializer) In[1]:=  prog = New[MLProgram,
               "NetworkProgramming`WindowObjects`wobjects`", LinkMode → Launch];
```

We follow the naming rule for the **Install[]** command.

```
(Serializer) In[2]:=  win = New[Window, prog]
```

```
(Serializer) Out[2]=  self$54
```

The instance of the window (here **self$54**) is assigned to **win**, and a new untitled window appears (Figure 11.4).

Figure 11.4. `New[Window, prog]` opens a new window.

Clicking the mouse in the window causes an event expression to be sent to the kernel. To monitor the exchange of front end packets, we use **PacketMonitor[]** (c.f. Section 10.6.2).

```
(Serializer) In[3]:=  PacketMonitor[]

          < -k : OutputNamePacket[Out[3] = ]
```

```
(Serializer) Out[3]=  1

          < -k : ReturnExpressionPacket[BoxData[1, StandardForm]]
```

When we click in the window, the resulting dialog is printed out in the Messages window (see Figure 11.5) because the expression is sent from the *MathLink* program, not from the front end.

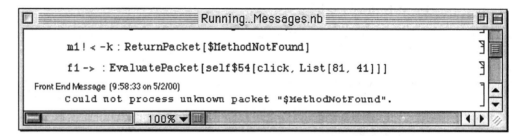

Figure 11.5. Dialog generated by a `click` event sent to `Serializer`.

self$54 is the instance symbol of the window. The kernel returns **$MethodNotFound** because the `click` method is not yet defined.

EvaluatePacket[self$54[dispose]] is sent when the close box is selected (see Figure 11.6), and the window is closed.

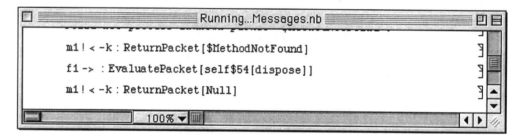

Figure 11.6. Selecting the close box sends an **EvaluatePacket[self$54[dispose]]** message.

We now turn off debugging.

```
(Serializer) In[4]:=  PacketMonitor[]

                      < -k : InputNamePacket[In[4]:= ]
                      f0 -> : EnterExpressionPacket[
                         MakeExpression[BoxData[RowBox[List[PacketMonitor, [, ]]]], StandardForm]]

(Serializer) Out[4]=  0
```

Checking how many instance symbols (i.e., of the form **"self$*"**) are in use,

```
(Serializer) In[5]:=  Names["self$*"]

(Serializer) Out[5]=  {self$, self$23}
```

we see that only the instance symbols of the program object (**self$23**) remain.

After creating two new windows, we again check to see how many instance symbols are in use.

```
(Serializer) In[6]:=  win2 = New[Window, prog]; win3 = New[Window, prog]; Names["self$*"]

(Serializer) Out[6]=  {self$, self$23, self$59, self$62}
```

Two new symbols—corresponding to the window objects **win2** and **win3**—have been created. Examining the definition of **win2** shows that it is a window object instance with methods **dispose**, **port**, and **receiver**.

```
(Serializer) In[7]:=  Definition[Evaluate[win2]]

(Serializer) Out[7]=  Attributes[self$59] = {Temporary}

          self$59[dispose] :=
           (CloseWindow[NetworkProgramming`MathLinkObject`Private`mylink$59,
             NetworkProgramming`MathLinkObject`Private`wport$59];
            Remove[NetworkProgramming`MathLinkObject`Private`wport$59,
             self$59, NetworkProgramming`MathLinkObject`Private`mylink$59])

          self$59[port] := NetworkProgramming`MathLinkObject`Private`wport$59

          self$59[receiver, NetworkProgramming`MathLinkObject`Private`s$_] :=
           SetWindowReceiver[NetworkProgramming`MathLinkObject`Private`mylink$59,
             NetworkProgramming`MathLinkObject`Private`s$,
             NetworkProgramming`MathLinkObject`Private`wport$59]

          self$59[NetworkProgramming`MathLinkObject`Private`selector$_,
             NetworkProgramming`MathLinkObject`Private`args$___] := findmethod[
            Window[self$59, NetworkProgramming`MathLinkObject`Private`selector$,
             NetworkProgramming`MathLinkObject`Private`args$],
            self$23[NetworkProgramming`MathLinkObject`Private`selector$,
             NetworkProgramming`MathLinkObject`Private`args$]]
```

11.5. More Additions to the Template

Two mouse-sensing functions are implemented. The template function **GetMouse[]** returns the current mouse location.

```
:Begin:
:Function:       getmouse
:Pattern:        GetMouse[$CurrentLink]
:Arguments:      {  }
:ArgumentTypes:  {  }
:ReturnType:     Manual
:End:
```

StillDown[] checks if the mouse is down.

```
:Begin:
:Function:       stilldown
:Pattern:        StillDown[$CurrentLink]
:Arguments:      {  }
:ArgumentTypes:  {  }
:ReturnType:     Manual
:End:
```

`getmouse()` and `stilldown()` call Toolbox routines.

```
void getmouse(void)
{
    int x[2];
    Point p;
    WindowPtr window;
    GrafPtr cp;

    if((window = FrontWindow()) != nil){
        GetPort(&cp);
        MacSetPort(window);
        GetMouse(&p);
        x[0] = p.h;
        x[1] = p.v;
        MLPutIntegerList(stdlink,x,2L);
        MacSetPort(cp);
    }
    else
        MLPutSymbol(stdlink,"Null");
}
```

```
void stilldown(void)
{
    if(StillDown())
        MLPutSymbol(stdlink,"True");
    else
        MLPutSymbol(stdlink,"False");
}
```

In addition, several drawing functions, similar to **MoveTo[]** and **LineTo[]** of Section 6.2, are defined. For the pen state **PenSize[]** is defined. **SetWindowTitle[]** sets the window's title.

11.6. Summary

In this chapter, we created a window object. User operation on a window produces events that are sent to the window object or program object as messages. The reaction to a message is defined as a method of the object in the kernel.

11.7. Objects Summary

In the following, a gray font is used to indicate optional arguments, for example, *opts*.

11.7.1 Window Object

A window object is an object within which the user can send events to that object.

New[Window, *prog*, *options***]**

This method creates a new window object and returns its instance. *prog* is a parent program object of the window. *title* is the window title, which is "untitled" by default. There are two options: **WindowTitle** and **WindowSize**. **WindowSize** determines the size of the window. Its default is {{0,0},{200,200}}, and new windows are stacked close to the location of previous windows.

wobj **[dispose]**

This function sends a **dispose** message to window object, *wobj*. The object closes the window and sends **dispose** messages to all objects in the window.

wobj **[port]**

This message returns the window index of the object, *wobj*.

wobj **[receiver,** *obj***]**

This message sets the event receiver object to *obj*.

11.7.2 Drawing Commands

MoveTo[{*x*, *y*}, *wobj* **]**

MoveTo[{*x*, *y*}, *wobj*] moves the current position of window *wobj* to {*x*, *y*}.

LineTo[{*x*, *y*}, *wobj* **]**

LineTo[{*x*, *y*}, *wobj*] draws a line from the current position to {*x*, *y*} in window *wobj*.

PenSize[{*x*, *y*}, *wobj* **]**

PenSize[{*x*, *y*}, *wobj*] sets the pen size to {*x*, *y*} in window object *wobj*.

SetWindowTitle[*string*, *wobj* **]**

SetWindowTitle[*string*, *wobj*] sets the title of window object *wobj* to *string*.

11.7.3 Program Object

A program object is an object of the *MathLink* program.

New[MLProgram, *name*, *options***]**

This function creates a new *MathLink* program object and returns its instance. *name* and *options* are the same as the options of **LinkOpen[]**:

- If **LinkMode** is **Launch**, *name* is the name of the *MathLink* program to be launched.

- If **LinkMode** is **Connect**, *name* is the link name of a *MathLink* program awaiting connection.

- **LinkProtocol** can be **TCP**, **PPC**, or **FileMap** depending on the operating system.

obj[dispose]

This function sends a **dispose** message to program object, *obj*. The object closes its link to Serializer and quits.

obj[link]

This function returns a link object of the *MathLink* program.

obj[elink]

This function returns the name of the eventlink (**elink**) connecting the program object, *obj*, and Serializer.

Chapter 12 — Window Object Applications

In this chapter, we make two applications using window objects developed in Chapter 11. The first is *Sketch*, a simple application that allows one to draw points and lines in a window. The second is an interactive interface to the *Forest Fire* simulation of Section 7.3. The purpose of this chapter is to show how easy it is to customize window objects for special purposes.

12.1. Simple Example: *Sketch*

First we start the `Serializer` kernel and launch `wobjects.exe`.

(Serializer) In[1]:= **prog = New[MLProgram,**
        "NetworkProgramming`WindowObjects`wobjects`", LinkMode → Launch];

No method for responding to a `click` event in a window object has been defined. As the result, the kernel will return **$MethodNotFound** (c.f. Figure 11.5). Here we add **click** and **drag** instance methods to a new window **w**.

(Serializer) In[2]:= **w = New[Window, prog];**

Clicking puts a point on the window, and dragging draws a freehand line. When the window object receives a `click` message, it moves the pen to {x,y} using **MoveTo[]** and draws a line to the same place using **LineTo[]**. This makes a single point at the clicked location.

(Serializer) In[3]:= **PenSize[{2, 2}, w];**

(Serializer) In[4]:= **w[click, {x_, y_}] := (MoveTo[{x, y}, w]; LineTo[{x, y}, w])**

When the window object receives a **drag** message, it moves the pen to the new location using **MoveTo[]** and starts monitoring the mouse state via **StillDown[]**. If the mouse is held down, a line is drawn using **LineTo[]** to the mouse location returned by **GetMouse[]**.

(Serializer) In[5]:= **w[drag, {x_, y_}] := (MoveTo[{x, y}, w];**
        While[StillDown[w[link]], LineTo[GetMouse[w[link]], w]])

(Serializer) In[6]:= **SetWindowTitle["Tsukuba", w];**

This process continues until the mouse is released and a curve following the mouse movement will be drawn. We can now draw points and freehand curves in response to click and drag events in the window object, **w**. Figure 12.1 shows a simple freehand picture drawn using `click` and `drag` messages. These messages are implemented as high-level kernel functions.

Sketch is a simple example of a drawing program, but one that has unique advantages over standard drawing software: it is *extensible* and *programmable*. To create a new special effect in a *Sketch* window, one just needs to define a new *Mathematica* function. With standard drawing software, it is rather tedious to draw 1000 lines using the mouse. In this example, we just write a simple **Do** loop that performs this operation. And the user can mix freehand drawings with more complicated recursive drawings. This mixture of mouse-driven interactivity with programmability makes it possible to create new and exciting drawing software.

Figure 12.1. Drawing points and lines in a window using `click` and `drag` messages.

12.2. An Interface to *Forest Fire*

In this section, we create an interface to the *Forest Fire* simulation of Section 7.3. There are two objectives for the interface:

[1] Cell states empty (**0**), tree (**1**), and fire (**2**) can be selected from a window palette using the mouse;

[2] Starting the simulation, and the number of time steps, can be controlled by selecting items from a menu.

12.2.1 Window Palette

We open up a small window of fixed size (150×20):

```
(Serializer) In[7]:=  cw = New[Window, prog,
                        WindowSize → {{0, 0}, {150, 20}} + 100, WindowResize → False];
```

On this window, we use **PutGraphicsObject[]** to paint brown, green, and yellow colors to represent the three states:

```
(Serializer) In[8]:=  SetColorList[cw[link], {
                        0 → RGBColor[0.380, 0.210, 0.050],
                        1 → RGBColor[0.240, 0.580, 0.110],
                        2 → RGBColor[1.000, 1.000, 0.170]}];
```

```
(Serializer) In[9]:=  PutGraphicsObject[IndexColor[{{0, 1, 2}}], cw];
```

Now we need to add some code so that clicking on one of the colors in this palette sets the current state. Then, when we click on a cell in the *Forest Fire* window, it will be set to the current color and, in this way, the simulation state can be prepared. To do this we have to work out which color is clicked from its {*x*, *y*} position. **findPos[]** returns the (scaled) coordinates of the clicked position.

(Serializer) In[10]:= **findPos[{x_, y_}, {{xdiv_, ydiv_}, {horiz_, vert_}}] :=**

$$\textbf{Quotient}\Big[\{x, y\}, \frac{\{horiz, vert\}}{\{xdiv, ydiv\}}\Big] + 1$$

Next, we set the value of the global variable **myclick** to be **0**, **1**, or **2**, according to the clicked position, by defining a method of the window **cw**.

(Serializer) In[11]:= **cw[click, {x_, y_}] := myclick = findPos[{x, y}, {{3, 1}, {150, 20}}][[1]] - 1**

Upon registering a click, this method sets the **myclick** value according to the clicked color. For example, if you click on the green color in the window palette, the value of **myclick** becomes **1**. Until a click is registered in the palette, **myclick** will remain unevaluated.

(Serializer) In[12]:= **myclick**

(Serializer) Out[12]= 1

To clearly indicate the current state — that is, empty, tree, or fire — we set the window title using **SetWindowTitle[]** to be the state name.

(Serializer) In[13]:= **showName[i_Integer] := SetWindowTitle[{"empty", "green", "fire"}[[i + 1]], cw]**

(Serializer) In[14]:= **cw[click, {x_, y_}] :=**
  showName[myclick = findPos[{x, y}, {{3, 1}, {150, 20}}][[1]] - 1]

Now, clicking on a color changes the current state and window title, as shown in Figure 12.2.

Figure 12.2. Clicking on the yellow color bar changes the window title to fire.

12.2.2 Forest Fire

We repeat the steps of Sections 7.3.1 and 7.3.2, now using the color index table (**IndexColor[]**) from Section 7.5. First we open a new window object.

(Serializer) In[15]:= **myforest = New[Window, prog, WindowTitle → "Forest Fire"];**

Next, we set the constants as in Section 7.3.1.

(Serializer) In[16]:= **n = 100; s = 0.3; k = 0; p = 0.05; f = 0.00025; g = 0; t = 100;**
  sprout = (1 + p); catch = (2 - g); spont = 1 + (1 - g) f;

The initial (random) state of the forest is a 100×100 matrix named **forestPreserve**.

(Serializer) In[17]:= **forestPreserve =**
  Table[Floor[1 + s - Random[]], {n}, {n}] /. 1 :→ Floor[1 + k + Random[]];

We display the current state in the window using **ShowForest[]**.

(Serializer) In[18]:= **ShowForest[lat_] := (PutGraphicsObject[IndexColor[lat], myforest]; lat)**

(Serializer) In[19]:= **ShowForest[forestPreserve];**

12.2.3 Changing State

If we click with the mouse in this window, we want to change the state to that currently selected in the palette, as shown in Figure 12.3. This is defined as the **click** method of this window object (**myforest**).

(Serializer) In[20]:= **myforest[click, {x_, y_}] :=**
               Module[{px, py, size = GetWindowSize[myforest]},
               {px, py} = findPos[{x, y}, {{n, n}, size}];
               If[forestPreserve⟦py, px⟧ =!= myclick,
               forestPreserve⟦py, px⟧ = myclick];
               paintCell[findRect[{px, py}, {{n, n}, size}], myclick, myforest]]

To update only the selected cell, we calculate the location of the cell using **findRect[]**,

(Serializer) In[21]:= **findRect[pindex_, {div_, size_}] := Round[{$\dfrac{(\text{pindex} - 1)\ \text{size}}{\text{div}}$, $\dfrac{\text{pindex}\ \text{size}}{\text{div}}$}]**

and color it with **paintCell[]**.

(Serializer) In[22]:= **paintCell[rect_, colornum_, win_] :=**
               PutGraphicsObject[IndexColor[{{colornum}}], win, FrameSize → rect]

Figure 12.3. Clicking on the Forest Fire window sets the state according to the state selected by the palette.

12.2.4 Evolution Rules

As in Section 7.3.1, **spread[**n**, __]** defines how the fire spreads using rule-based (*pattern matching*) programming.

```
(Serializer) In[23]:=   spread[0, _, _, _, _] := Floor[sprout - Random[]];
                        spread[2, _, _, _, _] = 0;
                        spread[1, a_, b_, c_, d_] :=
                          1 + Floor[catch - Random[]] /; MatchQ[2, a | b | c | d];
                        spread[1, a_, b_, c_, d_] := 1 + Floor[spont - Random[]];
```

This model has three cell states, indicated by the argument, *n*. The relationship, ▪▪▪, between the four nearest neighbors, ▪, of a specified cell, ·, is implemented as **VonNeumann[]** using list operations.

```
(Serializer) In[27]:=   VonNeumann[func_, lat_] :=
                          MapThread[func, Map[RotateRight[lat, #] &,
                            {{0, 0}, {1, 0}, {0, -1}, {-1, 0}, {0, 1}}], 2];
```

12.2.5 Start Evolution

To control the number of evolution steps, **fire[*n*]** evolves the current state *n* times and displays the *n*th state in the window.

```
(Serializer) In[28]:=   fire[n_] :=
                          (Do[SetWindowTitle["Running..." <> ToString[i], myforest];
                            forestPreserve = ShowForest[VonNeumann[spread, forestPreserve]],
                            {i, n}]; SetWindowTitle["Done", myforest])
```

Now we have an interactive interface to the *Forest Fire* program. Figure 12.4 shows a frame of the evolution of **fire[20]**.

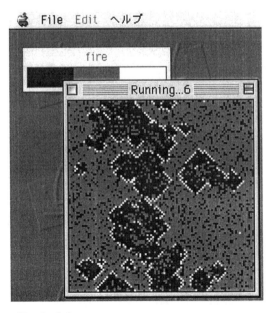

Figure 12.4. Interface to the *Forest Fire* simulation.

It was very easy to build this interface because only *Mathematica* functions were used. Once a program has such an interactive interface, the user no longer needs to worry about the program internals.

12.3. Summary

In this chapter, two programs were demonstrated — *Sketch* and an interactive interface to a *Forest Fire* simulation. Both programs only used *Mathematica* functions and, although these examples are simple, they indicate the power of combining programmability with interactivity. *Sketch* could be extended to have capabilities along the lines of more sophisticated applications such as NIH *Image* (http://rsb.info.nih.gov/nih-image/) or Adobe Photoshop (http://www.adobe.com/).

Chapter 13 — Writing an Interactive Graphics System

In this chapter, we introduce *point*, *line*, and *curve* objects as window objects. Using the event-driven mechanism introduced in Chapter 11, these objects provide real-time interactive graphics that the current front end does not support. Two applications — interactive geometry and interactive curve fitting — are demonstrated. Coupling *Mathematica*'s power with interactive graphics makes it easy to create sophisticated graphics applications.

13.1. Graphics Objects

In drawing software such as Illustrator, the drawing elements — point, line, curve, and so on — exist as window objects, which the user can move, duplicate, and erase. In comparison, painting software such as Photoshop only manipulates bitmap images in the window.

The set of graphics objects introduced here — generically referred to as a GraphicsObject — correspond to drawing software objects. Although each GraphicsObject is displayed in a window, it is defined as a kernel object. We summarize the concept of our GraphicsObject:

[1] Each GraphicsObject is represented as a kernel object (see Figure 13.1);

[2] Mouse events, such as a click or drag event, on a GraphicsObject are sent to the corresponding kernel object as messages;

[3] The kernel processes these messages and manipulates the GraphicsObject accordingly.

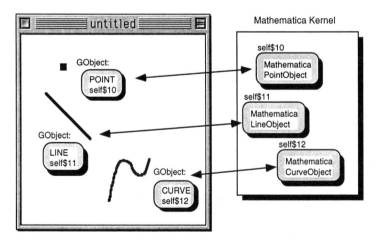

Figure 13.1. Each GraphicsObject in a window corresponds to a kernel object.

When a **Window** object receives a **dispose** message, it must send a **dispose** message to all GraphicsObjects. We map the **dispose** message over **ListAllGraphicsObject** to dispose of all the child objects of the **Window** object. Here is the definition of the **Window** class.

```
New[Window, super_Symbol, opts___Rule] :=
 Module[{wport, self, mylink = super[link]}, self[port] := wport;
  self[getwindow] := self;
  self[receiver, s_] := SetWindowReceiver[mylink, s, wport];
  self[dispose] := (Map[#[dispose] &, ListAllGraphicsObjects[mylink, wport]];
    CloseWindow[mylink, wport]; Remove[wport, self, mylink]);
  self[selector_, args___] :=
    findmethod[Window[self, selector, args], super[selector, args]];
  wport = OpenWindow[mylink, ReceiverObject /. {opts} /. {ReceiverObject -> self},
    opts]; If[wport === $Failed, Remove[wport, self, mylink]; $Failed, self]]]
```

The structure GObject holds the GraphicsObject information: type, symbol, and so on. Each GraphicsObject has this GObject structure.

```
typedef struct GObject {
    short type;      // type of the object
    Rect bbox;  // bounding box
    Point origin;    // origin of the object
    Boolean visible;// visible flag
    char * oSymbol; // symbol of the object
    void (*draw)(); // function to draw the object
    Boolean (*find)();  // function to find a object
    int (*dump)();  // dump the object information
    int (*dispose)();    // function to dispose the object
    char *winfo; // object's WindowIndexPtr, defined as char * for loop.
} GObject;

typedef GObject *GObjectPtr;
```

Each window has an array of pointers to GObject structures of size MAX_OBJECTS, which limits the maximum number of GraphicsObjects in a window.

```
#define MAX_OBJECTS 10000
```

All necessary window information is stored in the structure WindowIndex.

```
typedef struct WindowIndex{
    int dirty;  // dirty indicates to draw offscreen from objects.
    WindowPtr window;
    GWorldPtr offscreen;
    char * wSymbol;
    GObjectPtr gobjects[MAX_OBJECTS]; // array to hold all objects on the window.
    long ob_index[MAX_OBJECTS]; // index of gobjects array for update order.
    long ob_number; // number of objects on the window.
    GObjectPtr current_text; // pointer to the current_text.
} WindowIndex;

typedef WindowIndex *WindowIndexPtr;
```

`gobjects` is a list of objects, and `ob_index` indicates the visible order of these objects. Corresponding pointer references are shown in Figure 13.2.

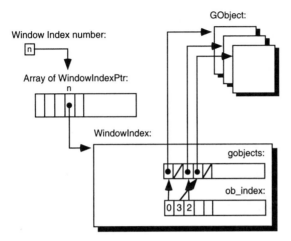

Figure 13.2. Structure of the pointer references of `WindowIndex` and `GObject`.

`newObjectSlot()` gets `WindowIndexPtr` as its argument, finds an empty slot in `gobjects` by linear search, and returns the index of `gobjects`.

```
int newObjectSlot(WindowIndexPtr windexptr)
{
    int i;
    char s[256];

        if(windexptr->ob_number >= MAX_OBJECTS){
            sprintf(s, "newObjectSlot:no more new object slot for window no %ld",
                windexptr);
            print_message(DEBUG_MESSAGE_WINDOW, s);
            return(-1);
        }
        for(i=0; i < MAX_OBJECTS; ++i)
            if((windexptr->gobjects)[i] == NULL)    // I found an empty slot.
                return(i);
        sprintf(s, "newObjectSlot:can't find new object slot for window no %ld",
            windexptr);
        print_message(DEBUG_PRINT, s);
        return(-2);
}
```

`disposeObjectSlot()` sets `gobjects`'s slot to `NULL` and rearranges `ob_index`.

```
void disposeObjectSlot(int oindex, WindowIndexPtr windexptr)
{
    int i, j;
    char s[256];

    windexptr->ob_number -= 1;
```

```
    windexptr->gobjects[oindex] = NULL; // clear the slot.
    for(i = 0;i <= windexptr->ob_number; ++i){
        if(windexptr->ob_index[i] == oindex){
            for(j=i; j < windexptr->ob_number; ++j)
                windexptr->ob_index[j] = windexptr->ob_index[j+1]; // shrink ob_index
            return;
        }
    }
    sprintf(s, "disposeObjectSlot:index %d is not in object's list of
        window no. %ld", oindex, windexptr);
    print_message(DEBUG_PRINT, s);
    return;
}
```

`putObjectSlot()` sets `GObjectPtr` information in `gobjects` and `ob_index`.

```
void putObjectSlot(WindowIndexPtr windexptr, int slot, GObjectPtr op)
{
    windexptr->gobjects[slot] = op;
    windexptr->ob_index[windexptr->ob_number] = slot;
    windexptr->ob_number += 1;
}
```

13.2. PointObject

The data structure of each `GObject` is manipulated by a set of template functions that are designed to:

[1] create data structures in the template program;

[2] manipulate data structures using template functions;

[3] wrap the template function as a definition of the object;

[4] use messages to access the data structure.

This is similar to the manipulation of window objects described in Section 11.3.

Here we define the template to create and dispose of a **PointObject**. `NewPointObject[]` creates a `PointObject` and returns its index. Its arguments are object position, object size, window index, and kernel symbol name.

```
:Begin:
:Function:        newpointobject
:Pattern:         NewPointObject[$CurrentLink, {x0_,y0_}, size_Integer,
                      windex_Integer, oSymbol_Symbol]
:Arguments:       { x0,y0,size,windex,oSymbol }
:ArgumentTypes:   { Integer,Integer,Integer,Integer,Manual }
:ReturnType:      Integer
:End:
```

The `PointObject` structure is identical to `GObject`. If the object needs to store more information—as is the case with `LineObject` (Section 13.4) and `CurveObject` (Section 13.6)—the `GObject` data structure needs to be extended.

```
typedef struct PointObject {
    short type; // type of the object
    Rect bbox;  // bounding box
    Point origin;   // origin of the object
    Boolean visible;// visible flag
    char * oSymbol; // symbol of the object
    void (*draw)(); // function to draw the object
    Boolean (*find)();  // function to find a object
    int (*dump)();  // dump the object information
    int (*dispose)();   // function to dispose the object
    char *winfo;    // object's windowIndexPtr.
} PointObject;

typedef PointObject *PointObjectPtr;
```

newpointobject() reads the symbol name of the object from the link using MLGetSymbol(). It then assigns winfo using getWindowSlotPtr(), calls newObjectSlot() to find a slot to save the PointObject pointer, allocates memory for PointObject, and then stores the information there and, finally, the pointer of these data is stored in gobjects using putObjectSlot().

```
int newpointobject(int x0, int y0, int size, int windex)
{
    Rect rec;
    int myslot;
    WindowIndexPtr winfo;
    char * symbol;
    PointObjectPtr op;
    Point pt;

    MLGetSymbol(stdlink, &symbol);  // get symbol of this object
    winfo = getWindowSlotPtr(windex);
    if(winfo == NULL){ // this windex is not used
        MLDisownSymbol(stdlink, symbol);
        return(-1);
    }
    if((myslot = newObjectSlot(winfo)) < 0){
        MLDisownSymbol(stdlink, symbol);
        return(-2);
    }
    MacSetRect(&rec,x0,y0,x0,y0);
    MacInsetRect(&rec,-size/2,-size/2);
    SetPt(&pt,x0,y0);
    if((op = (PointObjectPtr)NewPtr(sizeof(PointObject))) == nil){
        MLDisownSymbol(stdlink, symbol);
        disposeObjectSlot(myslot, winfo);
        return(-3);
    }
    op->type = OPOINT;
    op->bbox = rec;
    op->origin = pt;
    op->visible = true;
    op->oSymbol = symbol;
    op->draw = &drawpointobject;
    op->find = &findpointobject;
```

```
    op->dump = &dumppointobject;
    op->dispose = &disposepointobject;
    op->winfo = (char *)winfo;

    putObjectSlot(winfo, myslot, (GObjectPtr)op);

    invalidobjectrect(&rec, winfo);
    return(myslot);
}
```

invalidateobjectrect() sends an update request for the object to the system.

```
void invalidobjectrect(Rect *recptr, WindowIndexPtr winfo)
{
    GrafPtr cp;

    if(winfo->dirty <= 1){
        winfo->dirty = 1;
        GetPort(&cp);
        MacSetPort(winfo->window);
        InvalRect(recptr);
        MacSetPort(cp);
    }
}
```

The template function DisposePointObject[] erases oindex's GObject in window windex.

```
:Begin:
:Function:        disposepointobject
:Pattern:         DisposePointObject[$CurrentLink, oindex_Integer, windex_Integer]
:Arguments:       { oindex, windex }
:ArgumentTypes:   { Integer, Integer }
:ReturnType:      Integer
:End:
```

```
int disposepointobject(int oindex, int windex)
{
    PointObjectPtr gp;
    WindowIndexPtr winfo;

    winfo = getWindowSlotPtr(windex);
    if(winfo == NULL)
        return(-1);
    gp = (PointObjectPtr)winfo->gobjects[oindex];
    if(gp == NULL)
        return(-2);
    if(gp->type != OPOINT){
        return(-3);
    }

    invalidobjectrect(&(gp->bbox), winfo);

    MLDisownSymbol(stdlink, gp->oSymbol);
    DisposePtr((Ptr)gp);
    disposeObjectSlot(oindex, winfo);
```

```
        return(0);
}
```

The template function `MovePointObject[]` moves the object to the point {x0,y0} by calling `movepointobject()`.

```
:Begin:
:Function:          movepointobject
:Pattern:           MovePointObject[$CurrentLink,{x0_,y0_},oindex_Integer,windex_Inte-
ger]
:Arguments:         { x0,y0,oindex,windex }
:ArgumentTypes:     {Integer,Integer,Integer,Integer}
:ReturnType:        Integer
:End:
```

```
int movepointobject(int x0, int y0, int oindex, int windex)
{
    PointObjectPtr gp;
    WindowIndexPtr winfo;

    winfo = getWindowSlotPtr(windex);
    if(winfo == NULL)
        return(-1);
    gp = (PointObjectPtr)winfo->gobjects[oindex];
    if(gp == NULL)
        return(-2);
    if(gp->type != OPOINT){
        return(-3);
    }

    invalidobjectrect(&gp->bbox, winfo);

    MacOffsetRect(&(gp->bbox), x0 - gp->origin.h, y0 - gp->origin.v);
    gp->origin.h = x0;
    gp->origin.v = y0;

    invalidobjectrect(&(gp->bbox), winfo);
    return(0);
}
```

The move is performed by calling `invalidobjectrect()` twice. The first call assigns the current bounding box for updating. Then `movepointobject()` changes its position to the new location, and also changes its bounding box rectangle. Then it assigns the new location bounding box for updating. This is all that `movepointobject()` does. The rest of the drawing is done by the update function. The update function draws all objects using the object's draw function, `drawpointobject()`, on the erased offscreen. Because of this, the object's position is already updated and the object is drawn only in the new location, giving the appearance that the object has moved.

```
void drawpointobject(GObjectPtr obj, WindowPtr window)
{
    PaintRect(&obj->oBounds);
}
```

Only three template functions—for creation (`NewPointObject`), disposal (`DisposePointObject`), and movement (`MovePointObject`)—are defined for accessing a point's `GObject` data structure (see Figure 13.3).

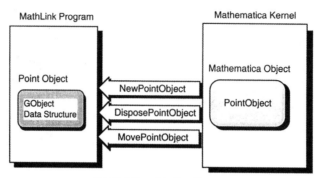

Figure 13.3. Three template functions are used to access a point's `GObject` structure.

Next, we define the corresponding kernel point object, **PointObject**. **New[PointObject,...]** creates a new **PointObject** using the template function **NewPointObject[]**. The **dispose** method uses **DisposePointObject[]**, and the **setposition** method uses **MovePointObject[]**.

```
New[PointObject, super_Symbol, opts___Rule] :=
  Module[{self, oindex, mypos, mylink = super[link], myport = super[port]},
    self[dispose] := (DisposePointObject[mylink, oindex, myport];
      Remove[self, oindex, mypos, mylink, myport]);
    self[index] := oindex;
    self[receiver, sym_Symbol] := SetObjectReceiver[mylink, sym, oindex, myport];
    self[getposition] := mypos;
    self[setposition, {x_, y_}] := (mypos = {x, y};
      MovePointObject[mylink, N[{x, y}], oindex, myport]);
    self[selector_, args___] :=
      findmethod[PointObject[self, selector, args], super[selector, args]];
    mypos = PointObjectPosition /. {opts} /. Options[PointObject];
    oindex = NewPointObject[mylink,
      N[mypos], (PointObjectSize /. {opts} /. Options[PointObject]),
      myport, ReceiverObject /. {opts} /. {ReceiverObject -> self}];
    If[! IntegerQ[oindex], Remove[self, oindex, mypos, mylink, myport];
      Return[$Failed]];
    self]
```

The **move** class method for **PointObject** sends a **setposition** message.

```
PointObject[self_, move, {x_, y_}] := self[setposition, {x, y}]
```

Here, we demonstrate **PointObject**.

```
(Serializer) In[1]:= prog = New[MLProgram,
                "NetworkProgramming`DrawObjects`draw`", LinkMode -> Launch];
```

MLProgram is introduced in Section 10.9. This uses the same method to load the package and install the executable as described in Section 11.4. Creating a **Window** object, **win1**,

(Serializer) In[2]:= **win1 = New[Window, prog, WindowTitle → "PointObject test",**
WindowSize → {{0, 0}, {200, 100}} + 100];

and a **PointObject** in this window,

(Serializer) In[3]:= **pt1 = New[PointObject, win1,**
PointObjectPosition → {20, 20}, PointObjectSize → 5];

a point appears in the window, as shown in Figure 13.4.

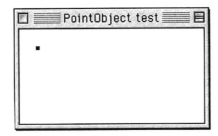

Figure 13.4. Creating a PointObject in a new window.

After moving **pt1** to **{50,50}**,

(Serializer) In[4]:= **pt1[move, {50, 50}];**

the point's location will have changed (see Figure 13.5).

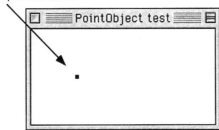

Figure 13.5. **move** message moves PointObject, **pt1**.

Sending a **getposition** message returns the current location.

(Serializer) In[5]:= **pt1[getposition]**

(Serializer) Out[5]= {50, 50}

All window events are sent to the appropriate kernel object as a message. For example, when the user drags a **PointObject** using the mouse, *self*[**drag,{x,y}**] is sent to the kernel, where *self* is the name (instance) of this

PointObject. Here is the definition of the **drag** method that performs dragging when a **PointObject** receives a **drag** message.

```
PointObject[self_, drag, {x_, y_}] := Module[{prev = {x, y}},
  While[StillDown[self[link]],
    If[prev =!= (prev = GetMouse[self[link]]), self[move, prev - {x, y}]]]]
```

This method sends a **move** message to the **PointObject** while the mouse is dragging the point. Using this **drag** method, dragging the **PointObject** with the mouse moves the point along with the mouse movement, as shown in Figure 13.6.

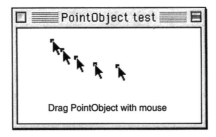

Figure 13.6. The selected **PointObject** moves along with mouse.

To modify the method we just redefine the function. For example, if we redefine the **drag** method for **pt1** as follows,

```
(Serializer) In[6]:= pt1[drag, {x_, y_}] := Module[{prev = {x, y}, pin = GetMouse[pt1[link]]},
              While[StillDown[pt1[link]], If[prev =!= (prev = GetMouse[pt1[link]]),
                pt1[move, {prev[[1]], pin[[2]]} - {x, y}]]]]
```

the motion of **pt1** (and *only* **pt1**) is restricted to move horizontally (see Figure 13.7).

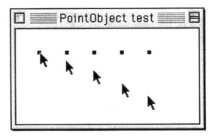

Figure 13.7. The **PointObject** instance **pt1** is restricted to move horizontally.

All GraphicsObject events are sent to the kernel, and the method for each event is defined as a *Mathematica* function (see Figure 13.8). This programming style enables dynamic modification of the method.

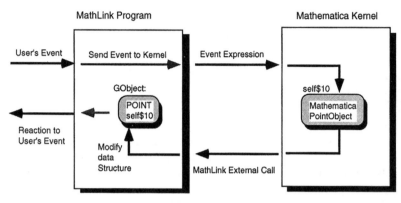

Figure 13.8. The relationship between a user's event and its action on a GObject.

13.3. Finding and Updating Graphics Objects

When the user clicks the mouse on some location, findobject() searches for a GObject whose area includes the mouse location and returns the pointer to the GObject. findobject() does a linear search starting with the latest object in ob_index, so, even if objects overlap, the latest object is returned. It gets WindowIndexPtr from the window and then searches the list of all the GObjects to see if they contain this location using each object's find() function.

```
GObjectPtr findobject(int x, int y, WindowIndexPtr windexptr)
{
    int i, olen;
    GObjectPtr *gp;
    char s[256];

    gp = windexptr->gobjects;
    olen = windexptr->ob_number;

    for(i = olen - 1; i >= 0; --i){ // search from end of the ob_index
        if((*(gp[windexptr->ob_index[i]]->find))(x, y,
            gp[windexptr->ob_index[i]]))
        {
            return(gp[windexptr->ob_index[i]]);
        }
    }
    return(NULL);
}
```

During execution of findobject, each object is searched using its corresponding find() function. For example, PointObject's find function, findpointobject(), searches a PointObject and checks whether or not the point is in its bounding box using the PtInRect() function.

```
Boolean findpointobject(int x, int y, GObjectPtr gp)
{
    Point pt;

    if(gp == NULL)
        return(false);
    SetPt(&pt, x, y);
    return(PtInRect(pt, &(gp->bbox)));
}
```

When the mouse is clicked, _handle_user_event() calls doMouseDown() which, in turn, calls, findob-ject() to locate the selected GObject. doMouseDown() waits 1/6 second (using the Macintosh Toolbox function Delay()) and, if the mouse is still down, then calls sendclick() or senddrag() (see Section 11.1.2) to send a message to that object.

```
void doMouseDown(WindowPtr window, Point point, EventRecord *event)
{
    GObjectPtr objectptr;
    char *name;
    Point p;
    unsigned long dummy;
    WindowIndexPtr windexptr;

    windexptr = getWindowSlotPtr(findWindowSlot(window));
    if(windexptr == NULL){
        return;
    }

    objectptr = findobject(point.h, point.v, windexptr);

    if(objectptr != nil){
        name = objectptr->oSymbol;
        p.h = point.h - (objectptr->origin).h;  // send relative coordinates
        p.v = point.v - (objectptr->origin).v;
    }
    else {
        name = windexptr->wSymbol;
        p = point;
    }
    Delay(10, &dummy);  // wait 1/6 sec and check...
    if(StillDown())
        senddrag(name, p.h, p.v, modifier(event));
    else
        sendclick(name, p.h, p.v, modifier(event));
}
```

Window updating is defined in doupdate(), which is called when an update event arrives. Each window has an offscreen buffer (offscreen), as explained in Section 11.2. For window updating there are two cases:

[1] when the window is exposed by the user, doupdate() only needs to copy offscreen to the window;

[2] when a GObject sends an update request to the system, all GObjects must be redrawn.

To indicate these two cases, the variable `dirty` is used. When the `dirty` flag is set to 1, all objects must be redrawn, otherwise `doupdate()` only copies `offscreen` using `flushoffscreen()`.

```
void doupdate(WindowPtr window)
{
    WindowIndexPtr windexptr;
    int wnum;
    CGrafPtr curport;
    GDHandle curdev;
    PixMapHandle offpix;
    char s[256];

    if((windexptr = getWindowSlotPtr(wnum = findWindowSlot(window))) == NULL){
        sprintf(s,"doupdate:can't find idex solt of %ld", window);
        print_message(DEBUG_DEFAULT, s);// On Mac, we can't execute MLEvaluate-
String during update process.
        return;
    }

    GetGWorld(&curport, &curdev);
    offpix = GetGWorldPixMap(windexptr->offscreen);
    LockPixels(offpix);
    if(windexptr->dirty == 1){  // we must redraw all objects on offscreen.
        updateAllGObjects(windexptr);
        windexptr->dirty = 0;
    }
    flushoffscreen(window, offpix);
    UnlockPixels(offpix);
    SetGWorld(curport,curdev);
}
```

`updateAllGObjects()` erases `offscreen` first, and then redraws all `GObjects` onto `offscreen` using each object's `draw` function. The `draw` function of `PointObject` was described in Section 13.2.

```
void updateAllGObjects(WindowIndexPtr windexptr)
{
    int i, olen;
    GObjectPtr *gp;

    if(gProgramDebug == DEBUG_UPDATE){
        char s[256];
        sprintf(s,"updateAllGObjects:windexptr=%ld", windexptr);
        print_message(DEBUG_DEFAULT, s);// for Mac.
    }

    SetGWorld(windexptr->offscreen,0);
    EraseRect(&((windexptr->offscreen)->portRect));
    gp = windexptr->gobjects;
    olen = windexptr->ob_number;
    for(i=0; i < olen; ++i){
        if(gp[windexptr->ob_index[i]]->type != OTEXT)
            (*(gp[windexptr->ob_index[i]]->draw))(gp[windexptr->ob_index[i]]);
    }
}
```

13.4. LineObject

LineObject represents a line segment. The template is similar to that of **PointObject** having create, dispose, and move functions. However, now there are two types of movement: MoveLineObject[] moves a line object and SetLineObject[] changes its slope or length.

```
:Begin:
:Function:        newlineobject
:Pattern:         NewLineObject[$CurrentLink, {{x0_,y0_},{x1_,y1_}},
                      size_Integer, windex_Integer, oSymbol_Symbol]
:Arguments:       { x0,y0,x1,y1,size,windex,oSymbol }
:ArgumentTypes:   { Integer,Integer,Integer,Integer,Integer,Integer,Manual }
:ReturnType:      Integer
:End:

:Begin:
:Function:        disposelineobject
:Pattern:         DisposeLineObject[$CurrentLink, oindex_Integer, windex_Integer]
:Arguments:       { oindex, windex }
:ArgumentTypes:   { Integer, Integer }
:ReturnType:      Integer
:End:

:Begin:
:Function:        movelineobject
:Pattern:         MoveLineObject[$CurrentLink,{x0_,y0_},
                      oindex_Integer,windex_Integer]
:Arguments:       { x0,y0,oindex,windex }
:ArgumentTypes:   {Integer,Integer,Integer,Integer}
:ReturnType:      Integer
:End:

:Begin:
:Function:        setlineobject
:Pattern:         SetLineObject[$CurrentLink,{{x0_,y0_},{x1_,y1_}},
                      oindex_Integer,windex_Integer]
:Arguments:       { x0,y0,x1,y1,oindex,windex }
:ArgumentTypes:   {Integer,Integer,Integer,Integer,Integer,Integer}
:ReturnType:      Integer
:End:
```

The structure of LineObject is an extension of the GObject structure; size and data[4] fields have been added.

```
typedef struct LineObject {
    short type; // type of the object
    Rect bbox;  // bounding box
    Point origin;   // origin of the object
    Boolean visible;// visible flag
    char * oSymbol; // symbol of the object
    void (*draw)(); // function to draw the object
    Boolean (*find)();  // function to find a object
    int (*dump)();  // dump the object information
    int (*dispose)();   // function to dispose the object
```

```
    char *winfo;    // object's windowindexptr. Defined as char * for defining loop.
    int size;       // special data storage for LineObject.
    int data[4];    // special data storage for LineObject.
} LineObject;
```

The C functions, `newlineobject()`, `disposelineobject()`, and `movelineobject()`, are similar to the **PointObject** C functions. `drawlineobject()`, which is called from the update function, is defined as follows. It moves to the start position using `MoveTo()` and then draws a line to the end position using `MacLineTo()`.

```
void drawlineobject(GObjectPtr gp)
{
    PenState pen;

    GetPenState(&pen);
    PenSize(((LineObjectPtr)gp)->size,((LineObjectPtr)gp)->size);
    MoveTo(((LineObjectPtr)gp)->data[0],((LineObjectPtr)gp)->data[1]);
    MacLineTo(((LineObjectPtr)gp)->data[2],((LineObjectPtr)gp)->data[3]);
    SetPenState(&pen);
}
```

Next, we define the corresponding kernel line object, **LineObject**:

```
New[LineObject, super_Symbol, opts___Rule] :=
 Module[{self, oindex, mypos, mylink = super[link], myport = super[port]},
  self[dispose] := (DisposeLineObject[mylink, oindexmyport];
   Remove[self, oindex, mypos, mylink, myport]);
  self[index] := oindex;
  self[receiver, sym_Symbol] := SetObjectReceiver[mylink, sym, oindex, myport];
  self[getposition] := mypos;
  self[setposition, {{x0_, y0_}, {x1_, y1_}}] := (mypos = {{x0, y0}, {x1, y1}};
   SetLineObject[mylink, N[{{x0, y0}, {x1, y1}}], oindex, myport]);
  self[setposition, {x_, y_}] := (mypos = MoveRect[mypos, {x, y}];
   MoveLineObject[mylink, N[{x, y}], oindex, myport]);
  self[selector_, args___] :=
   findmethod[LineObject[self, selector, args], super[selector, args]];
  mypos = LineObjectPosition /. {opts} /. Options[LineObject];
  oindex =
   NewLineObject[mylink, N[mypos], (LineObjectSize /. {opts} /. Options[LineObject]),
    myport, ReceiverObject /. {opts} /. {ReceiverObject -> self}];
  If[! IntegerQ[oindex], Remove[self, oindex, mypos, mylink, myport];
   Return[$Failed]];
  self]
```

The **dispose** method calls the **DisposeLineObject[]** template function. The **setposition** method calls **SetLineObject[]** or **MoveLineObject[]** depending on its arguments.

```
LineObject[self_, drag, {x_, y_}] :=
 Module[{l = self[link]}, While[StillDown[l], self[move, GetMouse[l] - {x, y}]]]
```

The **drag** class method sends the message *obj*[move, {{x0,y0},{x1,y1}}] if the mouse position is near the end of the line; otherwise, it sends an *obj*[move, {x,y}] message to translate the line.

```
LineObject[self_, move, {x_, y_}] :=
 If[! SameMoveQ[{x, y}, self[getposition]], self[setposition, {x, y}]]
```

Now we demonstrate **LineObject**. First, we open a new window.

(Serializer) In[7]:= **win2 = New[Window, prog, WindowTitle → "LineObject test",**
                    WindowSize → {{0, 0}, {200, 100}} + 100];

Then we create a **LineObject** in that window.

(Serializer) In[8]:= **line1 = New[LineObject, win2];**

A **LineObject** appears on the window, as shown in Figure 13.9.

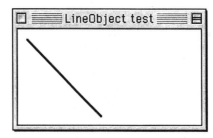

Figure 13.9. Creating a **LineObject** using **New[LineObject,** *window***]**.

Sending the following **move** message to the object translates it to a new location.

(Serializer) In[9]:= **line1[move, {80, 10}];**

If the user clicks on and drags the **LineObject**, it translates according to the mouse movement (see Figure 13.10).

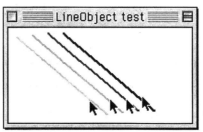

Drag LineObject with mouse

Figure 13.10. Dragging a **LineObject**.

Sending a **getposition** message returns the current location.

(Serializer) In[10]:= **line1[getposition]**

(Serializer) Out[10]= **{{94, 15}, {174, 95}}**

We close the open windows and then terminate the program.

```
(Serializer) In[11]:=  win1[dispose]; win2[dispose]; prog[dispose]
```

13.5. Defining Relationships between Objects

It is easy to define relationships between kernel objects. Here we use this capability to develop a simple *interactive geometry* application which displays, in real time, the perpendicular bisector of the line segment formed by two points using the graphics objects that we have defined. When the user moves either point, the position of the perpendicular bisector changes accordingly.

We invoke the program and create a new window.

```
(Serializer) In[12]:=  prog = New[MLProgram,
                "NetworkProgramming`DrawObjects`draw`", LinkMode → Launch];
```

```
(Serializer) In[13]:=  win3 = New[Window, prog, WindowTitle → "perpendicular bisector"];
```

Then two **PointObject**s, named **pt1** and **pt2**, are created.

```
(Serializer) In[14]:=  pt1 = New[PointObject, win3,
                PointObjectPosition → {60, 70}, PointObjectSize → 4];
```

```
(Serializer) In[15]:=  pt2 = New[PointObject, win3,
                PointObjectPosition → {130, 70}, PointObjectSize → 4];
```

A **LineObject**, **line3**, is created.

```
(Serializer) In[16]:=  line3 = New[LineObject, win3, LineObjectSize → 2,
                LineObjectPosition → {{55, 144}, {135, 144}}];
```

We now have two point objects and a line object in the window, as shown in Figure 13.11, and we can drag any object using the mouse.

Now we define a kernel function, **findline**[p_1, p_2, l], which returns the coordinates of the perpendicular bisector of the two points p_1 and p_2:

```
(Serializer) In[17]:=  findline[p1_, p2_, l_] :=
                Module[{p, x, y, sol, mid}, p = p1[getposition] - p2[getposition];
                sol = Solve[{{x, y}.p == 0.0, {x, y}.{x, y} == l}, {x, y}];
                mid = (p1[getposition] + p2[getposition]) / 2.0; {x, y} + mid /. sol]
```

$p = p_1 - p_2$ is the vector from p_1 to p_2. **Solve** finds *two* vectors, $\{x, y\}$, of (squared) length, l, which are perpendicular to p by solving the equation $\{x, y\}.p == 0$, subject to the constraint $\{x, y\}.\{x, y\} == l$. Adding $\{x, y\}$ to the midpoint of points p_1 and p_2 results in the perpendicular bisector coordinates.

After computing (one quarter of) the (squared) length of **line3**,

```
(Serializer) In[18]:=  len = Plus @@ (Subtract @@ line3[getposition])² / 4
```

```
(Serializer) Out[18]=  1600
```

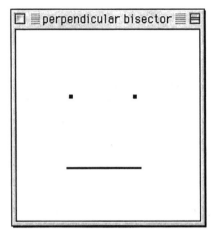

Figure 13.11. Two **PointObject**s and a **LineObject** in a new window.

findline[pt1,pt2,len] returns the endpoints of the perpendicular bisector for the current point positions, **pt1** and **pt2**.

(Serializer) In[19]:=   **findline[pt1, pt2, len]**

(Serializer) Out[19]=   {{95., 30.}, {95., 110.}}

Let's move the line to the perpendicular bisector position using a **move** message (see Figure 13.12).

(Serializer) In[20]:=   **line3[move, findline[pt1, pt2, len]];**

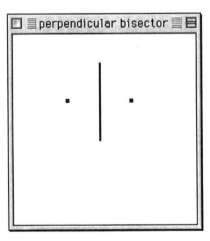

Figure 13.12. **LineObject** moves to the perpendicular bisector position.

It is straightforward to automate this process so that if either point is moved, the position of the perpendicular bisector is immediately updated. The required sequence of messages can be stated as follows: If either point receives a **move** message, it calculates the new perpendicular bisector position, moves the line to this location, and then sends **setposition** to itself. The required code is simply and directly implemented by redefining the **move** instance methods for both points.

```
(Serializer) In[21]:=  pt1[move, {x_, y_}] :=
                (line3[move, findline[pt1, pt2, len]]; pt1[setposition, {x, y}])
```

```
(Serializer) In[22]:=  pt2[move, {x_, y_}] :=
                (line3[move, findline[pt1, pt2, len]]; pt2[setposition, {x, y}])
```

With these definitions, if the user moves either **PointObject**, the perpendicular bisector moves accordingly (see Figure 13.13). From the method viewpoint, **move** is an external method and **setposition** is an internal method.

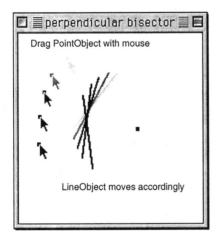

Figure 13.13. Moving either **PointObject** causes the perpendicular bisector to move accordingly.

Our code for computing the perpendicular bisector endpoints is somewhat slow because **Solve** is called each time.

```
(Serializer) In[23]:=  Timing[Table[findline[pt1, pt2, len], {100}];] // First
```

```
(Serializer) Out[23]=  0.966667 Second
```

We can speed up **findline[]** by solving the equations symbolically,

```
(Serializer) In[24]:=  {x, y} /. Solve[{{x, y}.{a, b} == 0, {x, y}.{x, y} == 1}, {x, y}]
```

$$(Serializer)\ Out[24]=\ \left\{\left\{-\frac{b\sqrt{1}}{\sqrt{a^2+b^2}},\ \frac{a\sqrt{1}}{\sqrt{a^2+b^2}}\right\},\ \left\{\frac{b\sqrt{1}}{\sqrt{a^2+b^2}},\ -\frac{a\sqrt{1}}{\sqrt{a^2+b^2}}\right\}\right\}$$

and modifying the code for **findline[]** accordingly.

(Serializer) In[25]:= **findline[p1_, p2_, l_] :=**

$$\text{Module}\Big[\{a, b, mid\}, \{a, b\} = p1[\text{getposition}] - p2[\text{getposition}];$$

$$mid = \frac{p1[\text{getposition}] + p2[\text{getposition}]}{2.0};$$

$$\frac{\sqrt{l} \; \{\{b, -a\}, \{-b, a\}\}}{\sqrt{a^2 + b^2}} + \{mid, mid\}\Big]$$

This gives the same result as before but is quite a bit faster, thus decreasing the mouse reaction time.

(Serializer) In[26]:= **Timing[Table[findline[pt1, pt2, len], {100}];] // First**

(Serializer) Out[26]= 0.5 Second

More complicated geometrical relationships are easily implemented by defining appropriate relationships between objects. Real-time implementation of such relationships is impossible with the current notebook front end or in existing interactive drawing applications.

13.6. CurveObject

Now we will add a curve object to our GraphicsObject elements. Our **CurveObject** consists of sequences of connected lines and can be used to represent various shapes, including circles, ellipses, polygons, and so on. Here is the definition of the kernel curve object, **CurveObject**:

```
New[CurveObject, super_Symbol, points_, opts___Rule] :=
 Module[{self, oindex, mypos, mylink = super[link], myport = super[port]},
  self[dispose] := (DisposeCurveObject[mylink, oindex, myport];
   Remove[self, oindex, mypos, mylink, myport]);
  self[index] := oindex;
  self[receiver, sym_Symbol] := SetObjectReceiver[mylink, sym, oindex, myport];
  self[getposition] := mypos;
  self[setposition, {x_, y_}] := (mypos = {x, y};
   MoveCurveObject[mylink, N[{x, y}], oindex, myport]);
  self[setdata, x_] :=
   SetCurveObject[mylink, N[mypos], N[Flatten[x]], oindex, myport];
  self[setdata, {x0_, y0_}, x_] := (mypos = {x0, y0};
   SetCurveObject[mylink, N[mypos], N[Flatten[x]], oindex, myport]);
  self[selector_, args___] :=
   findmethod[CurveObject[self, selector, args], super[selector, args]];
  mypos = CurveObjectOrigin /. {opts} /. Options[CurveObject];
  oindex = NewCurveObject[mylink, N[Flatten[points]],
    mypos, CurveObjectSize /. {opts} /. Options[CurveObject],
    myport, ReceiverObject /. {opts} /. {ReceiverObject -> self}];
  If[! IntegerQ[oindex], Remove[self, oindex, mypos, mylink, myport];
   Return[$Failed]];
  self]
```

The **setdata** class method redraws the **CurveObject** for new data.

The structure of CurveObject is an extension of the GObject structure; size, data, and len fields have been added.

```
typedef struct CurveObject {
    short type; // type of the object
    Rect bbox;  // bounding box
    Point origin;   // origin of the object
    Boolean visible;// visible flag
    char * oSymbol; // symbol of the object
    void (*draw)(); // function to draw the object
    Boolean (*find)();  // function to find a object
    int (*dump)();  // dump the object information
    int (*dispose)();   // function to dispose the object
    char *winfo;    // object's WindowIndexPtr. it is defined as char * for loop
defining.
    int size;       // special data storage for CurveObject.
    int *data;  // integer pointer to the coordinates data.
    long len;   // and its length.
} CurveObject;
```

CurveObject draws its data points using MoveTo() and MacLineTo().

```
void drawcurveobject(GObjectPtr gp)
{
    PenState pen;
    int i;

    GetPenState(&pen);
    PenSize(((CurveObjectPtr)gp)->size, ((CurveObjectPtr)gp)->size);
    MoveTo(((CurveObjectPtr)gp)->data[0], ((CurveObjectPtr)gp)->data[1]);
    for(i=2;i < ((CurveObjectPtr)gp)->len; i += 2){
        MacLineTo(((CurveObjectPtr)gp)->data[i], ((CurveObjectPtr)gp)->data[i+1]);
    }
    SetPenState(&pen);
}
```

13.7. Interactive Curve Fitting

Now we will implement an *interactive curve fitting* application using **CurveObject**. When the user moves data points, its fitting curve will change shape accordingly. First, we open a new window of size 400×400.

(Serializer) In[27]:= **win4 = New[Window, prog, WindowTitle → "Curve Fitting",
                WindowSize → {{0, 0}, {400, 400}} + 100];**

data is a list of 50 **PointObject**s that appear at random locations in the window, as shown in Figure 13.14.

(Serializer) In[28]:= **data = Table[New[PointObject, win4,
                PointObjectPosition → {Random[Integer, {50, 350}],
                    Random[Integer, {50, 350}]}, PointObjectSize → 4], {50}];**

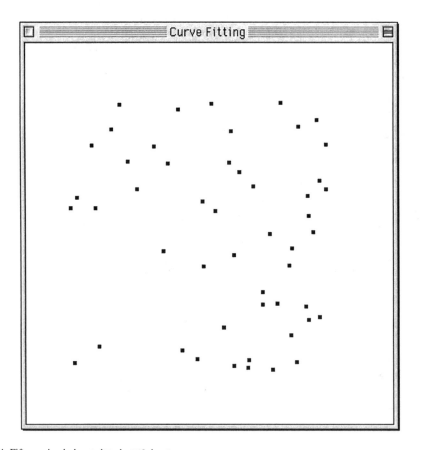

Figure 13.14. Fifty randomly located **PointObject**s.

fitpoints[*data*] finds the third-order polynomial best-fit curve using **Fit** and returns a list of 100 points, which lie on this curve.

```
(Serializer) In[29]:=  fitpoints[pts_] :=
                         Module[{f},
                           f = Fit[Map[#[getposition] &, pts], {1, x, x², x³}, x];
                             Table[{x, f} /. x → i, {i, 1, 400, 4}]]
```

We now display the best-fit polynomial curve as a **CurveObject** using points returned from **fitpoints**[data].

```
(Serializer) In[30]:=  fitcurve = New[CurveObject, win4, fitpoints[data], CurveObjectSize → 1]

(Serializer) Out[30]=  self$467
```

The best-fit curve appears in the window (see Figure 13.15).

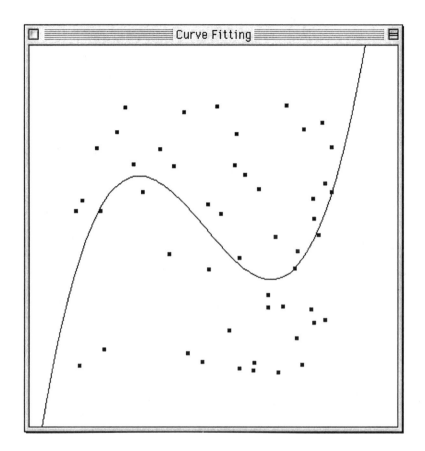

Figure 13.15. Third-order polynomial best-fit curve of fifty random points.

After defining the relationship between the data points, **data**, and curve (as we did above when displaying the perpendicular bisector),

```
(Serializer) In[31]:=  Map[(#[move, {x_, y_}] := (fitcurve[setdata, fitpoints[data]];
                          #[setposition, {x, y}])) &, data];
```

then moving *any* **PointObject** causes the best-fit to be recalculated and the new **CurveObject** to be displayed. **Map** allows us to define this relationship for all **PointObject**s at once. This simple implementation of interactive curve fitting allows the user to examine the influence of the location of a data point on the best-fit curve *dynamically*.

We conclude this section by closing the program.

```
(Serializer) In[32]:=  prog[dispose];
```

13.8. Summary

This chapter introduces three GraphicsObjects: **PointObject**, **LineObject**, and **CurveObject**. Defining relationships between such objects is straightforward, and this makes it possible to automate the interaction between objects. Integration of symbolic manipulation with interactive real-time graphics allows for a wide range of new applications.

13.9. Object Summary

In the following, gray font is used to indicate optional arguments, for example, *opts*.

13.9.1 PointObject

New[PointObject, *win*, *fend*, *opts***]**

This method creates a new PointObject instance in the window object, *win*, which is the super object of this object. *fend* is the front end object which receives the event for this object. When *fend* is Null this PointObject receives the event. The PointObjectSize option sets the point's size, and the PointObjectPosition option sets its location. The default values are PointObjectSize→2 and PointObject-Position→{{10,10},{90,90}}.

obj[**dispose**]

This function sends a **dispose** message to program object, *obj*.

obj[**index**]

This message returns the index number of *obj*.

obj[**getposition**]

This message returns the position of *obj*.

obj[**setposition, {x,y}**]

This message sets the position of *obj* to {*x*, *y*}.

obj[**move, {x,y}**]

This message moves *obj* to {*x*, *y*}. The move method uses setposition internally.

obj [drag, {*x*,*y*}]

This message is sent when the user drags *obj* with the mouse.

13.9.2 LineObject

New[LineObject, *win*, *fend*, *opts*]

This method creates a new LineObject in the window object *win*. *fend* is the front end object which receives the event for this object. When *fend* is Null this PointObject receives the event. The LineObjectSize option sets the line's thickness, and LineObjectPosition sets its location and length. The default values are LineObject-Size→2 and LineObjectPosition→{{10,10},{90,90}}.

obj [dispose]

This function sends a **dispose** message to program object, *obj*.

obj [index]

This message returns the index number of *obj*.

obj [getposition]

This message returns the position of *obj*.

obj [setposition, {*x*,*y*}]

This message translates *obj* so that its starting point becomes {*x*, *y*}.

obj [setposition, {{*x*$_0$,*y*$_0$}, {*x*$_1$,*y*$_1$}}]

This message translates *obj* to {{x_0, y_0}, {x_1, y_1}}.

obj [move, {*x*,*y*}]

This message calls *obj*[setposition,{*x*,*y*}] internally.

obj [move, {{*x*$_0$,*y*$_0$}, {*x*$_1$,*y*$_1$}}]

This message calls *obj*[setposition, {{x_0,y_0},{x_1, y_1}}] internally.

obj[**drag**, {*x*,*y*}]

This message is called when the user drags *obj* with the mouse.

13.9.3 CurveObject

New[CurveObject, *win*, *points*, *size*, *fend*, *opts*]

This method creates a CurveObject instance in window, *win*. *points* is a list of curve points, $\{\{x_0,y_0\},\{x_1,y_1\},...\{x_n,y_n\}\}$. *size* is the line thickness. *fend* is the front end object that receives the event. When *fend* is Null this CurveObject receives the event.

obj[**dispose**]

This function sends a **dispose** message to program object, *obj*.

obj[index]

This message returns the index number of *obj*.

obj[**setposition**, {*x*,*y*}]

This message translates *obj* so that its starting point becomes {*x*, *y*}.

obj[**getposition**]

This message returns the position of *obj*.

obj[**drag**, {*x*,*y*}]

This message is called when the user drags *obj* with the mouse.

obj[**setdata**, {{*x*₀,*y*₀}, {*x*₁,*y*₁}, ... {*x*ₙ,*y*ₙ}}]

This message updates the data of *obj* to $\{\{x_0,y_0\},\{x_1,y_1\},...,\{x_n,y_n\}\}$ and redraws it.

Chapter 14 — Interactive Geometry

In this chapter, we expand the interactive graphics described in Chapter 13 to a full-scale *Interactive Geometry* package. This package enables the user to construct geometrical systems and manipulate geometrical objects by mouse interactively, which is similar to the commercial packages such as Cabri or SketchPad. The main differences are:

[1] *Interactive Geometry* is written in *Mathematica*, which is more flexible and extensible;

[2] *Interactive Geometry* forces the user to define and manipulate geometry from two viewpoints — interaction and formal expression — whereas commercial software only supports the interactive aspect.

Software for interactive geometry should address both viewpoints equally. Also, we describe how our OOPS is used to implement the *Interactive Geometry* package.

14.1. Bidirectional Relation

In Chapter 13 we saw how the relation between objects can be defined to work interactively. For example, to create an interaction between a point and a line, we define the **move** method of the **point** like this; when the **point** receives a **move** message, it sends the **move** message to the **line**, then it sends **setposition** to itself (see Section 13.5).

```
point[move, {x_, y_}] := (line[move, {x, y}]; point[setposition, {x, y}])
```

This is a simple one-directional relation from **point** to **line**, but the relationship we want to implement is bidirectional. Consider two points (**point1**, **point2**) with a line (**line**) between them. When either point moves, we want the line to move; or when the line moves, we want both points to move with it (see Figure 14.1).

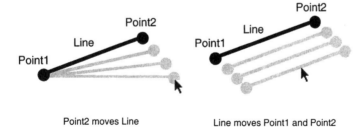

Point2 moves Line   Line moves Point1 and Point2

Figure 14.1. Two types of object movement for a line between two points.

If we try to implement this relationship using the previous method, it would look like this:

```
point1[move, {x_, y_}] := (line[move, {x, y}]; point1[setposition, {x, y}]);
point2[move, {x_, y_}] := (line[move, {x, y}]; point2[setposition, {x, y}]);
line[move, {x_, y_}] :=
 (point1[move, {x, y}]; point2[move, {x, y}]; line[setposition, {x, y}])
```

However, this definition can lead to an infinite loop, as shown in Figure 14.2.

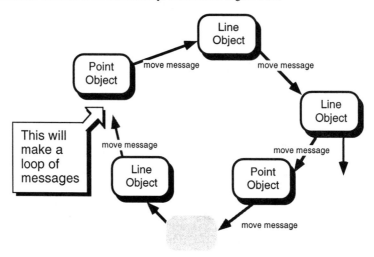

Figure 14.2. A chain of messages has a possibility of making a loop.

It is clear that the simple one-directional relation is not sufficient. We must define bidirectional relations without looping possibilities.

14.2. Master and Slave

The object class hierarchy we already have is like this: Graphical objects— **PointObject**, **LineObject**, and **CurveObject**—are inherited from the **Window** class, which, in turn, is inherited from the **MLProgram** class. Geometrical objects will be derived from the graphical objects class. The object hierarchy is shown in Figure 14.3.

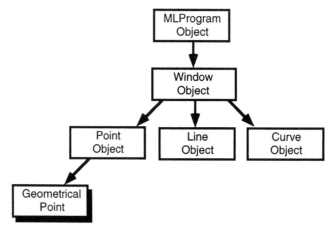

Figure 14.3. Hierarchy of the objects we build in this chapter.

In addition to the hierarchy, we create **master** and **slave** attributes for the objects according to the creation order. For example, suppose there are two points, and then a line is created between them. We give the line the two points as its **master**, and it does not have a **slave**. Neither point has a **master**, but we give each point the line as its **slave**. These attributes are indicated in Figure 14.4.

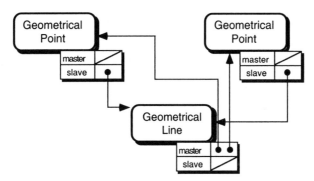

Figure 14.4. Master and slave attributes for each object.

In any geometrical system, all objects have **master** or **slave** attributes from the creation history. The *root objects* have no **master** attribute. All other objects are created from the root objects or other objects. For example, Figure 14.5 shows a triangle, its midpoints, and median lines between midpoints and vertices.

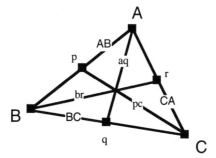

Figure 14.5. A geometrical system — triangle, midpoints, and medians.

Its **master** and **slave** relationships are displayed in Figure 14.6.

The vertices of the triangle — represented by three point objects **A**, **B**, and **C** — are the root objects of this system, and do not have any **master**. The endpoints of each line are the **master** objects of the lines. Each midpoint is a **slave** object of the sides, and so on. It is straightforward to apply this approach to *any* geometrical system to determine its **master** and **slave** relationships.

In our *Interactive Geometry* package, the **master** and **slave** relationships are defined using the **Geometrical-Relation** class, and each geometrical object is defined through multiple inheritance from the **GeometricalRelation** and graphical object classes (see Figure 14.7).

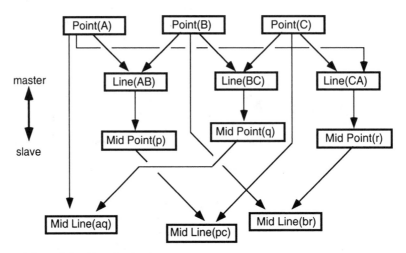

Figure 14.6. Master and slave relationships of a triangle.

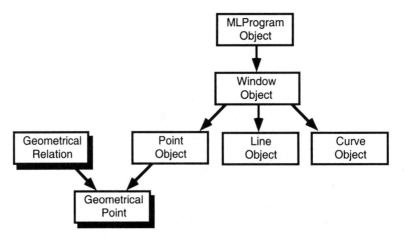

Figure 14.7. The **GeometricalPoint** class inherits from the **PointObject** and **GeometricalRelation** classes.

Next is the definition of the **GeometricalRelation** class. We assign the **master** object using **obj[master,{o$_1$,o$_2$}]**, and get the **master** object using **obj[master]**. **slave** is used in the same manner. First, we invoke the *MathLink* program draw.exe.

```
(Serializer) In[1]:=  prog = New[MLProgram,
                "NetworkProgramming`DrawObjects`draw`", LinkMode → Launch];
```

This command loads the package and installs the draw.exe executable, as described in Section 13.2. Here are the usage messages:

(Serializer) In[2]:=

```
debug::usage = "debug=True enables debugging. False disable it.";
request::usage = "obj[request,{x,y}] request the movement {x,y}.";
imove::usage = "obj[imove,{x,y}] makes obj move immediately." ;
mark::usage = "self[mark,{obj..}] includes obj in checked list.";
```

And here is the definition of the **GeometricalRelation** class:

(Serializer) In[3]:=

```
New[GeometricalRelation] :=
 Module[{self, mymaster = {}, myslave = {}, mymark = {}},
  self[dispose] := Remove[self, mymaster, myslave, mymark];
  self[master, x_] := mymaster = Flatten[Append[mymaster, x]];
  self[master] := mymaster;
  self[slave, x_] := myslave = Flatten[Append[myslave, x]];
  self[slave] := myslave;
  self[deleteslave, x_] := myslave = DeleteCases[myslave, x];
  self[mark] := mymark;
  self[mark, x_] := mymark = Flatten[Append[mymark, x]];
  self[deletemark, x_] := mymark = DeleteCases[mymark, x];
  self[selector_, args___] := $MethodNotFound;
  self]
```

14.3. Moving Objects

If an object receives a **move** message, its movement will affect both its **master** and **slave** objects. Also, its movement may be restricted by its **master** objects. To manage this, we require that an object only responds to a **move** message from its **master**. When an object receives a **move** message, it asks its **master** to **move**, and then the **master** sends a **move** message to the object, so that there is no inconsistency between the movement of **master** and object. Then the object sends a **move** message to its **slave** objects, and these **slave** objects move in the same manner.

Here is the movement procedure:

[1] If an object receives a **move** message, it sends a **request** message to its **master** objects;

[2] When the **master** receives a **request** message, it sends a **request** message to its **master** objects (see Figure 14.8). This recursive **request** process terminates when the root objects (objects without a **master**) are reached.

Once all requests reach root objects:

[3] Each root object moves according to its **request** message, and sends an **imove** message to its **slave** objects (see Figure 14.9);

[4] Each **slave** moves according to its **imove** message, and sends an **imove** message to its **slave** objects. This recursive **imove** process terminates when the *end objects* (object without a **slave**) are reached;

[5] If an object has multiple **master** objects, it can receive multiple **imove** message from its masters. In this case, the object moves according to the *last* **imove** message received. This is implemented using the **mark** message.

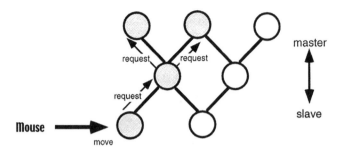

Figure 14.8. A **request** message is sent recursively.

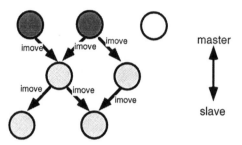

Figure 14.9. An **imove** message is sent recursively.

To summarize, a **move** message for an object generates recursive **request** messages, which, in turn, generate recursive **imove** messages, to resolve the movement. In this way, all movement is made without looping or inconsistency.

14.4. GeometricalPoint Class

14.4.1 Class Definition

We now construct a geometrical object based on the design described in Sections 14.2 and 14.3. The **Geometrical-Point** class inherits from the **PointObject** and **GeometricalRelation** classes.

```
(Serializer) In[4]:=   New[GeometricalPoint, win_Symbol, opts___Rule] :=
                       Module[{self, mypobj, myrel},
                         self[dispose] := (Map[#[deleteslave, self] &, myrel[master]];
                           If[myrel[slave] =!= {}, Map[#[dispose] &, myrel[slave]]];
                           Map[#[dispose] &, {mypobj, myrel}];
                           Remove[self, mypobj, myrel]);
                         self[selector_, args___] :=
                           findmethod[GeometricalPoint[self, selector, args],
                             findsuper[{mypobj, myrel}, selector, args]];
```

```
mypobj = New[PointObject, win, opts, ReceiverObject -> self];
myrel = New[GeometricalRelation] ;
self]
```

When the object receives a **dispose** message, it must ask the **master** object to remove itself. This is done by the following expression:

```
Map[#[deleteslave, self] &, myrel[master]]
```

A **GeometricalPoint** object creates a **PointObject** internally, and sets the **PointObject**'s receiver to **self** using the **ReceiverObject→self** option. In this way, event expressions, such as **click** or **drag** from the *Math-Link* program, are sent to this object.

We now define the **drag** method of the object. It is defined in the same way as the **drag** method of Section 13.2.

(Serializer) In[5]:=
```
GeometricalPoint[self_, drag, {x_, y_}] :=
  Module[{l = self[link], pp}, While[StillDown[l],
    If[pp != (pp = GetMouse[l]), self[move, pp - {x, y}]]]]
```

The **move** method checks the argument to see if it is different from its current location. If it is different, it sends a **request** message to itself.

(Serializer) In[6]:=
```
GeometricalPoint[self_, move, {x_, y_}] :=
  Module[{ex, win = self[getwindow]},
    If[{x, y} != self[getposition],
    ex = self[request, {x, y}];
    If[debug, Print[self, "(Point) move:", ex]];
    ReleaseHold[ex]]]
```

The **request** message is recursively sent to **master** objects. Eventually, the **request** message returns the **imove** message of the root object, wrapped in **Hold**. In the **move** method, these held expressions are assigned to **ex** (see Figure 14.10), and released using **ReleaseHold**, which invokes a chain of **imove** messages.

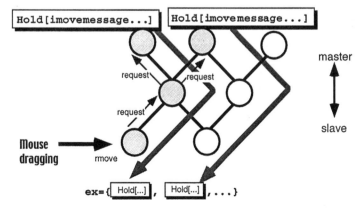

Figure 14.10. A **request** message returns a list of **imove** messages, wrapped in **Hold**.

The `GeometricalPoint` object is a root object, so the **request** method returns the expression
`Hold[self[imove,{x,y},self]]`, which makes itself move to the requested location.

```
(Serializer) In[7]:=    GeometricalPoint[self_, request, {x_, y_}] :=
                          Module[{m = self[master]},
                            If[debug, Print[self, "(Point) request:", {x, y}, m]];
                            If[m === {},
                             Hold[self[imove, {x, y}, self]],
                             Print[self, "(Point) should not have any master."]]]
```

The **imove** method performs the movement of the object. If the location is different from current location, it moves
itself using **self[setposition,{x,y}]**. After the move, if it has a **slave** object, it sends an **imove** message to
the **slave** object using `Map[#[imove,{x,y},self]&,s]`.

```
(Serializer) In[8]:=    GeometricalPoint[self_, imove, {x_, y_}, caller_] :=
                          Module[{s = self[slave]},
                            If[{x, y} ≠ self[getposition],
                             If[self[deletemark, caller] === {},
                              self[setposition, {x, y}];
                              If[debug, Print[self, "(Point) imove:", {x, y}, caller, s]];
                              If[s =!= {},
                               Map[#[imove, {x, y}, self] &, s], 0],
                              If[debug, Print[self, "(Point) imove:nomove:", self[mark]]]; -1],
                             If[debug, Print[self, "(Point) imove:ignore:", {x, y}]]; -2]]
```

NewPoint is a simple wrapper function for `New[GeometricalPoint, ...]`.

```
(Serializer) In[9]:=    NewPoint[w_, loc_, size_] := New[GeometricalPoint,
                          w, PointObjectPosition → loc, PointObjectSize → size]
```

14.4.2 GeometricalPoint Test

First, open a window:

```
(Serializer) In[10]:=   win0 = New[Window, prog, WindowTitle → "Point test"];
```

Create a `GeometricalPoint` object on the window (see Figure 14.11):

```
(Serializer) In[11]:=   z1 = NewPoint[win0, {180, 50}, 10]
```

```
(Serializer) Out[11]=   self$73
```

To see debug messages, we set **debug** to **True**.

```
(Serializer) In[12]:=   debug = True;
```

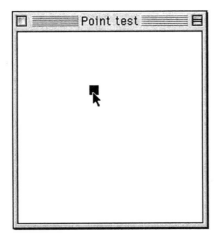

Figure 14.11. A **GeometricalPoint** appears on the window.

Here are the debug messages generated by a **move** message:

(Serializer) In[13]:= **z1[move, {20, 20}]**

self$73(Point)request:{20, 20}{}

self$73(Point)move:Hold[self$73[imove, {20, 20}, self$73]]

self$73(Point)imove:{20, 20}self$73{}

(Serializer) Out[13]=   0

We see that the **move** message sends a **request** message to itself, then receives an **imove** message (wrapped in **Hold**), and the **imove** messages moves the object. If you move the object by mouse, similar output appears on the **Messages** window, as shown in Figure 14.12.

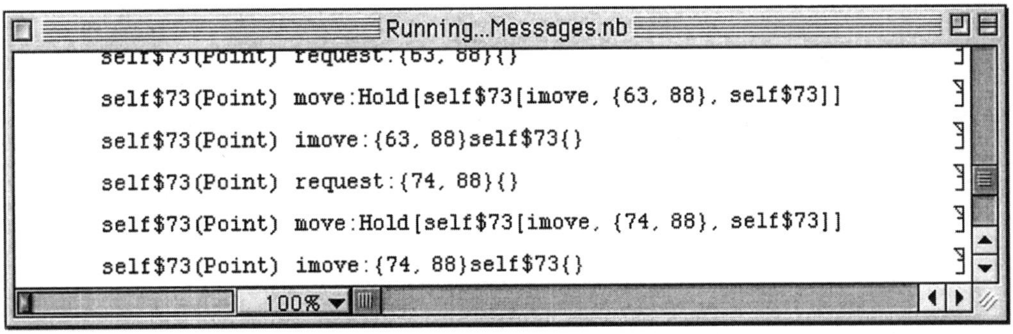

```
self$73(Point) request:{63, 88}{}
self$73(Point) move:Hold[self$73[imove, {63, 88}, self$73]]
self$73(Point) imove:{63, 88}self$73{}
self$73(Point) request:{74, 88}{}
self$73(Point) move:Hold[self$73[imove, {74, 88}, self$73]]
self$73(Point) imove:{74, 88}self$73{}
```
Running...Messages.nb   100%

Figure 14.12. Debug messages printed out when a **GeometricalPoint** object is moved by mouse.

We stop debugging and close the window.

(Serializer) In[14]:= **debug = False;**

(Serializer) In[15]:= **win0[dispose]**

14.5. GeometricalLine Class

14.5.1 Class Definition

The **GeometricalLine** class defines a line object between two endpoints. It has two **GeometricalPoint** objects as its **master** objects, as shown in Figure 14.13.

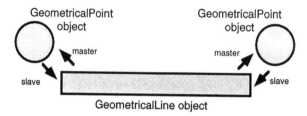

Figure 14.13. Schematic relationship between a line and its endpoints.

New[GeometricalLine,{p1,p2}...] creates a line object from two points, **{p1,p2}**. This line object creates a **LineObject** internally, and sets its receiver to itself using **ReceiverObject→self**. The line object sets its **master** to **p1** and **p2**, and uses **Map** to ask the point objects, **p1** and **p2**, to set the line object as a **slave** object.

(Serializer) In[16]:=
```
New[GeometricalLine, {p1_, p2_}, opts___Rule] :=
  Module[{self, myline, myrel}, self[dispose] :=
    (Map[#[deleteslave, self] &, myrel[master]];
     Map[#[dispose] &, myrel[slave]];
     Map[#[dispose] &, {myline, myrel}]; Remove[self, myline, myrel]);
    self[selector_, args___] :=
      findmethod[GeometricalLine[self, selector, args],
       findsuper[{myline, myrel}, selector, args]];
    myline = New[LineObject, p1[getwindow], opts, ReceiverObject → self,
      LineObjectPosition -> {p1[getposition], p2[getposition]}];
    myrel = New[GeometricalRelation];
    self[master, {p1, p2}];
    Map[#[slave, self] &, {p1, p2}]; self]
```

The **drag** method is the same as for **GeometricalPoint** (see Section 14.4.1).

(Serializer) In[17]:=
```
GeometricalLine[self_, drag, {x_, y_}] :=
  Module[{l = self[link], pp}, While[StillDown[l],
    If[pp != (pp = GetMouse[l]), self[move, pp - {x, y}]]]]
```

The **move** method is also the same as for **GeometricalPoint** (see Section 14.4.1). It sends a **request** message to its masters—the two point objects—when the argument, **{x,y}**, is different from its current location. Then it evaluates the expression returned by the **request** message using **ReleaseHold**.

```
(Serializer) In[18]:=   GeometricalLine[self_, move, {x_, y_}] :=
                        Module[{ex, win = self[getwindow]},
                         If[{x, y} ≠ self[getposition][[1]], ex = self[request, {x, y}];
                          If[debug, Print[self, "(Line) move:", ex]];
                          ReleaseHold[ex]]]
```

There are two ways to move a line object, and each motion is defined in the **request** and **imove** methods:

[1] When the line is dragged, both the line object and its endpoints will translate. In this case, the line object takes the action. This is implemented in the **request** message by asking the **master** objects to translate. When sending a **request** message to the point objects, the two **master** objects are listed in the marking list using a **mark** message to indicate that both objects will send an **imove** message. The last message in the marking list indicates which **imove** message should be performed. Then, the location of each endpoint is calculated from the **{x,y}** coordinates, and the **master** objects will send an **imove** message to the line.

```
(Serializer) In[19]:=   GeometricalLine[self_, request, {x_, y_}] :=
                        Module[{m = self[master], pos = self[getposition]},
                         If[debug, Print[self, "(Line) request:", {x, y}, m]];
                         self[mark, m];
                         {m[[1]][request, {x, y}],
                          m[[2]][request, {x, y} + pos[[2]] - pos[[1]]]}
                         ]
```

[2] When an endpoint is dragged, the point will move, and the line moves according to the position of the endpoint. In this case the point object—one of the **master** objects—takes the action. This is implemented in the **imove** method. If the position is different from the current location, and no object remains in its marking list, it sends a **setposition** message to itself to perform the movement. The movement is calculated from the current **master** object locations. Then, **imove** messages are sent to each **slave** object using **Map**.

```
(Serializer) In[20]:=   GeometricalLine[self_, imove, {x_, y_}, caller_] :=
                        Module[{s = self[slave]},
                         If[{x, y} != self[getposition][[1]],
                          If[self[deletemark, caller] === {},
                           self[setposition, Map[#[getposition] &, self[master]]];
                           If[debug, Print[self, "(Line) imove:", {x, y}, s]];
                           If[s =!= {},
                            Map[#[imove, self[getposition][[1]], self] &, s], 0],
                           If[debug, Print[self, "(Line) nomove:", self[mark]]]; -1],
                          If[debug, Print[self, "(Line) ignore:", {x, y}]]; -2]]
```

NewLine is a simple wrapper function for **New[GeometricalLine, ...]**.

```
(Serializer) In[21]:=   NewLine[w_, loc_, size_] :=
                          New[GeometricalLine, {NewPoint[w, loc[[1]], 8],
                            NewPoint[w, loc[[2]], 8]}, LineObjectSize → size]
```

```
(Serializer) In[22]:=   NewLine[{p1_Symbol, p2_Symbol}, size_] :=
                          New[GeometricalLine, {p1, p2}, LineObjectSize → size]
```

14.5.2 GeometricalLine Test

First, open a window:

```
(Serializer) In[23]:=   win0 = New[Window, prog, WindowTitle → "Line test"];
```

Create two **GeometricalPoint** objects, **z1** and **z2**, on the window.

```
(Serializer) In[24]:=   z1 = NewPoint[win0, {180, 50}, 10]
```

```
(Serializer) Out[24]=   self$82
```

```
(Serializer) In[25]:=   z2 = NewPoint[win0, {40, 150}, 10]
```

```
(Serializer) Out[25]=   self$85
```

Create a **GeometricalLine** object, **zz**, between these two points.

```
(Serializer) In[26]:=   zz = NewLine[{z1, z2}, 2]
```

```
(Serializer) Out[26]=   self$88
```

To see debug messages, we set **debug** to **True**.

```
(Serializer) In[27]:=   debug = True;
```

We move an endpoint:

```
(Serializer) In[28]:=   z1[move, {40, 20}]

                        self$82(Point)request:{40, 20}{}

                        self$82(Point)move:Hold[self$82[imove, {40, 20}, self$82]]

                        self$82(Point)imove:{40, 20}self$82{self$88}

                        self$88(Line)imove:{40, 20}{}
```

```
(Serializer) Out[28]=   {0}
```

The debug messages show that **move** calls **request**, returns an **imove** message, and creates two **imove** messages, one for the point and one for the line.

Now we move an endpoint:

(Serializer) In[29]:= **zz[move, {100, 80}]**

self$88(Line)request:{100, 80}{self$82, self$85}

self$82(Point)request:{100, 80}{}

self$85(Point)request:{100, 210}{}

self$88(Line)move:{Hold[self$82[imove, {100, 80}, self$82]],
   Hold[self$85[imove, {100, 210}, self$85]]}

self$82(Point)imove:{100, 80}self$82{self$88}

self$88(Line)nomove:{self$85}

self$85(Point)imove:{100, 210}self$85{self$88}

self$88(Line)imove:{100, 210}{}

(Serializer) Out[29]= {{-1}, {0}}

The **move** message to the line sends a **request** message to both endpoints. Then, **imove** messages for both points, wrapped in **Hold**, are returned. These **imove** messages move the endpoints and the line. The **imove** message from the line object to point self$82 is not executed because there is another **imove** message from self$85 remaining. This is indicated in the debug output by nomove.

We stop debugging and close the window.

(Serializer) In[30]:= **debug = False;**

(Serializer) In[31]:= **win0[dispose]**

14.6. MidpointOnLine Class

The **MidpointOnLine** class is derived from the **GeometricalPoint** class by modifying the **imove** and **request** methods. Its **master** is the line object on which the midpoint is located, as indicated in Figure 14.14. When the midpoint is moved, it sends a **request** message to its **master** to move. When the line is moved, it sends an **imove** message to the midpoint object to move it to the new position.

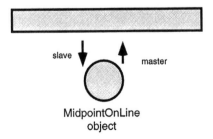

Figure 14.14. Relation between a line object and its midpoint.

The definition of the **MidpointOnLine** class follows. It uses **With** to override the **imove** and **request** methods of **GeometricalPoint**.

```
(Serializer) In[32]:=   New[MidpointOnLine, line_, opts___] :=
                         With[{self = New[GeometricalPoint, line[getwindow],
                             PointObjectPosition → Apply[Plus, line[getposition]] / 2, opts]},
                           self[imove, {x_, y_}, caller_] :=
                            Module[{s = self[slave]},
                             If[{x, y} ≠ self[getposition],
                              If[self[deletemark, caller] === {},
                               self[setposition, Apply[Plus, line[getposition]] / 2];
                               If[debug,
                                Print[self, "(MidPoint) imove:", self[getposition], s]];
                               If[s =!= {},
                                Map[#[imove, self[getposition], self] &, s], 0],
                                If[debug, Print[self, "(MidPoint) nomove:", self[mark]]]; -1],
                              If[debug, Print[self, "(MidPoint) ignore:", {x, y}]]; -2]];
                           self[request, {x_, y_}] :=
                            Module[{pos = line[getposition]},
                             If[debug, Print[self, "(MidPoint) request:", {x, y}, line]];
                             self[mark, line];
                             line[request, {x, y} + (pos[[1]] - pos[[2]]) / 2]];
                           self[master, line];
                           line[slave, self];
                           self]
```

NewMidpointOnLine is a simple wrapper function for **New[MidpointOnLine, ...]**.

```
(Serializer) In[33]:=   NewMidpointOnLine[line_, size_] :=
                         New[MidpointOnLine, line, PointObjectSize → size]
```

14.7. Triangle and Median

Figure 14.15 shows a triangle and its median lines. Any object in the window can be moved. For example, if you drag a vertex, the triangle changes the shape, or if you drag a median, all related lines are moved.

First, open a window:

```
(Serializer) In[34]:=   win2 = New[Window, prog, WindowTitle → "Triangle and Median"];
```

Next, create three points, **pA**, **pB**, and **pC**:

```
(Serializer) In[35]:=   pA = NewPoint[win2, {10, 10}, 8];
                         pB = NewPoint[win2, {180, 50}, 8];
                         pC = NewPoint[win2, {50, 180}, 8];
```

Then, create three lines, **AB**, **BC**, and **CA**:

```
(Serializer) In[38]:=   AB = NewLine[{pA, pB}, 2];
                         BC = NewLine[{pB, pC}, 2];
                         CA = NewLine[{pC, pA}, 2];
```

Then, create three midpoints, **p**, **q**, and **r**:

```
(Serializer) In[41]:=   p = NewMidpointOnLine[AB, 8];
                        q = NewMidpointOnLine[BC, 8];
                        r = NewMidpointOnLine[CA, 8];
```

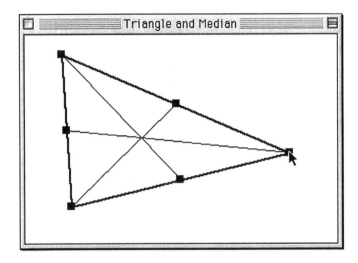

Figure 14.15. A triangle and median lines.

Finally, create three lines between the vertices and midpoints, **aq**, **br**, and **pc**:

```
(Serializer) In[44]:=   aq = NewLine[{pA, q}, 1];
                        br = NewLine[{pB, r}, 1];
                        pc = NewLine[{pC, p}, 1];
```

To see debug messages, we set **debug** to **True**.

```
(Serializer) In[47]:=   debug = True;
```

We examine the debug outputs generated by moving side **AB**:

```
(Serializer) In[48]:=   AB[move, {40, 20}]
```

```
self$115(Line)request:{40, 20}{self$106, self$109}

self$106(Point)request:{40, 20}{}

self$109(Point)request:{210, 60}{}

self$115(Line)move:{Hold[self$106[imove, {40, 20}, self$106]],
   Hold[self$109[imove, {210, 60}, self$109]]}

self$106(Point)imove:{40, 20}self$106{self$115, self$121, self$133}

self$115(Line)nomove:{self$109}

self$121(Line)imove:{40, 20}{self$130}

self$130(MidPoint)imove:{45, 100}{self$136}

self$136(Line)imove:{45, 100}{}
```

```
self$133(Line)imove:{40, 20}{}

self$109(Point)imove:{210, 60}self$109{self$115, self$118, self$136}

self$115(Line)imove:{210, 60}{self$124}

self$124(MidPoint)imove:{125, 40}{self$139}

self$139(Line)imove:{125, 40}{}

self$118(Line)imove:{210, 60}{self$127}

self$127(MidPoint)imove:{130, 120}{self$133}

self$133(Line)imove:{130, 120}{}

self$136(Line)imove:{210, 60}{}
```

(Serializer) Out[48]= {{-1, {{0}}, 0}, {{{0}}, {{0}}, 0}}

The line object sends a **request** message, and then each endpoint sends a **request** message. Then, the **move** method receives two held expressions that, in turn, generate a series of **imove** messages. One of the **imove** messages is not performed because it is not the final **imove** message. This is indicated in the debug output by nomove.

We stop debugging.

(Serializer) In[49]:= **debug = False;**

14.8. Packet Buffering

When dragging an object in Section 14.7, each object moves separately, and the motion looks jerky. This is because the move messages are sent separately. Moving one object can generate a large number of **imove** messages, and each **imove** message executed requires the program to move an object. As we found in Section 4.5, because of the overhead of link transfer, separate *MathLink* commands slow down the overall computation.

Each **imove** message generates a *MathLink* function like **MovePointObject**, and these functions return 0 if there is no error. So, it is safe to combine these *MathLink* functions and send them all at once. If the *MathLink* program processes a series of movements at once, it will speed up the drawing.

Each expression sent to the *MathLink* program is of the form **CallPacket[**n, args, ...**]** (see Section 3.9 and Section 2.12.14 of *The Mathematica Book*). We combine these **CallPacket[...]** expressions into a list and send it as a template function. Here is the template **MultiPackets**:

```
:Begin:
:Function:      multipackets
:Pattern:       MultiPackets[exp_List]
:Arguments:     {exp}
:ArgumentTypes: {Manual}
:ReturnType:    Manual
:End:
```

The C function multipackets copies the expression to the loopback link loop. Then, myDoCallPacket processes each **CallPacket[...]** expression. myDoCallPacket is a minor modification of MLDoCallPacket (see Section 3.9); it reads its arguments, calls the appropriate C function, and processes the return expression. All results are written to loop. multipackets transfers the list of return values in loop to the kernel as its return value.

```
void multipackets()
{
    const char *func;
    long i, len, len2, err;
    MLINK loop, save;
    int save_debug;

    save = stdlink;
    loop = MLLoopbackOpen(stdenv, &err);

    MLGetFunction(stdlink, &func, &len);     // read "List"
    for(i=0; i < len; ++i)      // read CallPacket[..], and send to loop,
        MLTransferExpression(loop, stdlink);
    MLPutFunction(loop, func, len);
    MLDisownSymbol(stdlink, func);
    for(i=0; i < len; ++i){
        MLGetFunction(loop, &func, &len2);
        if(strcmp(func,"CallPacket")==0)
            myDoCallPacket(loop);// CallPacket[..] on result, write to loop,
        else {
            MLAlert(stdenv,"illegal expression found in multipackets.");
            MLPutSymbol(loop,"$Failed");
            MLNewPacket(loop);
        }
        MLDisownSymbol(loop, func);
    }
    MLEndPacket(loop);
    stdlink = save;      // restore current stdlink now.
    MLTransferExpression(stdlink,loop); // return final result to stdlink,
    MLFlush(stdlink);
    MLClose(loop);
}
```

We now create a buffering mechanism for kernel functions. **$packetbuffer** will hold the list of **Call-Packet[...]** commands.

(Serializer) In[50]:= **$packetbuffer = {};**

$buffer is a flag that indicates buffering.

(Serializer) In[51]:= **$buffer = False;**

startBuffering sets **$MLPacketBuffer** and **$buffer** to **True**, and **$packetbuffer** to the empty list.

(Serializer) In[52]:= **startBuffering[win_Symbol] := If[$MLPacketBuffer === True,**
                 $buffer = True;
                 $packetbuffer = {};
                 SuppressUpdate[True, win]]

doBuffering appends **CallPacket[...]** expressions to **$packetbuffer**.

(Serializer) In[53]:= **doBuffering[exp_] := ($packetbuffer = Append[$packetbuffer, exp]; exp)**

endBuffering sends **$packetbuffer** to **MultiPackets** to process each **CallPacket[...]** in the *MathLink* program.

```
(Serializer) In[54]:=  endBuffering[win_Symbol] :=
                        Module[{n},
                         If[$MLPacketBuffer === True,
                          SuppressUpdate[False, win];
                          $buffer = False;
                          If[debug, Print["Flushing...:", $packetbuffer]];
                          If[$packetbuffer =!= {},
                           n = MultiPackets[$packetbuffer]];
                          $packetbuffer = {};
                          n]]
```

We modify the ExternalCall function (see Section 3.9) to do buffering when **$buffer** is **True**, otherwise it works as before.

```
(Serializer) In[55]:=  System`ExternalCall[link_LinkObject, packet_CallPacket] :=
                        Block[{ThisLink = link, $CurrentLink = link, $IterationLimit = ∞},
                         If[$buffer === True, doBuffering[packet],
                          If[LinkWrite[link, packet] === $Failed, $Failed,
                           System`Dump`ExternalAnswer[link, LinkReadHeld[link]]]]]
```

```
(Serializer) In[56]:=  $MLPacketBuffer = True;
```

We modify our **move** method to do buffering by adding the buffering functions **startBuffering** and **endBuffering** to **GeometricalPoint** and **GeometricalLine**.

```
(Serializer) In[57]:=  GeometricalPoint[self_, move, {x_, y_}] :=
                        Module[{ex, win = self[getwindow]},
                         If[{x, y} ≠ self[getposition],
                          startBuffering[win];
                          ex = self[request, {x, y}];
                          If[debug, Print[self, "(Point)move:", ex]];
                          ReleaseHold[ex];
                          endBuffering[win]]]
```

```
(Serializer) In[58]:=  GeometricalLine[self_, move, {x_, y_}] :=
                        Module[{ex, win = self[getwindow]},
                         If[{x, y} ≠ self[getposition][[1]],
                          startBuffering[win];
                          ex = self[request, {x, y}];
                          If[debug, Print[self, "(Line)move:", ex]];
                          ReleaseHold[ex];
                          endBuffering[win]]]
```

The reader can see how mouse dragging becomes smooth. What a dramatic change!

We set the **debug** flag to **True** and examine the debug outputs generated by moving side **AB**:

```
(Serializer) In[59]:=  debug = True; AB[move, {30, 30}]; debug = False;

    self$143(Line)request:{30, 30}{self$134, self$137}

    self$134(Point)request:{30, 30}{}

    self$137(Point)request:{200, 70}{}

    self$143(Line)move:{Hold[self$134[imove, {30, 30}, self$134]],
      Hold[self$137[imove, {200, 70}, self$137]]}

    self$134(Point)imove:{30, 30}self$134{self$143, self$149, self$161}

    self$143(Line)nomove:{self$137}

    self$149(Line)imove:{30, 30}{self$158}

    self$158(MidPoint)imove:{40, 105}{self$164}

    self$164(Line)imove:{40, 105}{}

    self$161(Line)imove:{30, 30}{}

    self$137(Point)imove:{200, 70}self$137{self$143, self$146, self$164}

    self$143(Line)imove:{200, 70}{self$152}

    self$152(MidPoint)imove:{115, 50}{self$167}

    self$167(Line)imove:{115, 50}{}

    self$146(Line)imove:{200, 70}{self$155}

    self$155(MidPoint)imove:{125, 125}{self$161}

    self$161(Line)imove:{125, 125}{}

    self$164(Line)imove:{200, 70}{}

    Flushing...:{CallPacket[18, {1, 0}],
      CallPacket[26, {30., 30., 0, 0}], CallPacket[30, {50., 180., 30., 30., 5, 0}],
      CallPacket[26, {40., 105., 8, 0}], CallPacket[30, {210., 60., 40., 105., 10, 0}],
      CallPacket[30, {30., 30., 130., 120., 9, 0}], CallPacket[26, {200., 70., 1, 0}],
      CallPacket[30, {30., 30., 200., 70., 3, 0}], CallPacket[26, {115., 50., 6, 0}],
      CallPacket[30, {50., 180., 115., 50., 11, 0}],
      CallPacket[30, {200., 70., 50., 180., 4, 0}],
      CallPacket[26, {125., 125., 7, 0}], CallPacket[30, {30., 30., 125., 125., 9, 0}],
      CallPacket[30, {200., 70., 40., 105., 10, 0}], CallPacket[18, {0, 0}]}
```

The output shows that the packets are buffered and sent as a list of **CallPacket[...]** functions.

We measure the effect of buffering using **Clock** by computing the transfer time with and without buffering.

```
(Serializer) In[60]:=  t0 = Clock[prog[link]]; AB[move, {30, 20}];
    $MLPacketBuffer = True; Clock[prog[link]] - t0
```

```
(Serializer) Out[60]=  0.116667
```

```
(Serializer) In[61]:=  $MLPacketBuffer = False; t0 = Clock[prog[link]];
    AB[move, {20, 30}]; $MLPacketBuffer = True; Clock[prog[link]] - t0
```

```
(Serializer) Out[61]=  0.75
```

The ratio of these results shows that buffered transfer is approximately 6 times faster than transfer without buffering. If a **move** message includes more **CallPacket[...]** functions, buffering will have an even larger effect.

14.9. PointOnLine and PointAtIntersection Classes

The **PointOnLine** class defines a point that is constrained to move only on a line. This class is derived from the **GeometricalPoint** class, and its **master** is the line (see Figure 14.16). This object has a local variable **myratio**, which is the parametric position of the point on the line. When a **request** message is received, **myratio** is updated and a held **imove** expression is returned. This object does not send a **request** message to its **master**, because moving the point does not affect the **master**.

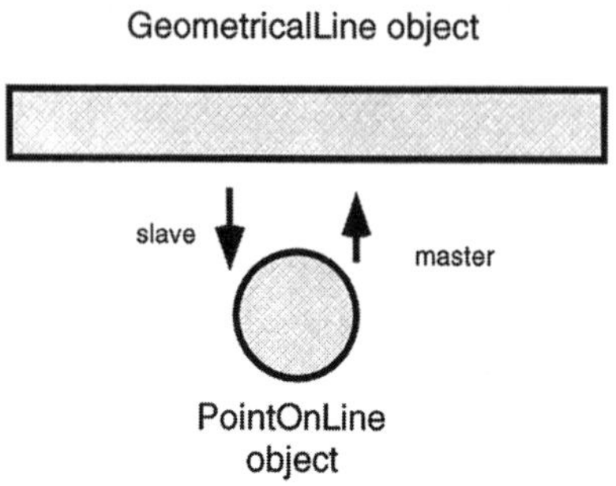

GeometricalLine object

Figure 14.16. Relation between a line and a point on the line.

```
(Serializer) In[62]:=    New[PointOnLine, line_, r_, opts___] :=
                         With[{self = New[GeometricalPoint, line[getwindow],
                             PointObjectPosition → getRatioPos[line[getposition], r], opts]},
                           Module[{myratio = r},
                             self[imove, {x_, y_}, caller_] :=
                              Module[{np, s = self[slave]},
                               If[{x, y} ≠ self[getposition],
                                If[self[deletemark, caller] === {},
                                 If[debug, Print[self, "(PointOnLine) imove:", N[{x, y}], s]];
                                 self[setposition,
                                  np = getRatioPos[line[getposition], myratio]];
                                 If[s =!= {},
                                  Map[#[imove, np, self] &, s], 0],
                                 If[debug,
                                  Print[self, "(PointOnLine) nomove:", self[mark]]]; -1],
                                If[debug, Print[self, "(PointOnLine) ignore:", {x, y}]]; -2]];
                             self[request, {x_, y_}] :=
                              (myratio = getRatio[line[getposition], {x, y}];
                               If[debug, Print[self,
                                 "(PointOnLine) request:", {x, y}, myratio, self[slave]]];
                               Hold[self[imove, {x, y}, self]]);
                             self[master, line];
                             line[slave, self];
                             self]]
```

getRatio calculates the parametric ratio from the line location to the new position **{x,y}**:

(Serializer) In[63]:= `getRatio[{p1_, p2_}, p0_] :=`
`Module[{r}, r /. Solve[(r (p2 - p1) + p1 - p0).(p2 - p1) == 0, r][[1]]]`

`getRatioPos` returns the calculated position from the location of the line and the value of **myratio**:

(Serializer) In[64]:= `getRatioPos[{p1_, p2_}, r_] := r (p2 - p1) + p1`

NewPointOnLine is a simple wrapper function for **New[PointOnLine, ...]**.

(Serializer) In[65]:= `NewPointOnLine[line_, size_, ratio_] :=`
`New[PointOnLine, line, ratio, PointObjectSize → size]`

The **PointAtIntersection** class defines a point at which two lines intersect. This class is derived from the **GeometricalPoint** class, and its **master** consists of two lines (see Figure 14.17). When either of the lines is moved, the intersection point also moves. When the intersection point moves, the point and both lines move.

(Serializer) In[66]:=
```
New[PointAtIntersection, {l1_, l2_}, opts___] :=
 With[{self = New[GeometricalPoint, l1[getwindow],
     PointObjectPosition -> getCrossPoint[l1, l2], opts]},
  self[imove, {x_, y_}, caller_] :=
   Module[{s = self[slave]},
    If[{x, y} ≠ self[getposition],
     If[self[deletemark, caller] === {},
      If[debug, Print[self, "(PointCrossLines)imove:", {x, y}, s]];
      self[setposition, getCrossPoint[l1, l2]];
      If[s =!= {},
       Map[#[imove, self[getposition], self] &, s], 0], If[debug,
       Print[self, "(PointCrossLines)nomove:", self[mark]]]; -1],
      If[debug, Print[self, "(PointCrossLines)ignore:", {x, y}]]; -2]];
  self[request, {x_, y_}] :=
   Module[{r = {x, y} - self[getposition]}, If[debug,
     Print[self, "(PointCrossLines)request:", {x, y}, {l1, l2}]];
    self[mark, {l1, l2}];
    {l1[request, r + l1[getposition][[1]]],
     l2[request, r + l2[getposition][[1]]]}];
  self[master, {l1, l2}];
  Map[#[slave, self] &, {l1, l2}];
  self]
```

getCrossPoint calculates the intersection position of two **GeometricalLine** objects.

(Serializer) In[67]:= `getCrossPoint[line1_, line2_] :=`
`Module[{x, y, formula},`
`formula[{{x1_, y1_}, {x2_, y2_}}, {x_, y_}] :=`
`(x1 - x2) y == x (y1 - y2) - (x2 y1 - x1 y2);`
`{x, y} /. Solve[{formula[line1[getposition], {x, y}],`
`formula[line2[getposition], {x, y}]}, {x, y}][[1]]]`

PointAtIntersection is a simple wrapper function for **New[PointAtIntersection, ...]**.

(Serializer) In[68]:= `PointAtIntersection[{l1_, l2_}, size_] :=`
`New[PointAtIntersection, {l1, l2}, PointObjectSize → size]`

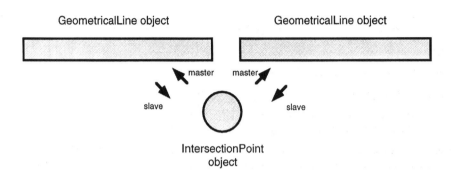

Figure 14.17. The relationship between two lines and the point of intersection.

14.10. Pappus's Hexagon Theorem

Here, we build an *Interactive Geometry* version of Pappus's hexagon theorem (see http://mathworld.wolfram.com/) using the classes we have defined. This theorem states that the three intersection points (joined by thin lines) in Figure 14.18 are colinear. This *Interactive Geometry* program enables the user to move each point and line to graphically verify the theorem.

First, open a window:

(Serializer) In[69]:= **win3 = New[Window, prog, WindowTitle → "Pappus Theorem"];**

Then, create a line **ab**, and put three points **p1**, **p3**, and **p5** on it:

(Serializer) In[70]:= **ab =**
**   NewLine[{NewPoint[win3, {12, 35}, 8], NewPoint[win3, {286, 97}, 8]}, 2];**
**   p1 = NewPointOnLine[ab, 8, 0.2];**
**   p3 = NewPointOnLine[ab, 8, 0.5];**
**   p5 = NewPointOnLine[ab, 8, 0.9];**

Now, create a line **cd**, and put three points **p2**, **p4**, and **p6** on it:

(Serializer) In[74]:= **cd = NewLine[**
**   {NewPoint[win3, {275, 277}, 8], NewPoint[win3, {24, 229}, 8]}, 2];**
**   p2 = NewPointOnLine[cd, 8, 0.2];**
**   p4 = NewPointOnLine[cd, 8, 0.9];**
**   p6 = NewPointOnLine[cd, 8, 0.7];**

Next, make the required connections between the points:

(Serializer) In[78]:= **l1 = NewLine[{p1, p6}, 2];**
**   l2 = NewLine[{p6, p5}, 2];**
**   l3 = NewLine[{p1, p2}, 2];**
**   l4 = NewLine[{p2, p3}, 2];**
**   l5 = NewLine[{p5, p4}, 2];**
**   l6 = NewLine[{p4, p3}, 2];**

Then, determine the cross points, **pp1**, **pp2**, and **pp3**, of these lines:

(Serializer) In[84]:= **pp1 = PointAtIntersection[{11, 16}, 8];**
pp2 = PointAtIntersection[{13, 15}, 8];
pp3 = PointAtIntersection[{12, 14}, 8];

Finally, create two lines from these three points:

(Serializer) In[87]:= **NewLine[{pp1, pp2}, 1];**
NewLine[{pp2, pp3}, 1];

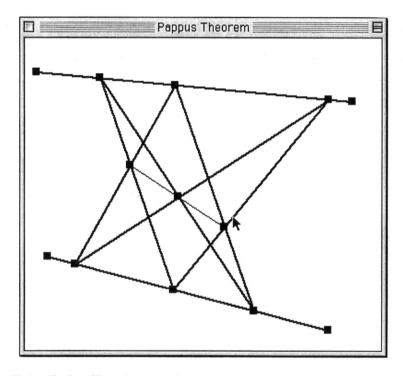

Figure 14.18. Graphical verification of Pappus's hexagon theorem.

If these two lines are colinear, the theorem is satisfied. You can move any point or line object using the mouse; graphically, it is clear that the theorem holds. To test for colinearity of three points, one can use the discriminant determinant. The next expression calculates the determinant and interprets the result:

(Serializer) In[89]:= **"These three points " <> If[Chop[Det[**
{Append[pp1[getposition], 1],
Append[pp2[getposition], 1],
Append[pp3[getposition], 1]}]] == 0,
"are colinear", "are not colinear"]

(Serializer) Out[89]= These three points are colinear

14.11. Summary

In this chapter, an *Interactive Geometry* package was created from the graphical objects described in Chapter 13. The *MathLink* program is used only for displaying points and lines in a window; the relations between objects are built on top using *Mathematica*. This is a good example which shows how the *MathLink* program and the kernel share the work.

Packet buffering is used to overcome the speed bottleneck. This technique is a general method for speeding up *MathLink* programs.

The *Interactive Geometry* package extends the classes of our OOPS system by adding **GeometricalPoint**, **GeometricalLine**, **MidpointOnLine**, **PointOnLine**, and **PointAtIntersection** classes. Adding menus, icons, and more classes would make this package superior to similar commercial applications.

Chapter 15 — Communication between Mathematica Sessions

This chapter shows how to link multiple `Serializer` sessions. Such a link enables us to send expressions between *Mathematica* sessions and assists cooperative work. For example, a user can copy and paste cell expressions to another session over the network, or exchange messages with other users. Hence `Serializer` becomes a communication tool between *Mathematica* sessions and is one powerful extension of this simple *MathLink* application.

15.1. Connecting Serializer Sessions

In this section, we will make a *MathLink* connection between two `Serializer` sessions, as indicated in Figure 15.1. Using this link allows us to send expressions to another *Mathematica* session. Such expressions will be evaluated by the partner's kernel in the same way as expressions from the front end or other *MathLink* programs.

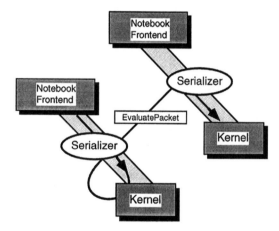

Figure 15.1. Sending `EvaluatePacket` expression from one *Mathematica* session to another.

To connect two `Serializer` sessions, the following basic capabilities are required: open a link, activate a link, close a link, read from a link, write to a link, and test to see if a link is ready. These primitives are defined as template functions: `SerializerLinkOpen[]`, `SerializerLinkActivate[]`, `SerializerLinkClose[]`, `EventLinkRead[]`, `EventLinkWrite[]`, and `EventLinkReadyQ[]`.

serializerlinkopen() opens a link and returns its connection port number and link name.

```
:Begin:
:Function:        serializerlinkopen
:Pattern:         SerializerLinkOpen[name_String, mode_Symbol, protocol_String]
:Arguments:       { name, mode, protocol}
:ArgumentTypes:   { String, Symbol, String }
:ReturnType:      Manual
:End:
```

```
:Begin:
:Function:       serializerlinklisten
:Pattern:        SerializerLinkOpen[ protocol_String ]
:Arguments:      { protocol }
:ArgumentTypes:  { String }
:ReturnType:     Manual
:End:
```

```c
void serializerlinkopen(const char *name, const char *mode, const char *protocol)
{
    long err;
    char *av[9], fullname[255];
    MLINK lp;
    int n0;

    av[0] = "-linkname";
    av[1] = (char *)name;
    av[2] = "-linkmode";
    av[3] = (char *)mode;
    av[4] = "-linkprotocol";
    av[5] = (char *)protocol;
    av[6] = "-linkoptions";
    av[7] = "MLDontInteract";
    av[8] = '\0';
    lp = MLOpenArgv(stdenv,av,av+8, &err);
    if(lp == (MLINK)0){
        MLPutSymbol(stdlink, "$Failed");
        return;
    }
    if((n0 = appendlink(lp, MLProg)) < 0){
        MLPutSymbol(stdlink, "$Failed");
        return;
    }
    MLFullName(fullname, lp, protocol);

    MLPutFunction(stdlink,"List",2L);
        MLPutInteger(stdlink, n0);
        MLPutString(stdlink, fullname);
    MLEndPacket(stdlink);
    bufferflag = false; // inhibit buffering until connection established.
}
```

```c
void serializerlinklisten(const char *protocol)
{
    long err;
    char *av[7], fullname[255];
    MLINK lp;
    int n0;

    av[0] = "-linkmode";
    av[1] = "Listen";
    av[2] = "-linkprotocol";
    av[3] = (char *)protocol;
    av[4] = "-linkoptions";
```

```
        av[5] = "MLDontInteract";
        av[6] = '\0';
        lp = MLOpenArgv(stdenv, av, av+6, &err);
        if(lp == (MLINK)0){
            MLPutSymbol(stdlink, "$Failed");
            return;
        }
        if((n0 = appendlink(lp, MLProg)) < 0){
            MLPutSymbol(stdlink, "$Failed");
            return;
        }
        MLFullName(fullname, lp, protocol);

        MLPutFunction(stdlink,"List",2L);
            MLPutInteger(stdlink, n0);
            MLPutString(stdlink, fullname);
        MLEndPacket(stdlink);
        bufferflag = false; // inhibit buffering until connection established.
}
```

serlializerlinkopen() opens a link and returns. In contrast, serliazerlinkactivate() waits for connection from its partner. While awaiting connection, if the user sends an Abort message from the front end, it will close the link. When the connection is established it sends its own instance symbol, self, to its partner as a string, reads its partner's instance symbol, and transfers it to the kernel as the return value.

```
:Begin:
:Function:          serializerlinkactivate
:Pattern:           SerializerLinkActivate[m_Integer, s_Symbol]
:Arguments:         { m, s }
:ArgumentTypes:     { Integer, Symbol }
:ReturnType:        Manual
:End:
```

```
void serializerlinkactivate(int m, const char *self)
{
    if(m < MAXLINK && eventlinks[m].link != (MLINK)0){
        while(MLReady(eventlinks[m].link) == 0){  // wait until link connected...
            MLCallYieldFunction(MLYieldFunction(stdlink), stdlink,
                (MLYieldParameters)0);
            if(MLAbort){
                removelink(m);
                MLPutFunction(stdlink, "Abort", 0);
                bufferflag = true;
                return;
            }
        }
    }
    else {
        MLPutSymbol(stdlink, "$Failed");
        bufferflag = true;
        return;
    }

    MLActivate(eventlinks[m].link);
```

```
        MLPutString(eventlinks[m].link, self);  // put my symbol name string
        MLEndPacket(eventlinks[m].link);
        MLFlush(eventlinks[m].link);

        MLTransferExpression(stdlink, eventlinks[m].link); // return partner's symbol
        MLNewPacket(eventlinks[m].link);      // make sure I read an expression
        bufferflag = true;
}
```

When `Serializer` attempts to disconnect a link using `serializerlinkclose()`, it first asks its partner to close its link, and then it closes its own link. It is for this reason that `Serializer` must send its own instance symbol to its partner at the link establishment phase.

```
:Begin:
:Function:        serializerlinkclose
:Pattern:         SerializerLinkClose[m_Integer, s_String]
:Arguments:       { m, s }
:ArgumentTypes:   { Integer, String }
:ReturnType:      Integer
:End:
```

```
int serializerlinkclose(int m, char *s)
{
    long en;

    if(0 <= m && m < MAXLINK && eventlinks[m].link != (MLINK)0){
        if((en = MLError(eventlinks[m].link)) == 0){
            MLPutFunction(eventlinks[m].link,"EvaluatePacket",1L);
            MLPutFunction(eventlinks[m].link, s, 1L);
            MLPutSymbol(eventlinks[m].link, "dispose");
            MLEndPacket(eventlinks[m].link);
            MLFlush(eventlinks[m].link);
            sleep(3);
        }
        MLClose(eventlinks[m].link);
        eventlinks[m].link = (MLINK)0;
        eventlinks[m].type = NotUsed;
        eventlinks[m].mode = NoMode;
        return(0);
    }
    else
        return(-2);
}
```

`eventlinkwrite()` uses `MLTransferExpression()` to transfer an expression from `stdlink` to the link, and it wraps the expression with `EvaluatePacket[]` to cause evaluation by the partner's kernel.

```
:Begin:
:Function:        eventlinkwrite
:Pattern:         EventLinkWrite[n_Integer, exp_]
:Arguments:       { n, Unevaluated[exp] }
:ArgumentTypes: { Integer, Manual }
```

```
:ReturnType:    Integer
:End:
```

```
int eventlinkwrite(int n)
{
    long en, len;
    char *f;

    if(n < MAXLINK && eventlinks[n].link != (MLINK)0){
        if((en = MLError(eventlinks[n].link)) == 0){
            MLGetFunction(stdlink, &f, &len);   // strip Unevaluated[]
            MLDisownSymbol(stdlink, f);       // disown it.
            if(len != 1){
                MLAlert(stdenv, "EventLinkWrite packet error");
                MLNewPacket(stdlink);
                return(-1);
            }
            else {
                MLTransferExpression(eventlinks[n].link, stdlink);
                MLEndPacket(eventlinks[n].link);
                MLFlush(eventlinks[n].link);
                return(0);
            }
        }
        return(en);
    }
    return(-2);
}
```

To read an expression from the link, `eventlinkwrapread()` uses `MLTransferExpression()` to transfer from the link to `stdlink` and then wraps the expression with head. For example, if head is `Hold`, the returned expression is wrapped with `Hold[]`. This prevents expression evaluation by the kernel. `LinkRead[link, Hold]` (see Section 2.12.6 of *The Mathematica Book*) uses a similar mechanism.

```
:Begin:
:Function:      eventlinkwrapread
:Pattern:       EventLinkRead[n_Integer, h_Symbol]
:Arguments:     { n, h }
:ArgumentTypes: { Integer, Symbol }
:ReturnType:    Manual
:End:
```

```
void eventlinkwrapread(int n, const char * h)
{
    if(n < MAXLINK && eventlinks[n].link != (MLINK)0){
        MLPutFunction(stdlink, h, 1L);
        if(MLReady(eventlinks[n].buf)){ //if there is an expression in buffer,
            MLTransferExpression(stdlink, eventlinks[n].buf);
            MLNewPacket(eventlinks[n].buf);
        }
        else {
            MLTransferExpression(stdlink, eventlinks[n].link);
            MLNewPacket(eventlinks[n].link);
```

```
            }
        }
        else {
            MLPutSymbol(stdlink, "$Failed");
        }
    }
```

`eventlinkread()` is similar to `eventlinkwrapread()`, except that it does not wrap the expression with a specified head. The difference between these functions is analogous to the difference between `LinkRead[link]` and `LinkRead[link,Hold]` (see Section 2.12.6 of *The Mathematica Book*).

```
:Begin:
:Function:       eventlinkread
:Pattern:        EventLinkRead[n_Integer]
:Arguments:      { n }
:ArgumentTypes:  { Integer }
:ReturnType:     Manual
:End:
```

`eventlinkready()` uses `MLReady()` to check if the link is ready.

```
:Begin:
:Function:       eventlinkready
:Pattern:        EventLinkReadyQ[n_Integer]
:Arguments:      { n }
:ArgumentTypes:  { Integer }
:ReturnType:     Manual
:End:
```

```
void eventlinkready(int n)
{
    if(n < MAXLINK && eventlinks[n].link != (MLINK)0){
        if(MLReady(eventlinks[n].buf) != 0)
            MLPutSymbol(stdlink, "True");
        else if(MLReady(eventlinks[n].link) != 0)
            MLPutSymbol(stdlink, "True");
        else
            MLPutSymbol(stdlink, "False");
    }
    MLPutSymbol(stdlink, "$Failed");
}
```

We now create a new **Serializer** class in which we wrap these template functions.

```
New[Serializer, lname_String, opts___Rule] :=
    Module[{self, myport, mypartner, lmode, lproto, myname, myserver = Null},
        self[dispose] := (
            SerializerLinkClose[myport[[1]], mypartner];
            Remove[self, myport, mypartner, lmode, lproto]);
        self[port] := myport[[1]];
        self[partner] := mypartner;
        self[nickname] := myname;
```

```
    self[send, exp_] := EventLinkWrite[myport[[1]], EvaluatePacket[exp]];
    self[eval, exp_] :=
SerializerEvaluate[{myport[[1]], mypartner}, exp, self];
    self[Hold[v_String]] := v;
    self[Hold[v_?NumericQ]] := v;
    self[Hold[v_]] := Hold[v];
  self[selector_, args___] :=
        findmethod[Serializer[self, selector, args], $MethodNotFound];
    SetAttributes[self, HoldAll];
    myname = NickName /. {opts} /. {NickName -> lname};
    lmode = LinkMode /. {opts} /. Options[Serializer];
    lproto = LinkProtocol /. {opts} /. Options[Serializer];
    If[$MSGLink === Null, MessageLinkCreate[]];
    myport = SerializerLinkOpen[lname, lmode, lproto];
    If[myport =!= $Failed,
    mypartner = SerializerLinkActivate[
  myport[[1]], FilterObject /. {opts} /. {FilterObject -> self}]];
    If[mypartner =!= $Failed, self, $Failed]]
```

self[send, *exp*] sends *exp* to its partner, but it does not return the result of the evaluation. **self[eval,***exp*]
sends *exp* to its partner and gets its return value using **SerializerEvaluate[]**.

```
SerializerEvaluate[{p1_Integer, p2_String}, exp_, f_] :=
    (EventLinkWrite[p1,
    EvaluatePacket[EventLinkWrite[ToExpression[p2][port], Evaluate[exp]]]];
        f[Evaluate[EventLinkRead[p1, Hold]]])
```

```
SetAttributes[SerializerEvaluate, HoldRest]
```

The expression returned from **self[eval,***exp*] has the form **self[Hold[***ret***]]**. Pattern matching is used to
process this (unevaluated) return expression, *ret*. If *ret* is a string or numeric, *ret* is returned. Otherwise *ret* is
wrapped with Hold, which prevents automatic evaluation. Figure 15.2 shows the hierarchy of messages sent to the
partner *Mathematica* session.

15.2. Testing the Connection

To test the Serializer connection, we first start two *Mathematica* sessions—here called **Jack** and **Jill**—with
kernels running on different machines and then connect these sessions using Serializer by running **New[Seri-
alizer,..]** on each machine (see Figure 15.3). The listening side, **Jack**, is blocked until the connecting side
connects.

```
(Jack) In[1]:=  Jill = New[Serializer, "3000",
            LinkMode → Listen, LinkProtocol → "TCP", NickName → "Jill"];
```

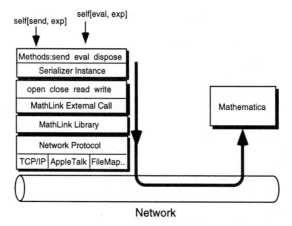

Figure 15.2. Message hierarchy between `Serializer` sessions.

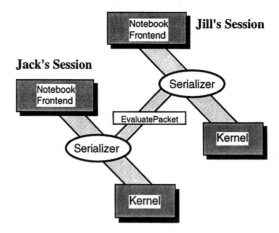

Figure 15.3. `Serializer` connection between *Mathematica* sessions **Jack** and **Jill**.

When the connecting side, **Jill**, evaluates the command shown in Figure 15.4 (192.168.0.2 is the IP address of Jack's machine), the **Serializer** instance is returned and, when both return values have been received, the connection is established.

If we evaluate **a=12** on **Jill**'s kernel:

(Jack) In[2]:= **Jill[eval, a = 12]**

(Jack) Out[2]= 12

12 is returned because the evaluation of **a=12** returns **12** on **Jill**'s kernel. However, the local kernel (**Jack**) symbol, **a**, is not assigned a value.

(Jack) In[3]:= **a**

(Jack) Out[3]= a

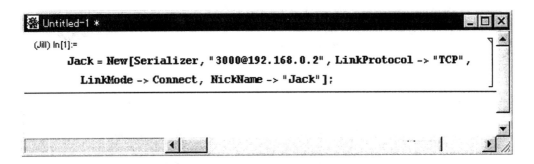

Figure 15.4. Serializer running on **Jill** connects to Serializer running on **Jack**.

Evaluating **ff[a]** on **Jill**'s kernel returns **ff[12]** wrapped with **Hold**.

(Jack) In[4]:= **Jill[eval, ff[a]]**

(Jack) Out[4]= Hold[ff[12]]

We will now examine the packets transferred between our two sessions by running **PacketMonitor[]** on the local kernel (**Jack**).

(Jack) In[5]:= **PacketMonitor[]**

     < -k : OutputNamePacket[(Jack) Out[5]=]

(Jack) Out[5]= 1

     < -k : ReturnExpressionPacket[BoxData[1, StandardForm]]

     < -k : InputNamePacket[(Jack) In[6]:=]

We are now waiting for expressions from our partner, **Jill**. Evaluating **Jack[send,NotebookCreate[]]** on **Jill**'s kernel first causes a set of debugging messages to be printed out on our messages window (Figure 15.5) and then the evaluation of **NotebookCreate[]** causes our front end to open up a new Notebook window.

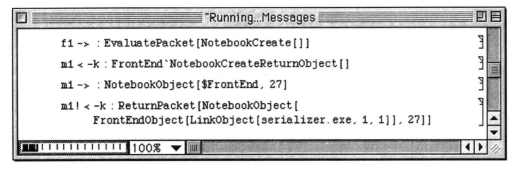

Figure 15.5. **PacketMonitor** messages generated by running **Jack[send,NotebookCreate[]]** on **Jill**'s kernel.

Figure 15.5 shows that Serializer got the expression EvaluatePacket[NotebookCreate[]] from the link **f1**, and it was evaluated on our kernel. We stop debugging.

```
(Jack) In[6]:=  PacketMonitor[]

          f0 -> : EnterExpressionPacket[
              MakeExpression[BoxData[RowBox[List[PacketMonitor, [, ]]]], StandardForm]]

(Jack) Out[6]=  0
```

15.3. NetCopy and NetPaste

Now we'll make functions **NetCopy[]** and **NetPaste[]**, which copy or paste clipboard content to or from their partner. **NetCopy** and **NetPaste** extend **Copy** and **Paste** to network applications, respectively. Since all notebook cells, including graphics and sounds, are simply ASCII text, **NetCopy** and **NetPaste** can transfer *any* object that can be represented as a notebook cell.

ClipboardRead[] reads cell expressions from the clipboard. It uses an invisible notebook, **$$clip**, internally.

```
ClipboardRead[] :=
(If[Head[$$clip] =!= NotebookObject,
    $$clip = NotebookCreate[Visible -> False]];
    clipread[$$clip])
```

The actual work is done by **clipread[]**, which sends a **FrontEndToken** (see Section 2.10.5 of *The Mathematica Book* for information on **FrontEnd`**) to **"Paste"** the clipboard content to **$$clip** and then reads it using **NotebookRead[]**.

```
clipread[nb_NotebookObject] :=
    (LinkWrite[First[$FrontEnd],
            Unevaluated[FrontEnd`FrontEndToken[nb, "Paste"];
    FrontEnd`SelectionMove[nb, All, Notebook]; FrontEnd`NotebookRead[nb]]];
  readfrom[First[$FrontEnd]])
```

readfrom[] reads cell expressions sent by **LinkRead**.

```
readfrom[link_LinkObject] :=
    Module[{exp},
        exp = LinkRead[link];
        If[LinkReadyQ[link],
            exp = {exp};
            While[LinkReadyQ[link],
                exp = Append[exp, LinkRead[link]]]];
        Flatten[exp]]
```

Using **ClipboardRead[]** we can define **NetCopy[z]**, which copies Serializer instance z's clipboard and pastes it into the notebook.

```
NetCopy[z_] := CellPrint[z[eval, ClipboardRead[]][[1]]]
```

The expression **CellPrint[z[eval,ClipboardRead[]]]** evaluates **ClipboardRead[]** on kernel z to read the clipboard, and returns it wrapped with **Hold[***exp***]**. The expression *exp* itself is extracted (it is part **[[1]]**), and **CellPrint** prints it in the notebook.

If our partner, **Jill**, copies some cells to the clipboard, say (Jill) In[3]:= **Jack[send,NotebookCreate[]]** and (Jill) Out[3]= 0, then executing **NetCopy[Jill]** copies these cells and inserts them into our notebook immediately below our input cell.

(Jack) In[7]:=   **NetCopy[Jill]**

(Jill) In[3]:=   **Jack[send, NotebookCreate[]]**

(Jill) Out[3]=   0

The implementation of **NetPaste[]** is similar. First, we define **SendCell[]**.

```
SendCell[m_, exp_] := m[send, Unevaluated[NotebookWrite[SelectedNotebook[], exp]]]
```

SendCell[*m***,***exp***]** sends a cell expression *exp* to Serializer instance *m*. **NotebookWrite[Selected-Notebook[],***exp***]** writes a cell expression *exp* in the currently selected notebook. **NetPaste[***z***]** pastes clipboard content to *z*'s notebook.

```
NetPaste[z_Symbol] := SendCell[z, ClipboardRead[]]
```

If *z* is a *list* of Serializer instances, **NetPaste[***z***]** sends the clipboard content to *all* instances.

```
NetPaste[z_List] := Module[{exp = ClipboardRead[]}, Map[SendCell[#, exp] &, z]]
```

If we copy this text cell, we can paste it in **Jill**'s notebook, as shown in Figure 15.6.

(Jack) In[8]:=   **NetPaste[Jill]**

(Jack) Out[8]=   0

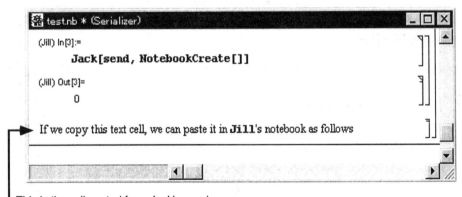

This is the cell pasted from Jack's session.

Figure 15.6. A screen snapshot of our partner's session.

The capabilities of our Serializer link, and the fact that notebooks are themselves defined as *Mathematica* expressions, enables us to develop more sophisticated communication programs along the lines of **NetCopy** and **NetPaste**.

15.4. Message Exchange Notebook

Next, we implement a notebook for exchanging cells between `Serializer` sessions.

15.4.1 An Example of Message Exchange

Executing the following command,

(Jack) In[9]:= `CellExchangeNotebook[Jill];`

opens a specialized notebook as shown in Figure 15.7.

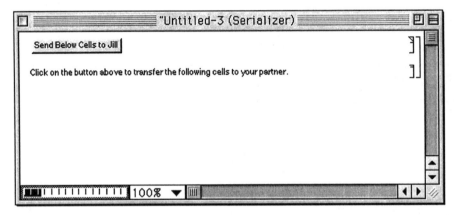

Figure 15.7. `CellExchangeNotebook[Jill]` opens a specialized notebook for exchanging messages with `Jill`.

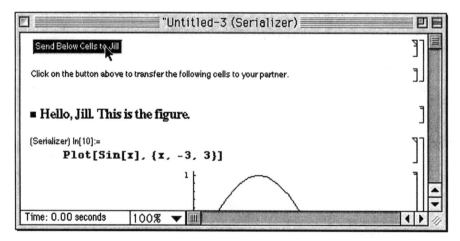

Figure 15.8. Sending notebook contents to `Jill`'s session.

Adding cells below the button cell and clicking on the Send Below Cells to Jill button causes all cells below the button to be sent to `Jill`'s session (see Figure 15.8). These contents, along with a suitably modified button (Send Below Cells to Jack), appear in `Jill`'s session (see Figure 15.9).

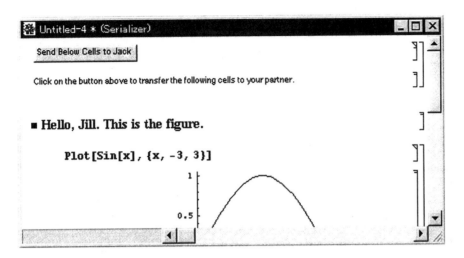

Figure 15.9. Notebook contents received by **Jill**'s session.

As either partner adds or modifies his or her notebook, the new contents can be sent to their partner by clicking the button. This is a simple message exchange system.

15.4.2 Implementation

The cell expression of the button Send Below Cells to Jill can be viewed by selecting the cell and using **Show Expression** under the **Format** menu (see Sections 2.8.3 and 2.10.1 of *The Mathematica Book*). The unformatted form is displayed next.

```
Cell[BoxData[
    FormBox[
      StyleBox[
        ButtonBox[
          RowBox[{"Send", " ", "Below", " ", "Cells", " ", "to", " ", "Jill"}],
          ButtonFunction:>CompoundExpression[
              myButtonFunction[ self$19,
                ExtractCells[ ]],
              NotebookClose[
                SelectedNotebook[ ]]],
          ButtonEvaluator->"Serializer",
          ButtonStyle->"Evaluate"],
        Active->True], TextForm]], "SmallText"]
```

Jill's instance, `self$19` in this session, is referenced in the `ButtonFunction`. When the user clicks on this button, the following expression is executed.

```
myButtonFunction[self$19, ExtractCells[]]; NotebookClose[SelectedNotebook[]]
```

`ExtractCells[]` selects the cell expressions below the button.

```
ExtractCells[] := Rest[First[NotebookGet[SelectedNotebook[]]]]
```

`myButtonFunction[z, cl]` is called with the `Serializer` instance, z, and cell expressions, cl, as arguments.

```
myButtonFunction[z_, cl_] := myButtonFunction[z, z[partner], cl]
```

```
myButtonFunction[z1_, z2_, cl_] :=
  z1[send, CellExchangeNotebook[ToExpression[z2], cl]]
```

This recursive function call sends the expression `CellExchangeNotebook[z, cl]` to `Serializer` instance y where z is the `Serializer` instance symbol in the partner's kernel. `CellExchangeNotebook[z, cl]` opens a notebook containing the cell expression that was sent from the partner.

```
CellExchangeNotebook[z_, cl_] :=
  NotebookPut[Insert[Get[$SerializerDef <> "ObjectDefinitions`MessageNote`"],
    Unevaluated[Apply[Sequence, cl]], {1, -1}] /.
    {self -> z, "str" -> "Send Below Cells to " <> z[nickname]}]
```

This works by opening the notebook **MessageNote.m** (we use a package name so that the machine-independent file specification, **Get[$SerializerDef<>"ObjectDefinitions`MessageNote`"]**, will work) shown in Figure 15.10, and uses replacement rules to replace **self** (which appears in the button code) by the `Serializer` instance, z, and replace the text string **"str"** with text appropriate for the partner's session (whose name is determined by the string z**[nickname]**).

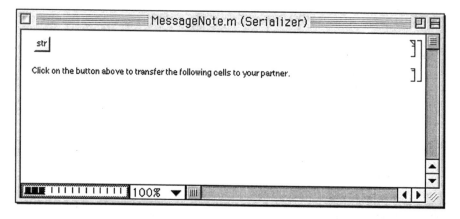

Figure 15.10. The notebook **MessageNote.m**.

Calling **CellExchangeNotebook** with no cell expression argument just opens a new notebook, as displayed in Figure 15.7.

```
CellExchangeNotebook[z_] := NotebookPut[
  Get[$SerializerDef <> "ObjectDefinitions`MessageNote`"] /. {self → z,
    "str" → "Send Below Cells to " <> z[nickname]}]
```

Exchanging messages is another simple application of the `Serializer` connection. It uses the **send** method internally, but all other functionality is achieved using ordinary *Mathematica* functions, making it easy to enhance or modify them to meet a user's specific requirements.

15.5. Summary

In this chapter, we extended `Serializer` to enable sending expressions between `Serializer` sessions through simple extensions of **LinkRead** and **LinkWrite** functions. Using these functions we implemented two utilities — **NetCopy/NetPaste** and **CellExchangeNotebook** — for exchanging information between notebooks. This chapter's pictures were created using these utility functions. Exchanging different system screen snapshot formats — here Microsoft Windows and Macintosh — is simplified. More complicated applications such as an "electronic whiteboard" — useful for classroom teaching or conferencing — can be implemented using multiple `Serializer` connections.

15.6. Future Directions

This book includes a wide range of *MathLink* programs. Starting with simple programs for adding two numbers (AddTwo) and transferring lists, we moved on to more interesting applications — *TurtleGraphics* and *Movie-Digitizer* — which used a collection of template functions. For these real-time interactive graphics applications, we developed an object-oriented programming style to hide the *MathLink* connection details and to allow us to create sophisticated applications using simple high-level code. This approach culminated with `Serializer`, which is a very general tool for linking multiple *Mathematica* sessions.

One recurrent theme throughout this book is the use of *Mathematica* expressions for exchanging information. Since *Mathematica* expressions can represent *any* form of data, the design of network programs is simplified because such expressions are a basic element of the *MathLink* transfer protocol. Now, we more deeply appreciate the basic idea of *MathLink* (see Section 2.12.1 of *The Mathematica Book*): *MathLink* is a mechanism for exchanging *Mathematica* expressions between programs.

We now indicate some future directions for *MathLink* programs that we are considering.

15.6.1 Special-purpose Front Ends

The *MathLink* programs presented here have considerable potential for further extension. For example, we could develop a suite of special-purpose front ends such as

[1] MovieDigitizer — for interacting with QuickTime movies;

[2] SpreadSheet — for editing, control, and display of tables;

[3] MathPaint — for creating paint-like graphics using *Mathematica*;

[4] MathDraw — for interactive editing of graphics objects under the control of *Mathematica*, etc.

Importantly, these front ends can interact with each other, because they can all share the same kernel, and all front ends are programmable using *Mathematica* functions. The environment would be similar to the concept of a lisp or SmallTalk machine.

15.6.2 Increased Portability Using Java

All applications presented here have portability problems. Such problems are especially critical for graphics and window operation primitives, which are, in general, machine dependent. Unless we have platform-independent libraries, we must write separate graphics functions for each platform.

Coupled to the dramatic rise of the Web, the Java programming language has become extremely popular. From our perspective, Java's most important characteristic is its platform independence. When a user compiles Java code, a binary program for a virtual machine is created that will run on *any* platform including Macintosh, Windows, and Unix. So, if we use Java for graphics and the user interface, we can easily create a platform-independent *MathLink* application. *J/Link*, available from http://www.wolfram.com/solutions/mathlink/jlink/, is a toolkit that integrates *Mathematica* and Java. It lets you call Java from *Mathematica* in a completely transparent way, and it lets you use and control the *Mathematica* kernel from a Java program.

In comparison with Java, *Mathematica* is much more suitable for an abstract, high-level, problem-oriented approach to programming. Hence it makes good sense to share the work between the two languages — using Java for the user interface and graphics, and using *Mathematica* for describing and implementing the model.

15.7. Serializer Summary

A `Serializer` object is a link object of the connection between `Serializer` sessions. In the following, gray font is used to indicate optional arguments, for example, *opts*.

New[Serializer, *name* , *options*]

This method makes a peer-to-peer connection with another `Serializer` object. *name* is the name of the link. There are `LinkProtocol`, `LinkMode`, and `NickName` options. One side opens a link with `LinkMode→Listen` and the other connects to it using `LinkMode→Connect`. `NickName` is a string used to associate a name with a `Serializer` instance.

obj[dispose]

This function sends a **dispose** message to program object, *obj*. When closing the connection, first a **close** command is sent to the other side, and then it closes itself.

obj[nickname]

This message returns the name assigned by the `NickName` option.

obj[send, *exp*]

This message sends *exp* to *obj* for evaluation by the partner's kernel. The result of the evaluation is not returned.

obj[eval, *exp*]

This message sends *exp* to *obj* for evaluation by the partner's kernel, and the result is returned. If the return value is a number or string, the value is returned, otherwise a held expression or the form *self*[Hold[*exp*]] is returned.

NetCopy[*obj*]

NetCopy[*obj*] copies *obj*'s clipboard content and pastes it into the currently selected notebook.

NetPaste[*obj*]

NetPaste[*obj*] pastes clipboard content into *obj*'s notebook. If *obj* is a list of Serializer instances, it pastes to all instances.

CellExchangeNotebook[*obj*]

CellExchangeNotebook[*obj*] creates a notebook for exchanging cells with its partner. When the user clicks on the button in this notebook, all cells below the button are relayed to its partner's notebook.

Index